ď 2.

BRITAIN'S NATIONAL PARKS

BRITAIN'S NATIONAL PARKS

Incorporating the
National Parks of England and Wales
Edited by **William S Lacey**

and the
National Scenic Areas of Scotland
by **Alan Hamilton**

Photographs by
Glyn Satterley

Foreword by
Lord Hunt,
President of the
COUNCIL FOR NATIONAL PARKS

WINDWARD

Created and produced by Robert Dudley and John Stidolph

Editorial assistant – Nicole Lanitis

Maps by John Flower

Index by Geraldine Christy

Designed by Norman Turpin

© Antler Books Ltd 1984

First published by Windward
an imprint owned by W H Smith & Son Ltd
Registered No 237811 England
Trading as W H S Distributors
St John's House, East Street, Leicester LE1 6NE

ISBN 0 7112 0325 3

Typesetting and illustration origination by Fakenham Photosetting Ltd
Printed in Spain by Grijelmo SA, Bilbao

Contents

Picture on page 1: *Wastwater in the Lake District*
Frontispiece: *Dry-stone walling on the slopes of Aonach Eagach, Glencoe*
Picture on page 4: *Sunset over Loch na Keal, Mull*
Below: *Water-lily ponds at Bosherton in the Pembrokeshire Coast Park*

The Contributors

WILLIAM S LACEY, a native of Leicestershire, studied botany in Reading University and was subsequently at University College Bangor, retiring as Professor Emeritus in 1982. He is Chairman of the North Wales Naturalists' Trust, which he helped to establish in 1963, and of the Association of Trusts for Nature Conservation in Wales, formed in 1974. In European Conservation Year 1970 he edited the book *Welsh Wildlife in Trust*. He has served on the Wales Committee of the Nature Conservancy Council and for ten years was a nominated member of the Snowdonia National Park Committee. He is a Council member of the Royal Society for Nature Conservation.

ALAN HAMILTON is a staff writer on *The Times* of London. He was born in Edinburgh in 1943, has travelled extensively in his native country, and is the author of *Essential Edinburgh*, the standard guide to his birthplace.

ROY CHRISTIAN retired early from teaching English at Derby College of Further Education to devote more time to writing and broadcasting, but he still lectures to adult classes in local history. Along with watching and commenting on cricket and soccer, exploring the countryside is one of his main hobbies. He has written books on his native Derbyshire and Nottinghamshire in the Batsford county series and on the Peak District. Many of his radio talks over more than thirty years have dealt with aspects of the Midlands rural scene, as have his articles for *Country Life* and other magazines. He became an MBE in 1976.

WILLIAM CONDRY is the author of numerous articles, broadcast scripts and books on wildlife and the countryside. Many of his articles have appeared in *Country Life* and he has been contributing a Country Diary to *The Guardian* since 1957. His books include such diverse subjects as a life of Thoreau, birdwatching in Africa, the ecology of woodlands and the natural history of Wales. He has long been involved in conservation in Wales and is a Vice-President of the North Wales Naturalists' Trust and President of Bardsey Bird and Field Observatory.

LEONARD CURTIS is Head of the Exmoor National Park Department. He was formerly Reader in Geography and Head of the Joint School of Botany and Geography in the University of Bristol, where he still holds an Honorary Senior Research Fellowship. His early work was in the field of soil studies as a member of the Soil Survey of England and Wales. An author of seven books concerned with soil studies, land use inventories and remote sensing applications using both aircraft and satellite observations, he is actively engaged in the development of policies for management of protected landscapes.

JOHN DAWSON is a Lancastrian by birth and a historian by training. He came to the Lake District in 1960 as first Headmaster of the John Ruskin School, Coniston. Unable to imagine a better place to live in, he has remained ever since, taking early retirement in 1982 in order to concentrate on his main hobby of historical research and to spend more time walking the Lake District hills. He has contributed articles of local, historical and topographical interest to many periodicals, particularly *Lancashire Life* and *Country Life*, and is currently working on a book about the Lakes and parish of Torver.

IAN MERCER is a geographer by training and has worked in Devon for twenty-five years. He established the Slapton Ley Field Centre, became County Conservation Officer, and was appointed the first Dartmoor National Park Officer in 1973. He sits on the England Committee of the Nature Conservancy Council and the Regional Advisory Committee of the Forestry Commission. He paints landscapes, watches birds and occasionally teaches fieldwork. He is Chairman of the Field Studies Council. His published work includes a *Nature Guide to the West Country* (1981) and contributions to *Environmental Education* and *Conservation in Practice*.

DEREK STATHAM is the National Park Officer for the North York Moors. He has a background of training in geography and planning and has occupied a number of posts in county council planning departments. As Assistant County Planning Officer for the former North Riding County Council he had responsibilities for advising National Park Committees for both the North York Moors and the Yorkshire Dales national parks. During 1971 he has awarded a fellowship with the Centre for Environmental Studies to explore the problems of rural land use, a topic in which he has a particular interest.

GEOFFREY WRIGHT was born and bred in north-east England, whose countryside he has explored extensively on foot and by cycle. After teaching in Wiltshire for twenty-six years, he retired early to concentrate on writing and photography, returning north to live in a restored eighteenth-century farmhouse in Wensleydale. His books include *The Yorkshire Dales, View of Northumberland, View of Wessex* and *The East Riding*. Books on *Stone Villages in Britain* and *Roads and Trackways in the Yorkshire Dales* are in preparation. He is an active member of the National Trust, the Yorkshire Dales Society and the Yorkshire Naturalists' Trust.

GLYN SATTERLEY, born in Kent, now lives in Edinburgh. He is one of today's leading landscape photographers. He has a number of successful exhibitions to his credit and is a regular contributor to most of the major magazines. He has completed two books, *Life in Caithness and Sutherland* and *Wild Britain*; he is currently working on a documentary on the Highland sporting estates and has been commissioned by the British Tourist Authority to photograph the Scottish islands.

Foreword

by **Lord Hunt of Llanfair Waterdine KG CBE DSO**
President of the Council for National Parks

IN HIS introduction to this book, Professor Lacey has recalled that a proposal to establish national parks was first considered by a British government in 1929. I have cause to remember that year for, as a teenager, I made my first visit to Snowdonia during the Easter holidays and, accompanied by my brother, made my first ascent of a Welsh mountain, Carnedd Llewelyn, by an unorthodox route up the steep slopes of the Nant Ffrancon from Ty Gwyn Farm.

As a boy I could not have foreseen the changes which would take place in that relatively remote and rugged corner of Wales during the next fifty years. There were few visitors around, even at Easter time, in such 'honeypot' areas as Pen y Pass, where my family stayed in the Gorphwysfa Hotel before climbing Snowdon. The proprietor Rawson Owen, had only recently ceased to drive his coach and four horses up and down the passes, untroubled by traffic on the narrow roads.

The history of our national parks is a success story which too many people who enjoy them today tend to take for granted. We have reason to be grateful to those enlightened pioneers referred to by Professor Lacey, who foresaw the need to protect our natural heritage of mountains, moorland, coastlines and inland waters from damaging land development, all those years ago. Today, the pressures bearing upon conservation of the wilder parts of our country are all too apparent, as the demands increase to exploit the resources of the land in order to meet the material needs of water and hydro-electric power, timber, minerals and food production. To these must be added the growth of tourism. This betokens a fairer distribution of wealth than when I was a boy; it also reflects the desire of many people from our own and other countries to escape for a while from the urban environments of industrialized societies, into the unspoilt countryside.

Not the least important aspect of the combined effects of all these pressures upon the national parks and, to a lesser extent, the highlands and islands of Scotland is that they also bear upon those people whose homes and livelihood are in those areas; for our parks have the unique characteristic of being areas which, over many centuries, have been inhabited, managed and landscaped by man's endeavours. To accommodate, modify and harmonize the diverse demands on their land usage without prejudicing the purposes for which the national parks were established following an Act of Parliament in 1949, is a task of formidable dimensions. In addition to the debt we owe to the pioneers of the 1930s we have reason also to be thankful for the work of the National Park Authorities, and to the many voluntary bodies which are variously dedicated to conserve them and to protect wildlife within them.

But, notwithstanding their efforts, more than this is called for. Nothing less will suffice than the same degree of enlightened foresight by the government of today as was displayed by its predecessors of 1939 and 1949, in upholding the original purposes of the national parks, establishing the appropriate priorities to that end and integrating the work of relevant government departments accordingly. The pace of change spells the urgency of the need.

It is up to all of us who value our natural heritage, encompassed within the national parks of England and Wales and in the highlands and islands of Scotland, to play some part in impressing upon the government that this precious asset must be safeguarded for the future and handed on without further damage for the next fifty years – and beyond.

John Hunt
President
Council for National Parks

Editor's Preface

THIS BOOK has been produced for all those who wish to explore unspoilt, remote or wild places in Britain. It indicates the opportunities for fuller enjoyment of the countryside by providing authoritative accounts of the physical features, archaeology and architecture, flora and fauna, and recreational facilities available in some of the most important landscape conservation areas in the country – indeed, in Europe. Of course, there have been earlier books describing our national parks. So why yet another? The justification lies in the more comprehensive nature of the present work and, in particular – distinguishing it from its predecessors – the inclusion of landscape conservation areas in Scotland. Since that country has, as yet, designated no national parks as such, but has legislated along lines different from those adopted earlier in England and Wales, separate treatment for Scotland is necessary.

The subject matter of the book is presented in two sections. The first section contains a general introduction dealing with the establishment, development and maintenance of national parks in England and Wales, followed by descriptions of the ten individual parks. The second section deals in like manner with Scotland. An introduction traces the different course of development which has taken place there and this is followed by descriptions of selected scenic areas of a status similar to national parks.

Individual contributors have been free to write in their own styles and to express views on any controversial topics which they wished to introduce. While every care has been taken to maintain a high standard of accuracy, the Editor and Publishers are not responsible for the statements and opinions of the contributors. Uniformity in the citing of names of plants and animals has been ensured by adopting the practice of using common English names with capital initials. In parts of the text dealing with geological and archaeological topics readers may detect apparent slight discrepancies. These reflect the state of knowledge in different parts of the country and hence the differing degrees of precision available to individual contributors.

Finally, the reader's attention is drawn to the lists of useful addresses at the end of each chapter and to the suggestions for further reading at the end of the book. These will enable advance enquiries to be made for information not contained in the book itself and will facilitate the planning of visits to some of the most attractive and varied open countryside in Britain.

William S Lacey
Penrhyn Bay, Llandudno
June 1983

COUNCIL FOR NATIONAL PARKS

THE COUNCIL for National Parks is a national voluntary organization whose aims are to promote the purposes for which our national parks were designated: namely, the conservation and enhancement of natural beauty, and the promotion of their enjoyment by the public.

The Council was established as an independent organization in 1977, out of the Standing Committee on National Parks, which was created in 1936 to campaign for legislation for National Parks. Since its success in 1949, the Committee – and subsequently the Council – has acted as a national 'watchdog' for national parks: speaking in defence of their purposes, ensuring that they are not forgotten when it comes to national policy and decision making, and fighting to protect them against specific threats.

Today the Council has over thirty constituent organizations, representing national and local amenity, recreation and wildlife interests. In order to provide a way for those millions of people who visit and enjoy the national parks to express their concern for their future, the Council has recently established the 'Friends of National Parks'. This enables individuals to support the work of the Council directly.

For a minimum annual subscription of £5, Friends receive a membership card and twice-yearly newsletter *Tarn and Tor*, which is full of information about the national parks, including visitor information and current issues and events.

Further details from:
The Secretary
Council for National Parks
4 Hobart Place
London SW1W 0HY

THE
NATIONAL
PARKS
OF

ENGLAND
AND WALES

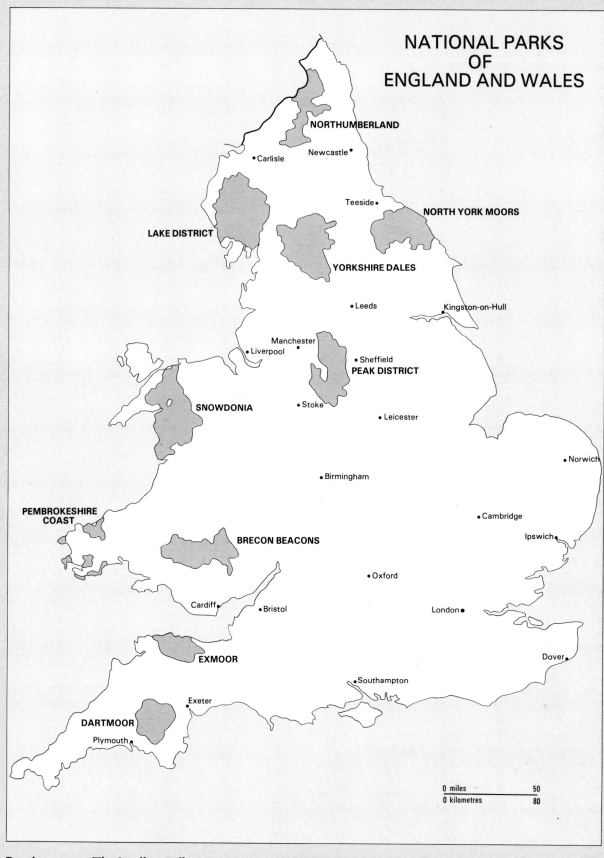

NATIONAL PARKS OF ENGLAND AND WALES

NORTHUMBERLAND

• Carlisle

Newcastle •

Teeside •

NORTH YORK MOORS

LAKE DISTRICT

YORKSHIRE DALES

• Leeds

Kingston-on-Hull

Manchester •
• Liverpool

• Sheffield

PEAK DISTRICT

SNOWDONIA

• Stoke

• Leicester

• Norwich

• Birmingham

PEMBROKESHIRE COAST

• Cambridge

Ipswich •

BRECON BEACONS

• Oxford

Cardiff •
• Bristol

London •

EXMOOR

Dover •

• Southampton

Exeter •

DARTMOOR

Plymouth •

| 0 miles | 50 |
| 0 kilometres | 80 |

Previous page: *The Swallow Falls near Betws-y-Coed, Snowdonia*

William S Lacey

Introduction

*A*DISTINGUISHED SCOTTISH naturalist, the late Frank Fraser Darling, once remarked that the United States had made a major contribution to world culture with the national park idea. It is true that America was the pioneer in this field, setting aside the Yosemite Valley as a protected area, the first national park in all but name, in 1864 and instituting the federal parks system with the designation of the Yellowstone Park in 1872. There is no doubt also that the early establishment of national parks in North America was in part responsible for the beginnings of the national park movement in Britain, but the systems adopted in the two countries differ fundamentally in many respects. In the United States it was national pride in the scenic wonders discovered as the West was opened up, rather than a concern for preserving whole environments, that originally led to the designation of the first national parks. The American parks were created in virgin lands acquired by the federal government and they are managed directly by government agencies. In Britain the impetus to create national parks came from two main sources – from those who wished to secure and improve access to the uplands, and from those who sought to protect beautiful countryside from unplanned and undesirable development. The fact that Britain was a densely populated and highly developed country, where almost every corner of the land was privately owned and much of it put to agricultural, industrial or residential use, ensured that our national parks would be different from those in America. In effect, a national park in Britain is an area of high landscape value, delineated on a map, within which practical steps are taken by negotiation and by all other appropriate means to provide and improve facilities for enjoyment of the countryside, to conserve and enhance its natural beauty and amenity, and to secure public access for open-air recreation.

In the event, more than three-quarters of a century was to elapse between the initiation of the American federal park system in 1872 and the setting-up of the first national park in Britain in 1951. However, it should not be thought that no action took place during this long period of time. On the contrary, there were many efforts, both by individuals and by voluntary bodies, directed towards the provision of increased access to and better protection for the countryside.

As long ago as 1884 James Bryce had introduced a bill into Parliament to secure for townsfolk easier access to the uplands. This early effort was abortive, but in later years the Commons, Open Spaces and Footpaths Preservation Society (formed in 1899 by the amalgamation of two earlier bodies) and the Ramblers' Association continued to press the access case. Some idea of the strength of feeling may be gained from the occurrence of a mass trespass by country lovers, organized from Sheffield, which took place on the Kinder Scout grouse-moors in 1932. The National Trust for Places of Historic Interest and Natural Beauty, incorporated in 1895, and the Councils for the Preservation (later Protection) of Rural England (CPRE) and Rural Wales (CPRW), established respectively in 1926 and 1928, were concerned primarily with the protection of both the natural and the man-made environment.

The access and protection arms of the movement were supported by the voluntary wildlife conservation organizations, notably the Royal Society for the Protection of Birds, established in 1889, and the Society for the Promotion of Nature Reserves (SPNR, now the Royal Society for Nature Conservation) set up in 1912.

In response to a suggestion from CPRE, the possible establishment of national parks was first examined by the government in 1929 and two years later SPNR recommended to Parliament the creation of 'national reserves and nature sanctuaries', but neither of these approaches was successful. In 1935 CPRE and CPRW jointly set up a Standing Committee to press for the establishment of national parks, but the worsening economic and political situation in the late 1930s ensured that the necessary legislation was postponed until after the Second World War. Then, at long last, pressure for access to and conservation of the countryside resulted in the Town and Country Planning Act of 1947 and the National Parks and Access to the Countryside Act of 1949.

The driving force for the all-important 1949 Act was the Report on National Parks in England and Wales, commissioned by the government and submitted by an architect, the late John Dower, to the Minister of Town and Country Planning in 1945. This report on the purpose and theory of national parks provided the basis for detailed proposals worked out by a government-appointed National Parks Committee, under the chairmanship of Sir Arthur Hobhouse, which reported in 1947. The Dower Report provided the following definition, accepted by Hobhouse, of a national park as applied to Great Britain:

'A National Park is an extensive area of beautiful and relatively wild country in which, for the national benefit and by appropriate national decision and action, (a) the characteristic landscape beauty is strictly preserved, (b) access and facilities for public open-air enjoyment are amply provided, (c) wildlife and buildings and places of architectural and historic interest are suitably protected, while (d) established farming use is effectively maintained.'

The 1949 Act established the National Parks Commission for England and Wales. It required the Commission to make orders designating national parks in suitable areas of high scenic quality and to advise the local planning authorities on their administration and development.

The Hobhouse Committee originally recommended the creation of twelve parks, but two, those for the South Downs and for the Norfolk Broads, have never been designated. (However, a Broads Authority, administering the area, was set up in 1978.) The ten parks were established between 1951 and 1957. As might be expected, they lie in the west and north of Britain. In the order of their creation they are: Peak District, Lake District, Snowdonia, Dartmoor, Pembrokeshire Coast, North York Moors, Yorkshire Dales, Exmoor, Northumberland and Brecon Beacons. Together they total about 13,600 square km (5,260 square miles) and cover about ten per cent of the total area of England and Wales.

The Countryside Act of 1968 replaced the National Parks Commission with the Countryside Commission, but that was much more than a simple change of name. The new Commission was given wider powers and functions, with increased responsibility for rural conservation and for recreation. Scotland already had its own Commission, established by the Countryside (Scotland) Act of 1967, but national parks on the England and Wales model have not been established there.

When the designation of a national park by the Countryside Commission has been confirmed by the Secretary of State for the Environment or for Wales, as appropriate, no change occurs in the ownership of the land. It does not become public property and there is no automatic right of access. The Commission advises on planning and management but the parks are administered locally.

The form of administration is not uniform throughout the national park system. In 1945 John Dower had strongly recommended the setting up of independent planning boards for the parks, rather than joint advisory committees of county councils. In the event, Joint Planning Boards were established only for the first two national parks to be designated, the Peak District and the Lake District, and even these differed from one another. The Peak Board had its own staff, headed by a director and planning officer, while the Lake District was administered on a part-time basis by officers of the county councils involved. The remaining multi-county parks, Snowdonia, Yorkshire Dales, Exmoor and Brecon Beacons, had separate National Park Committees for each county, together with joint advisory committees – a very cumbersome structure. The Dartmoor, Pembrokeshire Coast, North York Moors and Northumberland parks were wholly contained within single counties and each had its own National Park Committee.

Since 1974 each park has been the responsibility of a single executive board or committee. Park Planning Boards have been retained for the Peak District and the Lake District; elsewhere a separate National Park Committee, with delegated planning powers, has been established for the whole of each park.

On each park board or committee two thirds of the members are elected members of county and district councils and one third consists of persons appointed by the Secretary of State for the Environment or for Wales. The appointed members are selected for their specialist knowledge of different aspects of life in the park and include representatives of farming, tourism and recreation interests, the water authority, local natural history societies or wildlife conservation trusts. Each park has as its chief adviser a national park officer, a statutory post created by the Local Government Act of 1972, effective from 1974. One of his main duties is to prepare, and keep under review, the National Park Plan, which is primarily a management programme.

Since the parks exist for the benefit of all, a block grant is payable from the Exchequer towards the cost of administering them, conserving and enhancing their landscape, and providing for public enjoyment in them. This amounts to seventy-five per cent of total costs; the remaining finance comes from a charge on local rates (qualifying for rate support grant), augmented by income generated by various undertakings in the parks.

The year 1974 also saw the publication of the Report of the National Park Policies Review Committee (the Sandford Report), an important review of the working of the national parks during the previous twenty years. Many of the main proposals for change contained in this report, including the recommendation that over-riding priority should be accorded to conservation, were accepted in principle in 1976 by the two Secretaries of State. However, two recommendations were not successful. The first concerns public enquiries. Arising from a refusal in 1973 by the then Secretary of State for Wales to confirm a designation order for a Cambrian Mountains National Park in Mid-Wales – an action taken without consulting public opinion – the Commission recommended that there should be an automatic local public enquiry in the event of any sustained objection to the designation of a national park. The second recommendation concerned afforestation, an activity not requiring planning permission. In national parks control of this kind of development is exercised by 'gentlemen's agreements' arrived at in Forestry Consultative Committees, in which a wide spectrum of interests is represented. This consultative arrangement has sometimes proved to be an inadequate safeguard of national park interests. The Commission therefore proposed that forestry in national parks should be brought under normal planning control. Many people feel that it is a matter for regret that the Secretaries of State did not see fit to accept either of these two important recommendations.

The Wildlife and Countryside Act of 1981 provided for the status of the Countryside Commission to be changed, operative from 1982, to that of a grant-in-aid body within the public sector but outside the Civil Service and also conferred limited additional powers. The main addition was a matching of the Commission's long-standing independence in policy-making and promotional work with a new executive independence. The Act also carried with it some consequences for national park administration, in particular, the need for a more detailed approach to the conservation of moorland and heath within national parks; and the need for more extensive consultation before varying national park boundaries. It also gave statutory backing to the practice, hitherto voluntary, of including district council members on national park authorities.

The park authorities have the dual role of keeping the landscape unspoilt and making the necessary provisions for people to enjoy it. They are responsible for planning in the parks and work through the normal processes of planning control, but with specially high standards. Protection of the landscape involves the preservation and planting of trees, the removal of eyesores and clearing of derelict sites, and requires special attention to the design, materials, siting and screening of proposed developments within the park. Planning permission can be refused if a structure seems out of place in the environment, but a potential developer has the right of appeal to the appropriate Secretary of State. All the national park authorities now have comprehensive upland management schemes in operation. Provision for increased public enjoyment involves the construction of parking places, sites for caravans and camping, lay-out of footpaths and nature trails, negotiation of access agreements with landowners, establishment of information centres and residential study centres, and the operation of a warden service – all designed to enable people to gain the maximum enjoyment and benefit from their visit.

Although much of the land within the parks remains in private ownership, a few areas have been acquired by park authorities under various powers vested in them. Some properties within the parks have come into the care of the nation in other ways – for example, by purchase by the National Trust, as forest parks owned or leased by the Forestry Commission, and as national nature reserves owned and managed by the Nature Conservancy Council. In addition, many nature reserves within the parks are managed by the voluntary wildlife conservation trusts. The national park authorities cooperate closely with all such bodies.

The following ten chapters describe some of the features of the individual national parks in England and Wales, which now attract many millions of visitors every year.

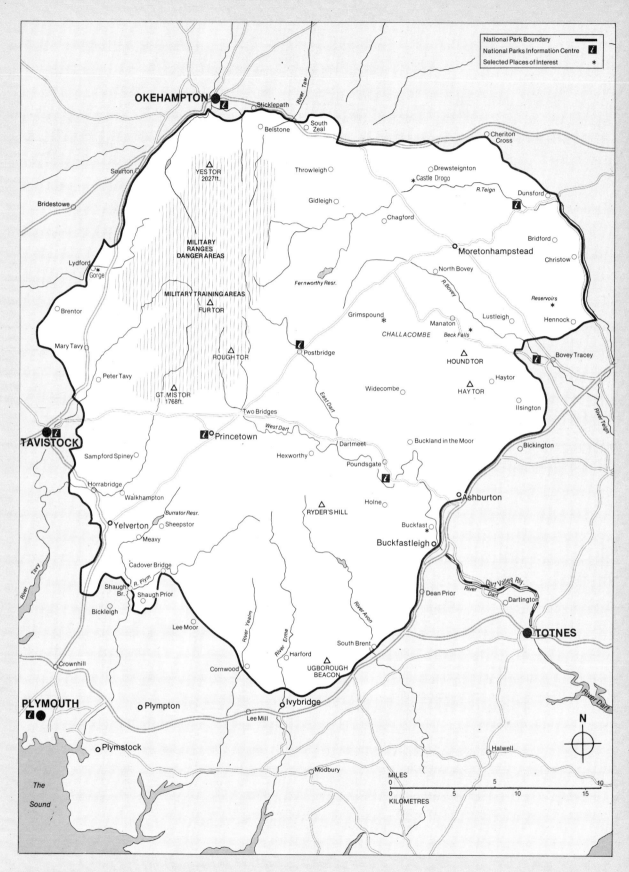

DARTMOOR NATIONAL PARK

Ian Mercer

Dartmoor

ING JOHN isolated it as a royal forest in 1204, Camden called it *'squalida montana'* as he passed it by, Risdon in 1630 said it was 'richer in the bowels than in the face thereof', Burnard knew it as the 'grand old moor'. It has meant, and offered, different things to different people throughout historic time. Since 1951 Dartmoor proper has been the core of a national park.

The Dartmoor National Park in plan is a compact, mirror image of Africa, 945 square km (365 square miles) in extent, twenty-three miles wide in its northern half, twenty-four miles from north to south. Okehampton, Tavistock, Ivybridge and Bovey Tracey lie just outside its boundary on the north, west, south and east respectively. Exeter is seven miles away to the east, Plymouth city boundary is only two miles from the south-western corner. The Torbay conurbation is within fifteen miles of south-eastern entrances to the park.

Geology and Landscape

Dartmoor is the largest exposed granite boss of the south-west peninsula of England. It is also the easternmost and highest of the procession running from the Scillies through Land's End, Carn Brea, St Austell, and Bodmin to Devon. They are probably all surface glimpses of a continuous granite mass beneath. 'The Dartmoor granite' is in a sense a collective phrase; some 400 different types of granite have been identified within the moor. The so-called 'giant' granite – with large, matchbox-size crystals of white felspar – is the type commonly seen in the tors which give parts of the landscape its singular character, while at the other extreme, dykes of fine-grained aplite penetrate the main mass and are visible in many places. At the south-western end the granite is kaolinized to varying degrees, chemically 'rotten' forming a sandy gravel of quartz and mica with the valuable kaolin. The granite is surrounded by a zone of the 'country' rock (slate, sandstone, limestone, grit and hornfels), altered by the physical intrusion and intense heat of the then molten granite. It is called the metamorphic aureole, is at least as tough as the granite, and possesses none of its chemical weaknesses.

'As hard as granite' may be a phrase applicable to the polished slab, or even the individual boulder at the roadside, but the vulnerability of the felspar crystals to the attack of even weak acids is a major factor in the development of the Dartmoor landscape. Rainwater is very dilute carbonic acid and is joined by humic acids as it passes through peat and peaty soils. As one of the three main components of such a coarsely crystalline rock is attacked, so disintegration of the whole rock is facilitated. To this chemical weakness must be added the fact that the granite is divided into blocks of varying size, by cracks, called joints. Many were undoubtedly formed as the molten granite cooled and contracted 250 million years ago well beneath the surface. Some are sub-parallel with the surface of the granite mass-sheet joints; others are roughly at right angles to the sheets. So concentric shells of granite are themselves broken up into rectilinear blocks. Because the granite was emplaced at depth in the earth's crust, a great weight of material then overlaid it. That weight has been eroded away between then and now, and the removal of its compressive effect has resulted in a second set of joints, due to 'unloading' and a springing apart of the rock, well seen in valley-side exposures of joints sub-parallel to the ground surface.

Both the tiny cracks between the loosened crystals and the major joints allow the passage of water. In extreme conditions that water freezes, in freezing it expands, and in expanding can lever away crystal or block, either accelerating disintegration of the rock, or changing the shape of the land. Only about 16,000 years ago, Dartmoor, with the rest of Southern England, was emerging from a long period of Arctic-type climate. In such a situation not only is freezing and thawing an effective sculpturing process, but in the brief summer, much that was split off in the preceding season, is sludged down-hill as a kind of peri-glacial porridge carrying boulders and mantling the lower slopes. So the profiles of the plateaux edges and the older valley sides have been determined. The interior of the two plateaux is largely mantled by blanket peat developed within the last 16,000 years, and in some places three or four metres thick. Most valley floors within the plateaux carry basin peat, as valley bogs, so that over parts of the landscape the peat is almost continuous.

Thus the details of the Dartmoor landscape – tors,

Lush pastureland with Chagford Common rising in the background

boulders, singly and in sheets called 'clitter', gravel in pits at roadsides and peat on high or low ground – owe their origins to the nature of granite and the climatic conditions applied to it during the last glaciation and since. The grand pattern of the landscape is older than that. Its altitude relates to the resistance of granite in the mass to erosion and weathering. The land within the park boundary ranges from 30–610 m (100–2,000 ft) OD. Its isolation at that altitude relates to the relative weakness of the older slates and shales around it, worked by substantial rivers like the Tamar and the Exe, their predecessors, and inundating seas before the Ice Age began.

All the summits of Dartmoor, plotted on a single graph, demonstrate a surprisingly consistent slope to the south. The northern plateau is drained largely by the Tavy, the headstreams of the Dart, and the Teign, all flowing off eventually to the south. The southern plateau is drained by the Plym, Yealm, Erme and Avon with similar directions. All this because the whole south-west peninsula was tilted to the south during the Alpine earth movements. There are of course exceptions to the pattern. At the local level a rectilinear pattern of valleys, reflecting the major joint pattern of the granite is evident – between Hennock and Moretonhampstead for instance. More obviously the upper Teign and the upper Dart and West Dart flow eastward for some miles, the former in a gorge along the granite edge, the latter in a wide, shallow, high level vale between the two plateaux. These two lines are probably all that remains of a pattern pre-dating the southerly tilt. There is some evidence that an early Tertiary landscape carried eastward-flowing tributaries to a proto-Rhine flowing north up the North Sea basin – Tyne, Tees, Trent, Thames may all be on lines inherited from such a pattern. In support of this theory there are Dartmoor pebbles and ball clay (kaolin produced by weathering) in Dorset south of Poole Harbour. They can only have been carried there by running water which, with those two valley lines on Dartmoor, points to a proto-Dart/Teign flowing along the line of the south coast from Teignmouth eastwards.

Where the contemporary rivers leave the granite they do so in a spectacular fashion. Pre-glacial seas, which temporarily isolated Dartmoor as an island, withdrew further and further, to lowest points during the glaciations (when seawater was locked up as ice). At each new lowering the rivers received a new incentive to cut down, and these cuts travelled upstream to accumulate at the edge of the granite. The physical symptoms of this are steep-sided gorges with sets of rapids, falls and pools in the rivers within them. The Dart falls 150 m (500 ft) from Dartmeet to Holne Bridge, the Teign 90 m (300 ft) from Chagford to Dunsford, the Tavy 120 m (400 ft) from the Rattlebrook confluence to Standon Steps. The gorges contain jumbles of boulders, clearly de-posited in times of torrential water flow; some have great fans of boulder-filled deposit immediately at their mouths – the Erme at Ivybridge is a good example – all of which demonstrates that they carried Ice Age melt water and must therefore pre-date the last glaciation.

Tors and gorges then coincide at the plateaux edges, bare rock and boulders loom largest here; elsewhere, as already noted, peat blankets the two plateaux; in a zone surrounding them podsolic soils with iron pans dominate the gentler slopes and flats, and outside that zone, especially in the drier east, round Widecombe and Moretonhampstead, a rich brown earth covers the parent rocks.

Flora and Fauna

The post-glacial development of the Dartmoor surface involves the fluctuating fortunes of natural vegetation, latterly at the hands of men. The optimum would appear to have brought the tree line to the edge of the blanket bog. Evidence of Alder, Birch, Pine and even some Oak occurs to about 520 m (1700 ft) OD. Neolithic, and more effective Bronze Age, human activity set back the edge of the forest to the steepest slopes and inserted what is now the true moorland between it and the summit bogs, by burning and other forms of clearance. Grazing and burning annually since have maintained the moorland, by preventing new thicket development. Because of the great variations in all the characteristics of the land between the steepest valley sides and the summit, there are a number of distinct communities of plants comprising the generalized 'moorland'.

The blanket peat is dominated by rushes, Cotton-grass, Deer sedge and Purple Moor-grass. Ling – the commonest of the heathers – occurs at the drier edges of peat bogs, and on patches of mineral soil showing through the bog. *Sphagnum* mosses take over in all the wettest hollows, and pools abound in the more level areas. At the other extreme, the driest slopes at the moorland edges support a short-cropped grassland with scattered European Gorse; Bracken on the thicker soils may take over completely. Between these two are great expanses of grass moor – dominated by Purple Moor-grass, with Flying Bent-grass and Mat-grass in the drier spaces – and heather moor, with Bell Heather and Crossleaved Heath as well as the dominant Ling, and Bilberry in places. On some slopes Western Gorse in dense low cushions is well mixed with heathers to the extent of overwhelming them occasionally. Here too in the east and at midsummer Dodder parasitizes the gorse and scrambles over whole tussocks as a pink web. Bracken is a choosy plant, indicating always the better soils, and is often most obvious and dominant where cultivation has occurred in the past. It tends therefore to be present in a zone around the moorland edge, especially in old fields. There is some evidence that it is advancing at the

Staple Tor, near Merrivale, consists of a series of piles of blocks of granite

pools and rivulets. On *Sphagnum* tussocks Round-leaved Sundew indulges in its occasional fly-catching; and on bare scrapes – ponies' hoof marks are good places – Pale Butterwort, the elegant Lusitanian cousin of the grosser common one from north of Bristol, tries the same exercise.

Valley bogs carry occasional Sallow thickets, and clumps of Bog Myrtle. At lowest levels Alder and Birch may shade the edge of the bog. Out on the drier slopes, but near the moorland boundary, scattered thorns and Rowan can add a distinctive dimension to the scene. The native woodland of Dartmoor proper is however confined to the steepest valley sides. Native trees may dominate it still, but man has managed it throughout history to a greater or lesser degree. It is still largely oakwood, mainly the Sessile Oak, and has invariably been coppiced. Coppicing involves regular cutting, and the encouragement of a number of stems from the ground-level stock. Firewood, charcoal, faggots and timber for building, fencing, gates, carts and wheels all came from coppice woods, but oak bark for tanning was a major product from these valleys. Leather was tanned in all the small towns around the moor, in the self-sufficient habit of most communities this far from the metropolis until the nineteenth century was well on. Coppicing had a rotational system, carried out by families, and the product removed by pack horse. Narrow zig-zag paths through the clitter beneath the tree canopy, climb the slopes. The boulders, covered with mosses, shelter ferns and Fumitory, Cowwheat, Woodrush, Dog's Mercury and Bluebell wherever there is room, but often the boulders touch each other, so that only the old charcoal burner's platform creates a tiny clearing for such plants in profusion.

The Oak has its tree companions. Ash and Birch are the true historic ones; where landowners followed fashion in the eighteenth century, Beech, Sycamore and Scots Pine have been inserted. The nineteenth century saw Sweet Chestnut and Larch added in places. On at least one site Small-leaved Lime and Wild Service-tree are present, and were coppiced

expense of other communities, and while local theory tries to tie this to changes in management practice, it appears to be happening throughout Europe, from Spain to northern Norway, so that there may be a more fundamental explanation. Purple Moor-grass, too, seems to be a fairly aggressive plant, and may be favoured against heathers under inexpert burning regimes, on damper soils. Heath and dry grass moorland are thus caught in a sort of pincer movement – Bracken from the dry side, and Purple Moor-grass from the wet. This vulnerability could mean substantial changes in the high Dartmoor scene during the next century.

The transition from wetter to drier soils can be very rapid, and on any route through one of the communities described so far, patchy change will become obvious. So at any time the bright yellow Tormentil, blue Milkwort and white Eyebright may take the eye. Lichens on boulders, heather stems and fence posts change the surface texture and colour, mosses and liverworts clothe the shaded overhang.

Throughout the whole moorland spectrum, and beyond its boundary in farmed valley bottoms, valley bogs of varying sizes punctuate the landscape. They can be simple mossy sheets round hillside flushes, or great quaking acres alongside streams. In all cases they have the richest floras of the Dartmoor scene. At lower altitudes, and early in the season, Bog-bean towers of white and pink may cover the shallow water; later, and higher, whole carpets of Bog Asphodel's yellow spikes can dominate an otherwise rush-filled saucer. In most, Bog Violet, Bog Pimpernel and Bog St John's Wort occur. Pond weeds, Star Wort and Water Crowfoot fill in

Dartmoor ponies and black-faced sheep on the Moor near Princetown

with the Oak. Holly, Rowan and Hazel form an understorey where there is room vertically, and the first two regenerate with more vigour than the Oak. Shade-tolerance is obviously the need, so the introductions – Beech and Sycamore particularly – tend to overtake the Oak too. Indeed in most valleys there is little or no sign of any young oaks.

There are three small 'high level' oakwoods in Dartmoor. They are primarily of the Pedunculate Oak, which is different from the oaks described so far. The woods appear to have been coppiced, and are noted for the gnarled, distorted shapes of their trees. The best known, Wistman's Wood, a National Nature Reserve requiring a permit from the Nature Conservancy Council to visit, has expanded in size within the present century. Mysterious they have always been; recent expansion intensifies the mystery.

Almost half of the park area is not moorland or woodland, but farmland with villages and roads. Stone walls, and the distinctive earth-and-stone hedge-banks of the West Country are the haven for animals and plants in the cultivated countryside. Primrose, Wild Daffodil, Red Campion, Stitchwort, Bluebell and Jack-by-the-hedge lead the early summer takeover of colours. Later Honeysuckle and Toadflax, Hogweed and Cow Parsley, Hemp Agrimony and Foxglove cause the banks to close on the lanes.

This farmland carries the populations of animals expected throughout the south-west of England. Badger and Fox are common, if rarely seen by the visitor. Deer are increasing all the time, and Red, Fallow, Sika and Roe breed in the park. Buzzard, Kestrel and Sparrowhawk are the breeding daytime predators, Tawny and Barn Owl hunt at night. In good vole years the Short-eared Owl and Hen Harrier may linger longer over the moor during spring and autumn. The woods carry all the common woodland birds. Their upland-edge position means that Redstart, Pied Flycatcher and Wood Warbler join the ubiquitous tits, woodpeckers and thrushes every spring.

Out on the moorland Skylark and Meadow Pipit crowd the hectares. Stonechat, Whinchat and Yellowhammer flit about the bracken and gorse mixtures. Ring Ouzel and Wheatear prefer the clitter and walls – western Dartmoor proves to be the national stronghold of the Wheatear. Lapwing, Curlew and Snipe are scattered thinly through the valley bogs, Red Grouse are even more thin in the heather moor. Deep in the high plateau a few Golden Plover and Dunlin nest. Raven and Crow scavenge over all, Magpie and Jay have booming populations in the valley woodland doing the same job.

Dartmoor rivers are clear but neutral to acid. Salmon and Sea-trout still move up them to spawn. Brown trout are here too, but the great growth of the fish of the chalk and limestone streams is not seen. The eight, fairly small, reservoirs carry varying stocks of fish, all introduced. They are

Looking south from Hound Tor towards Haytor Rocks

enjoyed by anglers, Heron, Cormorant and the odd energetic Black-backed Gull. Otters cling precariously to a habitat dominated by Feral Mink.

Six of the reservoirs have coniferous woodland closely associated with them, and there are three other sizeable plantations within the park. At maturity conifer woodland is not the richest habitat and the dark blanket is disliked intensely by some British landscape purists. But within any one forest a whole cycle of planting, thinning and harvesting is present, so that like a well-managed coppiced oakwood, all ages of tree should be there. In the shelter of a mature block, the newly planted area is actually far richer in insects, birds and small mammals than the moorland outside the forest. Dartmoor would not have its Redpoll or its Crossbill were it not for the plantings of the first half of this century. The Heron and even the odd Buzzard and Raven would be without alternatives to the more popular rock face or oak tree, for nesting purposes.

Man in the Park

Thus we have a landscape cultivated and thoroughly grazed in small fields at the edges, and up the broader valleys. A moorland fringe, rocky and jagged, with castellated tors and narrow, gorge-like valleys confronts the Devon farmscape creeping as far up the hill as it dares. Then beyond the fringe loom two moorland plateaux of long low profiles, but high enough to collect more than 2,540 mm (100 inches) of rain a year, with swirling mist on many days, snow and frost on rather more than the rest of Devon. In the higher valleys within the plateaux true moorland farms exist. Here farm-yards are steep with boulders lying between buildings, and trackways doubling-up as gullies for rainwater whenever necessary. From here the remaining real hill-farmers still set out to look at cattle and sheep on the moor. They are of course pursuing an art and a mystery that is more than 3,000 years old. Bronze Age man invented the system, historic men have merely tinkered with it. It is the lightest touch man has applied to a natural ecosystem, but only by continuing the application does he maintain the moorland. If the grazier withdraws, the thicket will advance. An interesting land-scape might develop, but moorland, wide horizons, the great bowl of the sky, the 360 degree uncluttered skyline would diminish, and eventually disappear, except from the blanket bog.

All of it then demands man's attention, and men have been varying that attention for a long, long time. Neolithic men seem to have been widely scattered – burial chambers exist in a number of places throughout eastern Dartmoor and even more elaborate sites exist in the Plym Valley and near Chagford. But Bronze Age men, judging by such of their work as has survived until now, flooded into the moor. Myriads of hut circles, pounds, stone rows, circles, and field boundaries cover the open moorland. It is their foundations which have survived. Vast boulders stand in tight circles, with an entrance away from the weather. Branches leant in from these low walls to a post, or in bigger huts a ring of posts, in the centre. Bronze Age men seem to have enclosed land, and divided the holdings of social groups one from another. In cases like the village of Grimspound, they diverted a stream to pass within the pound wall. That wall enclosed three acres or more, and its gateway was elaborate, paved and drained. The sixteen or so huts within it had hearths and sleeping benches.

Iron Age men seem to have stayed at the edges of the moor – at least there is far less evidence of their use of it than their predecessors left. Iron Age 'camps' exist on spurs above the Dart and Teign valleys, and are not uncommon out in the cultivated country of south Devon, so had they existed within Dartmoor they would surely have left some evidence. The Dark Ages are as dark here as anywhere, but clearly the Anglo-Saxons moved in as high up the valleys as they could. By Domesday most of the existing Dartmoor villages were in being. By then too, the general organization of the landscape we still know had been imposed upon the moor. There is, centrally, a rough ellipse from near Okehampton to north of Ivybridge, which is the Forest of Dartmoor – a hunting ground which technically should have become a 'chase', when King Henry III made it over to the Earl of Cornwall in 1239. (The Earl became the Duke, and a century later, in 1337, the Prince of Wales acquired the title Duke of Corn-

wall.) There abuts on to the Forest boundary a ring of com-mons, the Commons of Devon, and together Forest and Common land make the single great block of moorland described earlier. Other commons adjoin the Commons of Devon, and there are yet more detached from them as islands. In mediaeval times everyone with a hearth in the county, except those who lived in Totnes and Barnstaple, had the right to graze the Commons of Devon. Slowly that right contracted until only the hearths of the manors which also owned the common had those customary rights. Mean-time the commoners of certain parishes who paid dues to the Duke of Cornwall had a right to graze the Forest by day, and because there were no physical boundaries between them, the right, or at least the straying custom on to the Commons of Devon. These various rights are still in use. Surplus graz-ing in the Forest was let by the Duchy of Cornwall to agisters who sub-let it to others. Moormen monitored the system and the stock on the Forest, reeves supervised the commons. The commons were administered *inter alia* by Manor Courts, one or two of which still sit.

Some settlement had been allowed in the Forest by the thirteenth century, and the sites of the 'ancient tenements' in the East and West Dart valleys largely still exist as separate farms. It is clear however that during the last 700 years they have often been groups of much smaller holdings than the single one existing now. Outside the Forest, but at the same altitude as the ancient tenements, even more substantial settlements have disappeared except for the single farm remaining – Challacombe and Blackaton are the classic examples, and at Houndtor the remains of a fourteenth century village are easily inspected.

The Anglo-Saxons developed a pattern of building, housing men and cattle under one roof. Built often on the slope, the house was at the upper-end with a passage between it and the shippon. This pattern survives through the mediaeval period, evolving from wood to stone, and con-tinued into the seventeenth century. These buildings are called 'long-houses' and thatched, uncluttered examples still exist, as at Higher Uppacott in Poundsgate. Through all this time, wool was a major agricultural product. Cattle and sheep were summered on the moor, but their progeny normally went elsewhere for fattening or finishing. The Church, in its many mediaeval guises, owned a huge interest in the wool-producing world, and churches like Wide-combe, Sheepstor, Ashburton and Chagford, are in part analogous to those of East Anglia in their relationship with the wealth of wool. A woollen mill still operates in Buckfast, but others in Buckfastleigh and Ashburton have closed.

The ancient tenement dwellers were allowed, as each new tenant took over, to take another eight acres of the Forest into enclosure. Hence the 'newtake' which between 1750 and 1880 burgeoned through Act of Parliament, or

The East Dart river at Postbridge in the central part of the Moor

Duchy transaction. Large enclosures were made in that period, some as big as a 1,000 acres. These 'Forest newtakes' exist now as a belt of enclosed moorland across central Dartmoor, alongside the two main roads, though they sometimes lie between the in-bye land of the ancient tenements and the open moor. Other newtakes fringe the main moorland block, unrelated to the Forest. They were enclosed under Act of Parliament from common land by the owners; most lie up the west side of the moor, but there are some examples near Ilsington and Ashburton. Newtake vegetation is often indistinguishable from that of the common land outside the walls, but it represents to the contemporary farmer his private moorland, where his cows and ewes can be served by only his own bulls and rams, where he alone regulates the value of the 'bite' for his cows and calves, or ewes and lambs by the timing of their entry. Common grazing right he may have, and it may be very valuable to him, but it does not serve all the purposes of a newtake.

From the twelfth century on there are records of mineral working on Dartmoor, and the whole park is peppered with the remains of the various forms of extraction used in the intervening 800 years. Those first records were of tin-streaming, the search for pebbles containing tin ore in the deposits in valley floors. The angular excavations in these floors, and the heaps within their boundaries are commonplace on the open moor. Streaming developed into adit

mining in Elizabethan times, replaced in the nineteenth century by deep mining via shafts. Ruinous buildings and wheel pits remain from this last phase which extended into this century. Tin was always the most valuable product, but copper, lead and arsenic have been worked. Working and smelting were carried out close to source as evidence of structures and modifications to streams, for both power and washing purposes, show. While tin mines dominated central Dartmoor, large copper mines existed at Mary Tavy and Sticklepath in the nineteenth century, the former operating continuously from 1800 to 1925. Iron was worked in smaller mines especially on the east side of the park until well into this century.

Until the nineteenth century granite was picked up from the moor; sometimes boulders were cut where they lay and only part carried away. Clearly with so much, so readily to hand there can have been little incentive to quarry the stone. Nevertheless many churches and mediaeval long-houses are testimony to the fact that the moorstone was well worked by masons and intricate decoration achieved in this difficult medium. Troughs, gate posts, cider presses show its value domestically. By the nineteenth century, however, more sophisticated demands in volume were made. Quarries were

Brentor, a volcanic cone, rising on the western edge of the National Park

opened at Haytor, Foggintor and Merrivale, among others, to provide stone for Thames bridges in London, for Holborn Viaduct and Nelson's Column. Once concentrated specialization happened in this way, then machinery for cutting and polishing could be established as a reasonable investment. One granite quarry with associated machinery is still at work.

The value of Dartmoor's china clay was certainly recognized by the eighteenth century and was used in the Minton pottery before 1800. From 1830 onwards the extractive industry was developed at Lee Moor after the manner of the post-Industrial Revolution period. Victorian values meant industrial housing and even a mechanics institute at the newly-established settlement. Now china clay working is concentrated in, and dominates, that south-western corner of Dartmoor. Outposts of the nineteenth century working on the Avon and the Erme are long abandoned. The Lee Moor pit is one of the biggest pits in the world, and is still growing outwards. Clay is worked by high pressure hoses, and thus the handling of water controls the depths of pits and ensures their horizontal extension. Not only is the depth of the kaolin unknown, but methods of extraction at depth still elude the industry.

Peat, oakwoods and water have all played their part in the many other industries which have been associated with Dartmoor historically. Peat, burnt directly or converted to charcoal, was used in the smelting systems mentioned above;

it has always been a domestic fuel, and at various times in the last 150 years has been used to distill naphtha and petrol, and for horticultural and paper-making purposes. The 'ties' from which peat was taken are scattered all over the blanket and bigger valley bogs; they create very distinctive patterns seen from the air. Coppiced oakwoods produced charcoal and tanning bark in large quantities for tanyards at Okehampton, Moretonhampstead, Horrabridge, Tavistock and Sticklepath. Water, as a source of power, was crucial to all the industries mentioned so far, but for paper-making its purity was an added bonus. There were paper mills in most of the small towns including Princetown, and at more isolated sites like Shaugh Bridge and Lee Mill. It is still made at Ivybridge.

Water is now in demand for all the needs of a growing population well away from the hills where it falls in great abundance. Sir Francis Drake first tapped Dartmoor's water for his new dockyard at Devonport, and the Devonport Leat still diverts some nineteen million gallons a day from the Dart catchment to Plymouth, via Burrator Reservoir. Burrator was the first reservoir to be built (1898, enlarged in 1928) and now there are eight, supplying the Torbay towns, Newton Abbot and Teignmouth, as well as the South Hams and large areas of north-west Devon. Leats still in use, and many more dry, are to be found all over Dartmoor, constructed to 'lead' water for all its many purposes historically, but now normally only for drinking water to farms and fields.

Much of the late historic economic activity implied above could not have taken place had not the communication systems of the centre of Dartmoor been improved. The two major routes across the moor were turnpikes constructed near the beginning of the nineteenth century; they were built on landowning/agricultural capital, and encouraged the 'improvers' to attempt development. The railways to Princetown and Moretonhampstead offered the same encouragement. Agricultural aspirations found little fulfilment in the end, but new farms like Tor Royal, the development of Princetown itself, the conversion of the prison to civilian use, and the beginning of conifer plantations all followed. The Duchy began afforestation at Beardown and Brimpts, and as time went on Fernworthy, Bellever and Soussons became the major plantations taken over by the Forestry Commission. Planting had also begun in the catchment areas of Burrator and the Hennock reservoirs, and shelter belts had become a new part of the scene in the East Dart valley. Private plantings had taken place meanwhile in the lower Dart Valley at Ausewell and Buckland.

The human history of Dartmoor up to the mid-point of the present century would not be complete without reference to the military presence. Manoeuvres began early in the nineteenth century, more permanent camps and artillery firing became established near the end of that century, and there was great expansion of the training need during the Second World War. The pattern of modern use was created in the late 1940s, and consists of three live-firing ranges at Okehampton, Merrivale and Willsworthy, and a conglomeration of 'dry' training areas around Burrator Reservoir. Permanent camps exist at Okehampton and just outside the park at Bickleigh, but local troops train on Dartmoor by the day from various establishments in Plymouth and at Lympstone.

Dartmoor as a National Park

The compact hill, whose nature and human history have just been described, was, with a skirt of attendant footslope, designated a national park in 1951. That was only two years

The little church of St Michael on the summit of Brentor

after the year of the National Parks and Access to the Countryside Act, the year when the decline of soccer watching in the flesh began, and when television sets and Morris Minors started to proliferate. Mass landscape-visiting aspirations, opportunities and means, all coincided with the labelling of the targets and the first faltering steps of infant National Park Authorities, charged with preserving their natural beauty and promoting their enjoyment by people.

Southern Devonians had long regarded 'the Moors' as a regular visit – whether it was the Sunday School outing from a South Hams village, 'bus trip from Newton Abbot to Widecombe, week-end ride to Burrator or Roborough Down from Plymouth, or the early morning trek into the high plateaux from the railway station at Lydford. Still, in the 1980s, sixty-six per cent of the eight million visits a year are made by Devonian residents – largely to picnic in a favourite spot, or 'just for a ride', or to look at the view. For this they have their popular and regular target sites, indeed particular residential areas have their favourite congregating places on the moor, so that Plymouth people concentrate on Roborough Down, at Burrator and Cadover Bridge; Torbay and Teignmouth people in the lower Dart and around Widecombe. The majority, it is clear, want a change of environment (most of them live on the coast!), and are content with that part of it which is nearest to their start point. They do not on the whole seem to mind how many others share the place with them, as long as their activities are compatible.

So there are a number of heavily-used popular sites in the park – more in the east than the west, most associated with water, though exceptions like Haytor, Roborough Down and Widecombe stand out. The first two are the first natural moorland stopping places on the direct ways in from Torbay and Plymouth respectively, the third is the best known village in England by name, because of the song, 'Widecombe Fair'. Now, the National Park Authority tries to make sure that these popular places can cope with numbers, do not deteriorate, and remain satisfying to their regulars. At the same time a real attempt is made to stop the

The start of the Ten Tors Race from Okehampton Camp

Widecombe Church, often called the Cathedral of the Moor

unsightly spread of parked motor cars into moorland from these sites.

The great majority of visitors are not venturous; they may have bursts of energy, kicking a football or swimming for a short time, but otherwise remain passive. A much smaller number actually arrive in Dartmoor to walk seriously for any distance. But some do, and walks of nine or ten miles into the plateaux and back happen, as do walks of similar lengths on the network of footpaths in the farmland landscape. There are some 500 miles of footpath and bridle-way in the park, and the Ranger service of the National Park Authority maintains and signposts them. Giving advice and guidance to visitors is part of a Ranger's job, but he is backed by an information service operating at eight centres. Information can also be obtained from shops and post offices in some villages and the National Park Authority publishes annually a free compendium of information – *The Dartmoor Visitor*.

A number of more specialized recreational activities are also pursued in the park, though it is rather better suited to some than to others. There are one or two rock-climbs, but all fairly short. Some reaches of the Dart, the Teign and the Tavy provide good canoeing at certain times of the year. Hang-gliders find the odd site for take-off, but none are spectacularly good. Many more people ride horses – especially in pony-trekking strings, and a substantial number fish, more on reservoirs than on rivers. Organized competitive sports occur from time to time – endurance riding, motor-rallying and orienteering are the commonest, but the number of such events in a year can be counted on the fingers of two hands. On the other hand 'mass' walks, usually for some worthy purpose like raising money for a medical charity, seem to be increasing in number – to the extent of clashes of timing and venue occurring, when organizers have omitted to inform anyone of their plans. There is a long-standing event of this kind called the 'Ten Tors Expedition' whose purpose is to provide a challenge for young people.

All these activities are enjoyed in a living landscape. Its development is the result of the processes which have been described here, and they are still going on. National park designation poses two problems: how to ensure that the enjoyment does not interfere with the living processes – the working of that landscape; and how to ensure that those processes under human control do not destroy the enjoyable qualities of the landscape as it continues to evolve. These two problems are in the lap of the authority which is charged with promoting the enjoyment, with ensuring social and economic well-being, and with conserving the landscape beauty of the park. Government has advised that, where there is a conflict between objectives, conservation of landscape beauty must take precedence and this advice, if followed, should help. Where the conflict is between conservation and recreation it does help, but where the conflict is between conservation and the aspirations of a farmer then a whole set of questions is exposed. How to define landscape beauty? How to quantify and evaluate the beauty put at risk? How to decide what should be done and who should foot the bill? In short, how to arrive at an agreement acceptable to all interested parties?

The landscape which accommodates most recreation, including the passive kind – picnicking, sitting in a parked car, or looking at a view – is the moor and heath in one form or another. The natural stopping places along the roads are either the edges of large moorland areas, or tiny enclaves of gorse and bracken. But the unique quality of Dartmoor is the total extent of its largest blocks of moorland. South of the Peak District, there is nothing bigger in England. That size alone allows a moorland character to develop in the interior, which cannot exist in a smaller compass. Thus it is that the changes made by farming or forestry, by water works, or mineral extraction, have to be seen as a diminution of the totality of Dartmoor, an attack on its whole beauty. Mineral working for the time-being is confined, reservoir builders have other sites in mind, foresters have agreed about the protection of moorland. Agriculture remains the chief agent of change. The farmers' circumstances vary enormously. Some cannot be blamed for increasing the value of their assets if the government pays half the cost. Others may have no farm debt and be happy to coast along, collecting subsidies, but wreaking no change in the landscape. They are increasingly rare, and market forces can change rapidly.

The National Park Authority and a hesitant government search for protective systems and ideas. Somehow the 5,000 years of landscape development and maintenance overseen by farmers has to be kept in their hands – they have the skills, and there is no alternative – but the wilful, the unnecessary, the anti-social acts have to be restrained. The Ministry of Agriculture will have to provide grant aid for landscape maintenance – optimum flocks and herds, annual programmes of burning, wall, bank and copse management; and the National Park Authority will have to add bonuses for quality workmanship, for burning patterns achieved, for new heather, for good walls, and so on.

By these means, and with work in kind by the Authority and the myriad of volunteers who come forward each year already, the resource for recreation, for the enjoyment which makes life in the late twentieth century livable may be conserved. Sustaining this yield of pleasure, of contentment derived from the hills year by year is becoming as important to a modern society as its need for the contribution to food production from the marginal lands. For the essential character of Dartmoor to survive the farmer needs his independence, but the visitor also needs the freedom to explore that character in order to appreciate it fully. Independence for the farmer and freedom for the visitor both carry responsibilities and, if these responsibilities are met by both communities, then Dartmoor will continue to provide for both. Somehow the community of farmers and the community of those who enjoy visiting the farmed uplands must merge their objectives. The need is for them to share in the aim of conserving Dartmoor, but they need also to be able to make contact with each other to stay sane. Dartmoor provides an aid to sanity, and much more, for both.

Useful Addresses

Dartmoor National Park Authority Headquarters: 'Parke', Haytor Rd, Bovey Tracey, Newton Abbot, Devon TQ13 9JQ

Dartmoor National Park Information Centres at:
Newbridge, Okehampton, Plymouth, Postbridge, Princetown, Stepsbridge and Tavistock

Devon Trust for Nature Conservation: 35 New Bridge Street, Exeter

National Trust Regional Office: Killerton House, Broadclyst, nr Exeter

Pleasure boats in the small harbour of Lynmouth, so devastated by the great flood of 1952

Leonard Curtis

Exmoor

E XMOOR IS the more diverse of the two southern National Parks. It contains an intimate, rich and varied patchwork of rolling moorland set against green, beech-hedged, pastures and is laced through with deep, wooded valleys. To the north this splendidly varied terrain ends abruptly in the magnificent Exmoor coastline, containing England's highest coastal viewpoints, sweeping down to the sea-bird colonies and the surging tides of the Bristol Channel. The whole is encompassed in a mere 694 square km (265 square miles), and only Pembrokeshire Coast National Park, seen distantly across the channel, is smaller in size.

A stag's head in black on a green triangle is the symbol which marks entry into the National Park. This is an apt reminder that the core of Exmoor was one of the sixty-seven royal forests where deer were reserved for the King. Throughout Exmoor, the wild and secretive hollows, heather slopes, wooded and bracken-strewn valleys and swift moorland streams, support a rich variety of wildlife. Here is a landscape which quickens the heart with excitement yet wraps itself with a quiet spell of emotive beauty. It drew the poets such as Coleridge and Southey, provided the setting for Blackmore's epic story of Lorna Doone, and was the home of Williamson's Tarka the Otter.

The Physique of Exmoor

At the highest point of Exmoor on the heather dome of Dunkery Beacon, 520 m (1,706 ft) the eye scans an area of broad summits and level skylines from which gentle slopes stretch in all directions to the margins of deeply incised valleys. These 'upland plains' represent levels where the underlying rocks were planed off by the action of ancient seas or rivers. They are characteristic of much of south-west England. Indeed, if one looks south-west from the heart of Exmoor towards Barnstaple Bay, it is as if a giant staircase descended towards the town of Instow. Some would distinguish a series of planation surfaces extending from the uppermost 'Exmoor' surface (1,600–1,250 ft), downward to the 'Lynton' surface (1,225–1,000 ft), then to 'Molland' (925–850 ft), 'Anstey' (750–700 ft), 'Buckland' (675–500 ft),

'Georgeham' (425–308 ft) and eventually reaching the 'Instow' surface at 280–200 ft.

No one has yet given a fully satisfying account of the formation of each of these surfaces. If they are due to erosion by the sea this would imply a sea-level falling since Cretaceous times (190 million years ago) because some academic studies support the view that the uppermost 'Exmoor' surface was cut by the sea early in the Cretaceous period, whereas the 'Lynton' surface may be a marine surface of Late Miocene age. In all probability, however, some of the levels we now see have been shaped by ancient rivers flowing into the ancient seas which once stood at much higher levels.

All of these plateau-like surfaces are fragmentary but they are all the more remarkable because there is no accord with the underlying geological structure and the rocks beneath have been intensely folded. Exmoor consists mainly of ancient sedimentary rocks affected by Armorican folding in Permo-Carboniferous times (about 350 million years

The top of Dunkery Beacon, at 1706 ft it is the highest point on Exmoor

ago). These earth movements rumpled the rocks so that most are dipping at an angle of about thirty degrees to the south with the lines of folding striking south-east to north-west. These lines are well seen if one looks at modern satellite pictures taken when the angle of the sun is low.

Most of the rocks are part of the Devonian and Carboniferous sediments that form a huge downfold that crosses the south-west peninsula. Locally the surface expression of rock types is made complex by fractures leading to fault lines. These are especially important in the Minehead region when softer and younger sediments (Permian, Trias and Lias) are preserved in low lying areas enclosed between more resistant ancient blocks.

Although the broad features of Exmoor were hewn out in the distant past, the facial expression it wears now arises from its experiences in the more recent Ice Age. We cannot be sure about precise dating of events but it seems likely that the Ice Age was drawing to a close about 14000 BC. Immediately before this, for some hundreds of thousands of years, northern Britain beyond a line roughly between the Severn and the Thames, was held in the grip of the ice sheets.

At this time pack ice floated in the Bristol Channel and in the warmer months ice floes were moved with currents and wind along the Exmoor coast. Some sea ice carried boulders from as far north as Scotland. When the ice floes stranded on the beach they melted, leaving rocks in unfam-

iliar surroundings as erratics. The pink granite boulder at the junction of beach and cliff beneath Saunton Down is one such remnant of the Ice Age.

Inland, the hills of Exmoor bore snowfields and patches of ice which waxed and waned with the seasons. In the summers powerful rock-laden meltwaters thundered down, deepening the existing valleys of the Exe, Barle, East Lyn and West Lyn. Side valleys were newly created by water erosion and all tributaries combined to carry masses of debris down from the hills to fan out as gravel or silt spreads in the lowlands. In the Aller and Horner valleys some of the gravel terraces probably date back to these times.

Meanwhile the soils formed in the warmer Pre-Glacial periods became sodden by snow melt and slipped or flowed downslope, shaping hillsides into unusual forms like that in the Punchbowl beside Winsford Hill. On rocky slopes, water freezing in cracks split open joints, so that fragments or large blocks of stone slid down the valley side, only to become further split by the frosts of subsequent winters. In this way Late Glacial stone screes were formed which now lie, grey and lichen covered, in valleys such as those of the East and West Lyn. Often these ancient screes are partly hidden from view beneath fern, scrub and woodland which have colonized large areas, as can be seen at Watersmeet near Lynmouth.

Rock buttresses with deep clefts wrought by frost action

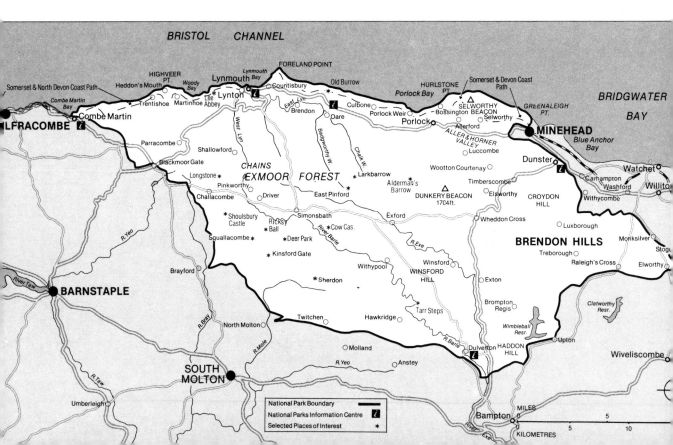

stand above many screes. Sometimes they are shaped in the form of small tors. They are well seen in the Valley of the Rocks west of Lynton. Larger blocks are usually rectangular and follow joint systems. When sky can be seen behind fallen or tilted blocks on the summits, the mind creates images from the outline. A famous example of this is the 'White Lady', formed by rock weathering near Castle Rock.

The Valley of the Rocks is now a dry valley, and it seems that the East Lyn river once flowed through it westwards towards the valley where Lee Abbey lies, and then beyond towards Crock Point. It is thought that this ancient river was progressively dismembered by the sea breaking into it at Heddon's Mouth, Woody Bay, Wringcliff Bay and Lynmouth Bay. The Lynmouth capture is so recent that the West Lyn, once a quieter tributary of the ancient river, now plunges dramatically some 400 ft within the last mile through the Glen Lyn gorge.

The coast of Exmoor is both dramatic and topographically unusual. Characteristically, a long convex slope extends down almost to sea-level before it is eroded to form a marine cliff. The stretch between Greenaleigh and Hurlstone Point near Porlock gives an example, which is repeated in the tree-clad cliffs of Culbone and the splendid headland of Foreland Point. West of Lynmouth the coast becomes more rugged, its seaward face fretted by the elements from the Ice Age onwards. Steep cliffs bound the outer wall of the Valley of the Rocks and westward between Lee Bay and Combe Martin there are great contrasts in coastal scenery. Sea-birds abound. Heddon's Mouth is a deep ravine with extensive screes stretching down to the sea. Beyond lies the high ground of Martinhoe and Trentishoe, 323 m (1,060 ft), and then the 'hogs-back' cliffs rising to 315 m (1,043 ft) where the Great Hangman and Little Hangman form a grand symmetry. Between Trentishoe and Hangman lies stony Holdstone Down where stones were cast up in circular patterns by frost action in the Ice Age, and heather-clad declivities show where ice sapped the rocks on this exposed northern coast. Here too Sherrycombe Water forms a good waterfall and then, at the westernmost boundary of the national park, Combe Martin Bay marks the point where a drowned river valley runs out to sea.

As the ice caps waxed and waned, the sea levels fell and then rose again, thereby drowning forests which had formed at the land margins. The remains of submerged forests still exist off Minehead beach and in Porlock Bay. Evidence of variation in sea levels also occurs in the raised beach deposits preserved at sheltered places as in Lee Bay. In modern times, however, it is the great tidal range which builds features such as the massive pebble beach in Porlock Bay. Its sweeping curve and stepped profile, well seen from Hurlstone Point, stands in front of marshes and pools where migrant birds tarry for a while on their long journeys.

Tarr Steps, an ancient stone footbridge across the River Barle

Plants, Animals and Early Man

It was on this varied landscape bounded by the sea and on its rocks and soils, that plants, animals and early man began to establish themselves following the Ice Age. At first, there was an open arctic tundra with copses of Dwarf Willow and Birch, as an improvement of growing conditions began around 14000 BC. At the time the Continent was still connected to southern Britain by land bridges, and Reindeer and Arctic Fox were amongst the early animal inhabitants. The early horse, from which the Exmoor pony is descended probably appeared at this time. Certain details of the teeth and bones of the Exmoor pony are thought to be adaptions to these early environments.

Gradually, a succession of woodland established itself. First Birch and Pine, then Oak and Hazel, with Alder in the wetter places. From about 6000 BC to 2000 BC a warm moist climatic phase allowed early man to penetrate the uplands.

The Middle Stone Age (Mesolithic) people, at about

8000–4000 BC relied on hunting, fishing and food gathering, and settled in places on and around the moor. Sites rich in their flint implements have been found, for example, near Hawkcombe Head. By the time of the New Stone Age (Neolithic) primitive agriculture and pasture had been introduced by people who were potters (circa 4000–2000 BC). Arrowheads uncovered in the sheltered and productive vale of the Selworthy–Minehead area were made by these folk.

It was, however, in the Early Bronze Age (about 1750–1250 BC) that the more obvious landmarks of early man began to appear. These people could make fine pottery beakers and discovered the art of alloying copper with tin to produce bronze. They lived in circular dwellings of turf, wattle and daub, and brushwood. Their dead were buried in small round barrows and most of the barrows, stone circles and stone settings of Exmoor are thought to be of Bronze Age.

Although not always obvious to the casual observer, archaeological sites are numerous, and recent surveys using air photographs reveal a very rich inheritance. Stone circles can be well seen on the heaths of Porlock Common and Withypool Hill, whereas stone-rows are best seen on Wilmersham Common. Other stone settings remain on magnificent wild moorland at Great Tom's Hill and East Pinford, recently purchased by the National Park Committee. Perhaps the most famous standing stone of this age is that of the Longstone high on the grass moor in the west near Challacombe. It stands nine feet high not far from the site of Woodbarrow. Barrows on the moor are numerous and when seen on the skyline, as at Five Barrows near Kinsford Gate, they form constant reminders of the early Exmoor folk.

These early Bronze Age people mostly lived on south facing slopes, particularly near rivers and streams. Settlement sites occur at places such as Valley of the Rocks, Shallowford Common and Great Hill, but others will doubtless be discovered as a result of recent aerial surveys.

The great open moorland of Brendon Common

The way of life changed in the succeeding Iron Age. Apart from the use of iron for the production of weapons and implements in great numbers, these tribes built impressive hill forts to protect their territories. Shoulsbury, at the western side of Exmoor, Cow Castle beside the River Barle and Wind Hill at Countisbury near Lynmouth, are examples of their work and their eye for defensive positions. There are many other remains which reflect life at this time. For example, there are stock enclosures at Sweetworthy on the slopes beneath Dunkery Beacon and at Bury Castle above Selworthy. Further archaeological survey will probably reveal other enclosures and evidence of field systems which often persisted into the Dark Ages.

Prior to the Dark Ages and the Saxon period (410–1066 AD) there is little remaining evidence of the Roman

Heddon's Mouth, a great cleft in the rocks, owned by the National Trust

period. Yet the Romans were concerned to protect themselves from the tribes of the Silures in South Wales. One can understand their fears, for on a clear day, following showers, the Welsh coast seems remarkably close to Exmoor. Two small coastal forts were built at Old Burrow and Martinhoe. They were constructed around 48–60 AD and abandoned about 75 AD when the Silures were eventually subjugated. The Old Burrow site lies on the Glenthorne Estate, through which the coastal footpath runs.

In the Dark Ages and Saxon period, Exmoor inhabitants would have lived in fear of raids or invasions. Some traces of ramparted enclosures with rounded corners may be remnants of fortified homesteads built between 400–600 AD. The best preserved is at Stock Castle near Lynton.

Caratacus Stone, on the heather-clad moorland of Winsford Hill, is one of the most visited relics on Exmoor. It is inscribed *CARATACI NEPUS* (Kinsman of Caratacus), who may have been a war chief in the early years of Roman occupation. The Stone – now enclosed in a protective shelter – is likely to have been in its present position at least since 1219, when it is mentioned as one of the forest boundary stones.

Another inscribed memorial stone stands in the garden of Six Acre Farm, Lynton. This is inscribed *CAVUDI FILIUS CIVILI* (Cavudus, son of Civilus). It was discovered in 1913, serving as a gatepost near Caffyn Cross, and moved to its present position for protection. Possibly this stone dates back to the sixth century.

In the Saxon period we look for place names ending in worthy (Saxon worthig), indicating Saxon settlement. In the heart of Exmoor the National Park Committee has acquired land at Pinkworthy and Elsworthy. Other places near the high moor such as Elworthy, Sweetworthy and two Radworthys can also be found. At this time, names often included the element 'ton' and 'ham' both meaning a farm, eg

Dulverton, Langham. The plant cover at this time must have been largely heath and grass moor with boggy places, grassy lower slopes and thickly wooded valleys with some copses. It was a struggle to maintain all of the settlements and some villages became deserted in mediaeval times.

The best known of the abandoned villages is Badgworthy. At the end of the twelfth century it belonged to the Pomeroy family, and records show they gave to the Brethren of the Hospital of Jerusalem 'the church of Brendon with its appendages and the land of the hermits of Bagwordia'. The ruins of the so-called Doone's house which we now see at Badgworthy, may be either hermitages or remnants of peasant houses. They include, however, longhouses typical of Norman times which probably replaced buildings of the tenth and eleventh centuries. For the visitor to Exmoor, Badgworthy provides a visual image to link with Blackmore's epic story of Lorna Doone and the earlier legends of Sir James Ensor Doone, thwarted kinsman of the Earl of Moray, who was exiled from Scotland, and whose family existed as raiders of the Exmoor countryside.

At the heart of Exmoor lies the parish of Exmoor Forest, which embraces some 8000 hectares (20,000 acres) of the higher ground. The land was one of the sixty-seven royal forests of England, in which deer and certain other wild animals were reserved to the King and protected by Forest Law. The protection and administration afforded by the crown virtually excluded agricultural activities for several centuries. The chronicler MacDermot wrote in 1911,

> . . . *if we except the small enclosure made at Simonsbath in the middle of the seventeenth century, we find nothing to negative in any way and much to confirm the inherent probability that the present parish of Exmoor was in the same state in the year 800 as in 1800, and as regards a large portion of it, in 1900, save for a few fences and drainage gutters.*

The Valley of the Rocks forms the backdrop to a game of cricket

A valuation in 1289 indicates that the herbage on Exmoor was valued, but records suggest that woodland did not exist on the higher ground. Only fringing woodlands at places like Selworthy are mentioned. John Leland's journey in 1540 also bears this out and by pleadings of 1617 that the royal forest had no woods or covert but was,

> *a large ground many thousand acres in extent and thirty miles round at least, time out of mind used for the pasture of great numbers of sheep, cattle and horse beasts.*

Yet there was a hint of changes to come in a memorandum of the survey of Exmoor Chase (1651) as follows.

> *Memerendum that the said Chace is a Mountenous and cold ground much be Clouded with thick Foggs and Mists . . . a verrye great part theirof is overgrowne with heath, and yielding but a pore kind of turf of Litle vallue . . . the Residue theirof being only some of the Balls or Hills, if they were inclosed might bee capeable of Improvement being a good soyle.*

It is clear that heathland, sedges, moss and acidic grassland have been the dominant components of the moorland cover for at least 800 years. Burning, grazing and turf cutting have been the chief agents modifying the vegetation during this time. Evidence of burning is afforded by Forest Inquisitions of Edward III (circa 1333–1338). Free suitors of Withypool and Hawkridge had a right to carry away as much turf, heath and fern as they could consume on their tenements. In addition the 'foresters' sold turf, or rather invited people to cut turf at established rates.

The most common land use over much of Exmoor was summer pasturing of sheep, cattle and horses. At the end of the sixteenth century animals grazed within the royal forest were estimated as 40,000 sheep, 1,000 cattle and 400 horses. It may be supposed that such grazing, coupled with browsing by deer, inhibited tree growth in areas where woodland might otherwise have been established.

Where they existed, particularly in the valleys, woods were used for feeding of livestock on acorns or beech mast (pannage) and leaf fodder. Building materials, tools, charcoal for smelting and tanbark for curing skins were other woodland products. Since prehistoric times man has gradually reduced the woodland areas so that the bulk now remains in the deep combes and steep hillsides.

Coppicing became a dominant style of management from the Middle Ages through to the mid-nineteenth century. Coppice is achieved by cutting down a tree and allowing shoots to spring from the stump. When grown for a period of seven to thirty years the new growth could be cropped for charcoal, tanbark, fuel or fencing materials.

Oak coppices grew well, but the rural population also depended on Hazel, Ash, Birch, Lime, Alder and Willow for besoms, baskets, hurdles and a host of other things. By mediaeval times Sweet Chestnut and Walnut were also present, and so a great variety of wood products was available. Some trees were subjected to a form of raised coppicing known as pollarding, leaving the new crop of shoots beyond the reach of livestock. Oak pollards of great girth remain on Exmoor and they are clearly very old.

The observant visitor will detect old, decaying, stools of coppice in many Exmoor woods. The labour requirement for coppicing became too great and many of these old coppice woods are now slowly degenerating into scrub – woodland without specimen trees or commercially useful species. Regeneration of broadleaved woodland is hindered by the browsing of livestock and deer. The latter are essentially creatures of the woods.

Coppicing of the past gave succulent food for the deer of those earlier times, and in woods reserved for the King's pleasure it was an offence to interfere with the vert or greenwood which sheltered and fed the deer. The derelict woods of today with their scrub undergrowth harbour the deer equally well. Despite their lack of marketable timber, many of these woods present varied habitats for fungi, ferns and ground flora and their associated small mammals, birds and butterflies. In spring and autumn they form colourful glades.

Nineteenth Century Reclamation of the High Moorland

It will be evident to the reader that man has gently moulded the Exmoor landscape and vegetation cover from the earliest times. In the nineteenth century the hand of man became bolder and sought out reclaimable areas of moorland. His power was to grow apace in the twentieth century as machines and chemical technology aided human efforts.

The stirrings of modern reclamation began in the heart of the old royal forest. A fascinating story of investment of external capital, reclamation and land use change began, following inclosure and sale of the royal forest in 1819. John Knight, a Shropshire iron-master, initiated reclamation works which were continued by his son Frederic.

John Knight began by attempting to farm his property on a large scale from a base at Simonsbath House. This house was built by James Boevey, and the visitor may see the date 1654 cut in an old oak beam within. Now a hotel lounge, the wood panelled room must have been used by the Knight family in earlier days.

The building of boundary walls and roads, cutting of drains and reclamation of some 2,500 acres by paring off turf, ploughing and burning the land, marked the beginning of the Knight reclamation. Shortly after the death of John in 1850, his son Frederic discontinued the practice of farming as a single unit. Instead he created allotments and built farms for letting to tenants. During this period the number of farms increased to fifteen comprising about 2,000 hectares (5,000 acres) of improved and inclosed lands.

These must have been exciting days. The modern visitor travelling from Simonsbath towards Challacombe may look towards Titchcombe, Driver, Duredown and the moorland edge, and try to imagine the scene when steam engines ploughed these slopes in the 1870s. The Sutherland plough consisted of two shares and a subsoiler resting on wooden rollers. It was drawn by ropes drawn by the steam engines and once set to work, ploughed furrows twelve inches deep and two feet wide. The subsoiler, a hook like the fluke of an anchor, was dragged beneath the surface to break up the thin iron pan, and so improved the soil drainage.

Other areas were reclaimed slowly by traditional means and gradually the farmsteads of the high moor were established. Few have lost their place as farms, but Larkbarrow and Tom's Hill have since been ruined by wartime shelling on the practice ranges of World War II. Pinkery, after a period of shepherding, has become a field studies centre.

Springtime in Bossington at the north end of Porlock beach

Present-day Wildlife and its distribution

Existing patterns of moorland vegetation are largely determined by local variations in the moisture holding capacity of the soils, together with the effects of burning and grazing. There is a central grass moorland which runs from Alderman's Barrow westward through the Pinfords and Exe Plain to the Chains and Challacombe. South-eastward from this point, another high grass moor plateau extends through Shoulsbarrow, Squallacombe, Ricksy Ball and Deer Park to Horsen.

The rolling grass moors are more suited to riding than walking. On the level summits where peat is deepest, the vegetation is dominated by Deer Grass and tussocks of Purple Moor-grass and Mat-grass. Patches of white set against dark green mark wetter places where Common Cotton-grass and Hare's Tail Cotton-grass occur, together with several different species of sedge and rush. The Heath Spotted Orchid is one of the showier flowers in this sea of grass, which changes its mood and colour according to season, cloud, wind and sky. Within the grass moor occasional drier slopes carry Bents, Fescues and Wavy Hair-grass and, infrequently, the blue Ivy-leaved Bellflower.

Boggy areas are of two kinds – valley bogs and blanket bogs – the latter fed by the heavy rains (seventy inches or more annually) on the flattish summits. Both types of bog include Round-leaved Sundew, an insectivorous plant growing amongst the *Sphagnum* moss, and with the stiff yellow spikes of the Bog Asphodel showing brightly in July.

Crowberry is fairly common and Cranberry rather rare. Besides the two kinds of Cotton-grass one can find occasional patches of Bog Pondweed growing in the standing water of old peat diggings. In the valley bogs sedges abound and Western Butterwort, another insectivorous plant, may be found occasionally.

The heather moors occur as islands within areas of reclamation or forestry. It may be convenient to refer to them separately according to their geographical location but they have a great deal in common, particularly so far as wildlife is concerned.

Along the coast from North Hill, near Minehead, to Combe Martin there are tracts of heather standing at about 300 m (1,000 ft) on rounded hills which often run down to the sea cliffs. The species include Common Heather or Ling, but in these coastal areas Bell Heather is more prominent than on other moors. This reflects the stoniness and free draining character of many of the coastal hills. The low-growing Western Gorse with its curved spines is strongly represented, and yellow competes with purple in the autumn. The Whortleberry (called the Bilberry in the North of England), Tormentil, Milkwort, Heath Bedstraw and the larger, straight-spined Common Gorse form part of this attractive moorland. Scattered, wind-pruned Hawthorns bear testimony to the constancy of the coastal winds, and there are patches of Fescues and Bents giving grassy patches on footpaths and heavily grazed areas.

Inland, the slopes flanking the central grass moorland extend up to about 425 m (1,400 ft). The soils here are rather wetter in places, and so Ling and the Cross-leaved Heath are the dominants, with patches of Moor Rush and Deer Sedge marking the wettest areas. This is an extensive area of heather stretching from Challacombe in the west, across the spurs such as Ilkerton Ridge which run down between the northward draining valleys, and on to Porlock Common and Crawter Hill. It includes the Dunkery Beacon and Alderman's Barrow moors.

To the south there are several heather-capped ridges rising above the surrounding farmland. These include Withypool Common, Winsford Hill, Molland and Anstey Commons, and Haddon Hill which overlooks the waters of the Wimbleball Reservoir. Ling and Cross-leaved Heath are the dominant heath species. The effects of grazing and extensive burning are well seen on these moorlands. In many stretches the heaths have not survived the pressure, and Purple Moor-grass, Cotton-grass and Deer Sedge are more evident, together with the all pervasive Bracken.

On the eastern side of the park, towards the Brendon Hills, the remnants of the formerly more extensive heaths are small. Most have been reclaimed for agriculture or afforested. There are, however, beautiful views to be gained from vantage points such as Grabbist Hill, Rodhuish Common and within the forested area of Croydon Hill. This is an area steeped in history, and the intimacy of the Exmoor landscape is well seen around Dunster, Luxborough, Timberscombe and Withycombe.

The moorland areas are the habitats for a wide range of breeding birds. These include Merlin, Red Grouse, Snipe,

A competitor in the Golden Horseshoe Ride passes Pile Mill, Holnicote

Curlew, Ring Ouzel, Wheatear, Stonechat, and the Whinchat, for which Exmoor is a national stronghold.

Skylark and Meadow Pipit are the most common breeding birds on Exmoor, but others include Kestrel, Cuckoo (using the Meadow Pipit as its host) and Grasshopper Warbler. Although Buzzards are often seen sweeping over the moor, they breed mainly on the moorland edge and in lowland sites. Some species such as Wren, Dunnock, Whitethroat, Willow Warbler and Yellowhammer are particularly associated with sites where gorse and heather occur together.

The migratory and wintering species making use of the moorland areas include Peregrine Falcon, Hen Harrier, Short-Eared Owl, Golden Plover, Woodcock, Common Sandpiper, Fieldfare and Redwing. The richest bird communities are to be found in moorlands which are diverse in both type of vegetation and the age structure of the plant community. Some stretches such as Molland and Cussacombe Common have very productive bird habitats with a mixture of heathers, Bracken, Purple Moor-grass, gorse, scattered Hawthorn and rushes.

Gentle slopes and improvable soils led to considerable areas of moorland being reclaimed for agriculture with the aid of substantial government grants through the Ministry of Agriculture. Earlier methods of ploughing and reseeding are now being overtaken by modern techniques of herbicide spraying, sometimes using helicopters.

There is little of Exmoor which could not be improved by a determined thrust of agricultural interests. Indeed, some see the retention of moorland as sentimental attachment to land which could be made to support greater numbers of sheep. Yet the National Park Committee is required by government to 'protect and enhance the natural beauty' of the Park. In these circumstances the National Park Authority finds itself trying to seek a balance between the farming interests and those of the community having interest in the preservation of wildlife and areas of special landscape quality.

The reclamation of some 4,800 hectares (12,000 acres) of moorland between 1947 and 1976 focused attention on Exmoor. As a result, following a public inquiry, a report by Lord Porchester published in 1977 recommended action to conserve remaining areas of outstanding landscape quality. The National Park Authority has now published maps of moorland, and made assessments which identify areas which the Park Committee would wish to see conserved for all time. In parallel with the preparation of these maps, the Park Committee negotiated with farming interests in order to set up guidelines for financial compensation to the farmers where conservation constraints were placed on the land. By the end of 1982 some thirty eight per cent of the moorland area considered by Lord Porchester to be at risk had been protected, and further areas were subject to negotiation. The agreements so far negotiated on Exmoor can be regarded as the first administratively practical steps towards ecologically sound management of the moorland. Emphasis has been placed on maintenance of existing soil and vegetation conditions, and protection of food sources for wildlife by maintaining production of biological material and nutrient cycles.

Recreation

Apart from its opportunities for touring and sightseeing, Exmoor offers several opportunities for recreational activities. Its landscape probably offers the most enjoyable riding country in England. Riders are to be seen engaged in a wide range of pursuits including pony-trekking, hunting, point-to-point races, and special events such as the Golden Horseshoe Ride. This is a test of long distance and endurance riding for which both horses and riders must qualify in preliminary rides. The final on Exmoor in May consists of a fifty mile ride on the first day, and a further twenty-five on the second. Veterinary supervision is exercised throughout, and to gain a coveted gold medal a minimum speed of eight mph and maximum veterinary marks are demanded.

Another popular feature of the Exmoor park is the waymarked walk system. Notice boards or signposts with the tip of the arm pointed in the appropriate 'route colour' have been erected at the beginnings and ends of the paths. Other marks occur on walls, trees, stakes and cairns where the route is not obvious. Booklets published by the Park Department include maps, a brief description of each walk and, in some cases, suggestions for alternative return routes. Many of the paths on Exmoor are 'permissive' paths freely granted by farmers and landowners.

Trout fishing can be enjoyed on many stretches of the Exmoor rivers. The Horner Water, Badgworthy, Oare Water, Chalk Water, Exe, Barle, Sherdon and Danes' Brook are some of the many sources of pleasure for trouting. Salmon fishing is also popular, together with sea fishing from the beach, as at Bossington, or from boats.

The completion of the scenically attractive Wimbleball Reservoir, just within the southern boundary of the park near Dulverton, has provided both fishing and sailing opportunities. The reservoir is stocked with trout, and fishing is available either from the bank or from hired boats.

Sailing in the Bristol Channel is popular, but care is needed along the Exmoor coastline with its strong tides. In the past many of the small coves were used for imports of coal, limestone and culm. Smugglers also found the Exmoor coast to their liking. In 1827 a smuggler's haul, consisting of some 202 tubs of brandy, was found at Trentishoe concealed in a farm building shortly after being landed at Heddon's Mouth from a small craft.

Sheep may safely graze at the Castle Hotel, Lynton

Nowadays pleasure craft, consisting of privately-owned yachts, fishing boats and motor boats, are mostly centred on Lynmouth, Porlock Weir and Minehead. The best way of seeing the Exmoor coastline and its bird life is from the sea. Boat trips can be made from the coastal resorts, and colonies of sea birds are particularly well observed between Lynmouth and Heddon's Mouth. Gulls, Cormorant, Fulmar, Shag, Guillemot and Razorbill are amongst the birds most commonly seen.

Bird watching is a rewarding pursuit on Exmoor. Apart from the moorland and coast, a wide range of habitats occurs in the woodlands and beside streams. The ancient oak woodlands, such as Horner Woods, offer the best homes for woodland birds. These include Green Woodpecker, Nuthatch, Tree Creeper and Pied Flycatcher as well as the common species. Beside the streams, one can often see Dippers, and in a few places, such as around Winsford, a few pairs of Kingfishers nest each year. Grey Wagtails reside through much of the year, and Herons occur near Winsford and on the edge of Porlock Marsh.

Other pursuits such as hang-gliding at Hurlstone Point, motor-cycle scrambles on Haddon Hill, and occasional motor rallies and raft races are minor activities. For the most part the car-borne visitor seeks the viewpoints on the moorland or the coast. There are, however, many opportunities to seek out the history of Exmoor within the settlements and churches.

There are several ancient churches dedicated to the early Celtic missionaries. The beautiful churches at Parracombe

(St Petrock) and Porlock (St Dubricius) are examples but one of the most famous is Culbone (St Beuno). Culbone is the smallest parish church in England – the length of the nave is 6·5 m (21 ft 5 ins). Exmoor has a rich endowment of churches with Norman associations, including some seventeen Norman fonts, and at Dunster and Hawkridge there are Norman doorways, which together with Norman features at Monksilver and Exton, point to the antiquity of the settlements.

A great variety of features of historical interest can be observed. These range from picturesque villages such as Selworthy with the white church set above, to the remains of the nineteenth century iron mining at Wheal Eliza mine near Simonsbath. The associations of people and places range from the Ship Inn at Porlock where Southey wrote a sonnet (Porlock also has associations with Coleridge), to the bridge at Exford where the highwayman Tom Faggus escaped his captors. The changing aspect of the countryside can be understood at Dunster Castle, a fourteenth century building on eleventh century foundations, which once stood over an inland seaport on the River Avill. All of these, and many more too numerous to mention, flavour the landscape with history.

The picturesque village of Winsford beside the River Exe

For those with an interest in mining and industrial archaeology, there are the remains of old shafts, mounds and slag heaps with traces of the old mineral railways. Places such as Molland, North Molton and Combe Martin appear in the early records. The principal ores were silver, lead and iron. Combe Martin silver mines were active when Edward I licensed miners, but suffered various periods of inactivity until 1796 when some 9,393 tons of ore were sent to Wales. There were other brief periods of interest in mining copper, lead and silver, but the major interest was in iron mining which led to a burst of activity on the Brendon Hills, and the construction of the inclined railway from the mines near Raleigh's Cross down to the port of Watchet. This small port – now enjoying another period of commercial use – saw some 550 vessels clearing it each year in the 1880s. Much of the trade was with the iron works in South Wales. This fell away by the end of the century when cheaper Spanish ore became available.

Frederic Knight became interested in the mining possibilities on his estate in Exmoor Forest, and signed an agreement in 1855 with the Dowlais Iron Company of South Wales for its development. It was recognized that a tramway would be needed to transport the ore. By 1857 Knight had the ground prepared along some two-thirds of the route, but

The Devon & Somerset staghounds being exercised on the road during the off-season

before a rail was laid, it was found that the ore deposit did not live up to early promise. The scheme was abandoned, but the traces of the projected railway can be found running across heather and grass moorland from Hawkcombe Head, past Maddacombe and Larkbarrow, to Elsworthy and Warren Farm.

Although the motorist and walker can gain much pleasure from tracking down the different aspects of the history of Exmoor, there is little doubt that the greatest thrill still comes from the sight of the Red Deer. They are the largest wild animals found in Britain, and a stag with a good pair of antlers stands about six feet tall. The Red Deer are widespread on Exmoor, totalling perhaps 800, and concentrations occur near the ancient oak woodlands and river valleys. Almost every evening they come out to the more open ground on the moor or on fields. Here they browse, and sometimes will settle down among the heather and gorse, particularly in sheltered positions on the leeward sides of the hills. The mating or rutting season is towards the end of September, when each stag gathers several hinds and keeps off other stags with much 'belling' (roaring) and clashing of antlers. The calves are born each year during the early weeks of June. The calf is covered with large light spots which give it a dappled appearance, and provides a beautiful form of camouflage. By the time a stag is eight years old he should have three points, 'brow, bay and trey', on each main stem or 'beam' of the horn. Yet the stag sheds its horns each year in the spring, and then regrows them in the summer months. It is in this regrowth period that the new antlers are covered in 'velvet' – a skin, grey in colour and velvety to the touch.

There are smaller numbers of Fallow, Roe and Sika deer which can be seen occasionally. The small Roe Deer is native to Britain, and is chiefly a woodland animal. It flourishes well near big Forestry Commission plantations. The Fallow Deer probably came to England with the Romans. They are mainly to be found in the eastern part of the park, particularly around Dunster. They are probably descendants from the deer parks at Dunster Castle and Nettlecombe Court. The Japanese Sika deer were introduced as park deer in 1874, and the few Sika deer in the southern parts of Exmoor have spread from Pixton, near Dulverton, to the woods of the Mole and Bray valleys.

Exmoor remains today, as it has been for centuries, a place where the wild Red Deer and Exmoor pony, along with the Fox, Badger and thousands of plants and smaller creatures survive to breed for the future. These, together with the birdlife, give enjoyment to the visitor and the Exmoor folk throughout the seasons. It is not only a summer playground. Some of its most attractive moods are to be seen in the late autumn and on sunny winter days.

The National Park now seeks to maintain that heritage into the twenty-first century, and preserve its wildlife and landscape in the face of the pressures of modern developments. The enjoyment of Exmoor springs from its diversity of form, colour and activity – all contained within a small space.

Useful Addresses

Exmoor National Park Dept: Exmoor House, Dulverton, Somerset

Exmoor Natural History Society: 24 Staunton Rd, Minehead

Exmoor Society: The Parish Rooms, Dulverton, Somerset

West Country Tourist Board: Trinity Court, Southernhay East, Exeter

Somerset County Council Tourist Officer: County Hall, Taunton

Devon County Council Tourist Officer: County Hall, Exeter

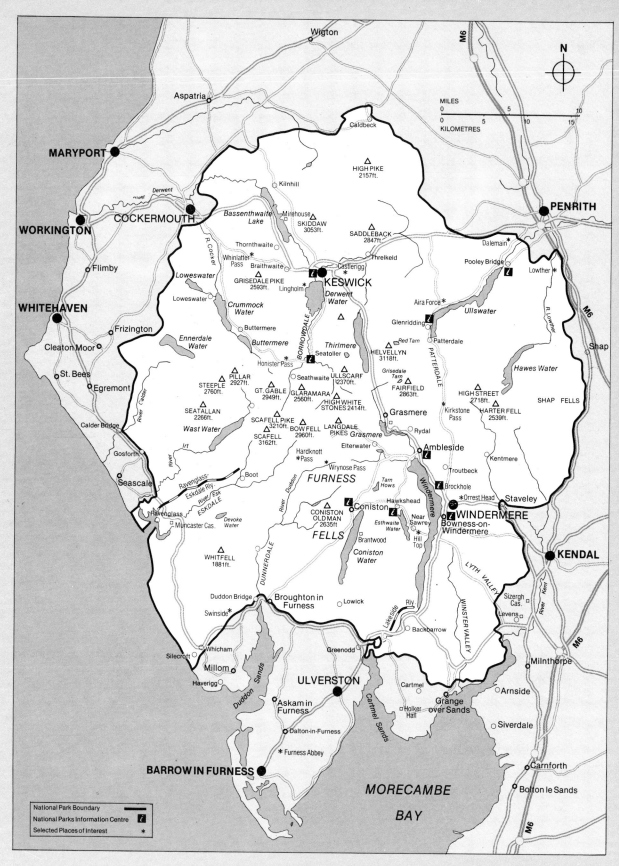

THE LAKE DISTRICT

John Dawson

Lake District

THE LAKE DISTRICT NATIONAL PARK consists of 2,280 square km (880 square miles) of land within the county of Cumbria. Just outside the park boundary, and forming the points of a St Andrew's cross, are the towns of Penrith, Kendal, Millom and Cockermouth. The only towns of any size inside the park are Keswick and Bowness/ Windermere. The principal roads through the park are the A66 from Penrith to the coast at Workington, and the A591 which runs through Windermere, Ambleside and Grasmere to join the A66 at Keswick, thus forming a rough T-shape. All the Lake District mountains are included in the park, together with all the lakes and a stretch of coastline from Ravenglass to Silecroft. Within the park the Lake District Special Planning Board is responsible for the control of new development which would alter the appearance of the countryside; not an easy task, since the needs and interests of farmers, industrialists, holidaymakers, ordinary residents and wildlife, whether fauna or flora, seldom coincide, and the uncontrolled pursuit of private gain or pleasure has usually destroyed the fragile balance on which the beauty of this unique area depends.

Geology and Landscape

The basic elements of the Lake District landscape have been created by geological action over unimaginable aeons of time to produce the astonishing variety within a small compass which is one of the principal attractions to the millions of visitors who pour in from every corner of the world. This is a region composed mainly of very old, hard rocks, none less than 200 million years old, and the majority at least twice that age. All traces of younger rock have been completely eroded from the main mountain dome, but leaving a fringe of limestone or sandstone, which may be seen round Kendal and St Bees respectively outside the park boundary, and remaining south of Ravenglass as a sandy coastline.

The oldest rocks in the Lake District are the Skiddaw Slates. These were laid down as mud about 500 million years ago during the Ordovician period, in a shallow sea which contained the graptolites and trilobites which remain as fossils today. Most of the northern part of the area consists of this dark rock, usually blue or black, from Saddleback (Blencathra) and Skiddaw itself, round by Derwentwater to Buttermere, Crummock and Loweswater, with Black Combe overlooking Duddon sands as an outlier. The shapely peaks south-west of Keswick, such as Grisedale and Causey Pikes, therefore owe their outlines to the slate which, being very fine grained, weathers into tiny pieces, and creates smooth slopes by the gradual downward creep of eroded material.

By contrast, the Borrowdale Volcanics of the central Lake District owe their origin to geological cataclysm, and still give an impression of violence by their harsh and craggy appearance. About 400 million years ago fierce volcanic activity poured out vast quantities of ash and lava. The ash solidified and was often converted by later pressures into slates, of a much finer cleavage than the Skiddaw Slates. There are no fossils in these rocks, which have been weathered by frost and rain, and battered by ice into the magnificent peaks and steep buttresses of such mountains as Fairfield, Bowfell, Pillar, Great Gable and Scafell. The crag just south of Keswick, known as Castle Crag, was a volcanic plug which solidified in one of the vents through which these mountains were first cast up. The mineral wealth, later to be exploited by mining, especially for copper and lead, was created when other masses of igneous rock later intruded into the Borrowdale Series.

Continuing to move south, the third large area within the Lake District consists of the Silurian rocks, laid down after the explosions which had created the central mountains. These are gentler rocks, softer in outline, again usually dark in colour, blue grey or black. They contain marine fossils, from the study of which it is possible to deduce whether particular strata were laid down in deeper or shallower water. The countryside round Hawkshead is characteristically Silurian; the moderately energetic pedestrian may appreciate its qualities as he follows the Silurian Way which has been marked round the Grizedale valley by the Forestry Commission.

Dividing the Borrowdale Volcanic from the Silurian rocks is the narrow band of Coniston Limestone, running from near Duddon Bridge to Shap. This is the exposed edge

Sheep on the lower fells, near Blea Tarn in the Langdales

of a much larger bed now otherwise buried by earth movements or eroded away. It is not very exciting rock, visually; indeed, it is often difficult to recognize, but it is so unusual and so rich in fossils that the better known sites have been considerably eroded by the hammers of over-zealous geologists. There is no danger of the Ennerdale granophyre, of which Buttermere Red Pike is made, and the Eskdale granite being similarly plundered; there is so much of it, and it contains no fossils. In geological terms, these two rocks represent an igneous intrusion, dating from the Caledonian orogeny.

This 'Caledonian' upheaval, which can be dated to about 400 million years ago, was a time of mountain building which raised chains of mountains of Alpine, or larger, proportions across what is now northern Britain. The subsequent geological history of the Lake District has been of the gradual destruction of these mountains, halted, rather less than 300 million years ago, by another period of uplift, the Hercynian orogeny, so that we may imagine them reduced to something like their present height at the end of the Tertiary era, approximately two million years ago.

The changes brought about in recent geological times have been due to the action of ice during the periods when the relatively drastic cooling of earth has brought a series of ice ages, the latest of which ended about 12,000 years ago. The ice dismantled the mountain slopes, plucking away pieces of rock, then carrying them down to grind out rock basins, now often containing mountain tarns, such as Red Tarn on Helvellyn; and gouging the steep-sided, flat-bottomed valleys, of which Langdale is a classic example. The glacier deepened the floor of the main valley, leaving the smaller side valleys hanging high above, so that the tributary streams, like Mill Gill, now descend as waterfalls. When the ice retreated, it left behind heaps of debris, known as drumlins, which give parts of the valley floor an attractively hummocky appearance. Most important of all, however, for us, was the way in which the action of the glaciers created the lakes by depositing quantities of drift material in such a way as to modify former patterns of drainage, and bring into being those magical stretches of water, as varied in character as Ennerdale and Coniston, Buttermere or Esthwaite.

Man in the Lake District

Only during this latest inter-glacial period has human activity begun to influence the face of the landscape. The evidence produced by the interpretation of pollen analysis and by archaeological finds combines to indicate that significant settlement did not take place until the Neolithic period, some 5,000 years ago; although people had been living near the coast round Ravenglass a millenium and a half earlier still.

They had been hunting and food-gathering people, but the Neolithic settlers were farmers who made their homes on the lighter soils at the perimeter of the main mountain massif. The 'axe factory' in Langdale dates from this period. On the scree below Pike o' Stickle, and at sites on Scafell and Glaramara, pieces of the fine-grained hard volcanic tuff were selected and roughed into shape to become axe heads after further trimming and polishing in some less inhospitable situation. These Lakeland stone axes were the area's earlier export, for they have been found in other parts of England, in Scotland, Man and Ireland.

The peoples of the Stone and Bronze Ages have left a few traces of their presence either in the form of burials, or settlement sites. Their most obvious memorials are the mysterious stone circles of which the best examples are to be seen at Castlerigg, near Keswick, and Swinside, above the road to Millom, about two miles beyond Duddon Bridge. The evidence of pollen analysis suggests that whatever kind of tools the farmers used, their way of life changed little until the second century AD.

By this time the Lake District had been occupied by the Romans. They had driven a road through the heart of the mountains from Watercrook at Kendal to Ravenglass, with intermediate forts at Ambleside and Hardknott. Another road from Ambleside ran over High Street to Brougham, an important fort on the main road to Carlisle. Archaeological work has revealed civil settlements (*vici*) at many of the forts in Cumbria, so for the first time there would be a demand for

The first new settlers to succeed the Romans were Anglians who entered the Lake District from the east in the late seventh century. Place names are the best guide to the eventually widespread distribution of these newcomers. As arable farmers, they naturally made for the area best suited to the way of life they already knew, so their 'hams' and 'tuns' are to be found mainly round the edges of the national park, in Low Furness, or along the Cumberland coastal strip – Aldingham, or Workington. Keswick, however, 'the dairy farm where cheese was made', brings them right into the mountains, as do the surviving 'mere' names for some of the lakes.

During the late ninth century, Scandinavians began to settle in the Lake District. Again, we must not think of this as a sudden ferocious onslaught, so much as a gradual infiltration, with different peoples often living side by side. Some place names, such as Coniston, look to be a combination of Scandinavian and English elements. By their thwaites and riggs, their becks and tarns, their fells and dales, they have left a strong imprint on the steep wooded valleys of the western fells. This countryside was ideal for their combination of pastoral and arable subsistence farming, basically the same as that of the Neolithic farmers who had first colonized the uplands.

The only physical remains from this period, however, are religious, in the form of the crosses and tombs which have survived in and around the Lake District. One of the best examples is at Gosforth, where the great wheel-headed cross in the churchyard combined Christian symbols with Norse mythology.

In the context of these earlier settlements, the Norman conquest was not an event of great immediate significance. The ancient pattern of agriculture had been gradually modified over the centuries to serve the needs of the small, fiercely independent communities of the upland valleys. Domesday Survey stopped short of trying to enumerate them, but eventually the Norman kings established the most efficient civil administration since Roman times, in the hands either of their feudal barons or the religious houses which were situated round the circumference of the mountains.

The abbeys, Furness, St Bees, Holm Cultram, to name the three best known, were not simply religious institutions; they were big business organizations, and the principal commodity in which they dealt was wool. By the end of the thirteenth century they owned vast tracts of land. Furness, for instance, held all the eastern part of the Furness fells between Windermere and Coniston Water, right to the old Lancashire boundary along the River Brathay, Borrowdale, and all the wild country which constitutes upper Eskdale. Much of this land they converted into sheepwalks, and exploited for the sake of the profits to be made from the wool trade. The consequences for the appearance of the Lake

whatever food the local farmers could produce, from the non-productive inhabitants of the *vici* and from the Roman military authorities. This increased demand is sufficient to explain the great expansion of agriculture which took place both on the more easily cultivated fertile ground round the fringes of the Lake District, and on the intermediate uplands, where, on Burnmoor, for example, the oak forest was irretrievably destroyed. Cereal crops, which have left their pollen in the sediments of the tarn, took their place. Although this evidence of settled life and busy economic activity is a wonderful illustration of the far-reaching effect of the *Pax Romana*, the methods of these farmers unfortunately brought about tremendous erosion, so that during the 'dark ages' there was a gradual withdrawal, as the fertility of the soil declined.

During the years following the collapse of the Roman administration in the fifth century, the Lake District formed part of the British kingdom of Rheged, which stretched from the Ribble to north of the Solway. Early Welsh sources refer to the people of Rheged as *Cymry* – 'Fellow-countrymen' – the first known use of the word which has become 'Cumbria'. Real evidence is still so scarce that we know little of life at this time. The survival of British river names – Derwent, or Esk – argues continuity from Roman days, or beyond. In his account of the life of Cuthbert, Bede tells how the saint, on a visit to Carlisle in 685 AD, marvelled at the, presumably Roman, fountain which he saw in the course of his tour of the town walls.

The Swinside stone circle dating from late Neolithic times

District were far reaching. They established 'granges', known also as 'herdwicks' – the farms where the herdmen were based – throughout their domains. Many of these herdwicks took their name from the fact that the abbot had enclosed, or emparked, what had hitherto been a tract of forest. Water Park at the foot of Coniston Water is one illustration. The land was cleared to provide grazing for the sheep, which themselves would gradually increase the area of open country by preventing the regeneration of all woodland from which they were not rigorously excluded.

Towards the end of the Middle Ages tenants, not only of the monasteries, were sometimes allowed to enclose areas which had been open common land; a process which has given many farm names to High Furness especially, as the 'ground' enclosed was named after the original encloser – Atkinson, maybe, or Dixon. After the dissolution of the monasteries these men continued where the monks had left off. Wherever the high pastures were not stinted, overgrazing slowly caused the quality of the land to deteriorate. The bare and desolate aspect of many Lake District uplands is a direct consequence of centuries of exploitation.

Nevertheless, sheep have remained the foundation of the Lakeland economy. The farmer no longer takes his oats or corn to be ground at the local mill, and he has no need to keep any cows for milking; but he is still tied to the routine imposed by his flock, and the pattern of life in the dales reflects the rhythms of the shepherd's year. Herdwick sheep,

the little agile ones with bright, grey faces and hairy-looking wool, are no longer the dominant breed. Many flocks now consist of Swaledales or cross-bred sheep which are almost as hardy as the Herdwicks, and produce a greater quantity of meat more quickly.

The sheep were not allowed to nibble away the whole of the Lake District woodlands because these also represented a valuable economic resource. The Furness monks managed considerable areas as coppices for producing charcoal to use in iron smelting, or bark for the tanneries. These industries, and others based on the lower level woods, such as bobbin making or basket weaving, continued into the twentieth century. Indeed, the Victorian cotton mills created a boom in bobbin making, and many a converted country residence today is on the site of an old bobbin mill. Although most of the coppices have become neglected and overgrown, it is still possible to see the circular pitsteads of the charcoal burners, especially in High Furness.

The forests, as distinct from the woods, have been completely transformed. When William de Lancaster shared out the Furness fells with the Abbot of Furness in the twelfth century, he wanted the forest for hunting. 'Forest' meant land set aside for the chase, not necessarily tree-covered. Sheep farming eventually put an end to practically all the Mediaeval forest. Only on one or two estates, such as Martindale, did the old order survive; then during the twentieth century, the Forestry Commission began to re-establish large areas of forest.

Exploitation of the mineral resources to be found within the national park had already begun in the later Middle Ages, when there were bloomsmithies – at Cunsey near Windermere, for example, where iron ore from Low Furness was smelted. After a lull in Elizabethan times, the iron industry expanded again, so that in the eighteenth century the great furnaces at Backbarrow and Duddon Bridge came to be of national importance. Copper mining began on an economic scale in the Keswick area during the sixteenth century, under the aegis of the Company of Mines Royal. Soon the activity was extended to Coniston, which in the nineteenth century became a mining boom town. Two other once-flourishing mining areas were Glenridding, above Ullswater, where lead ore was extracted, and Eskdale, where the miniature railway was originally built for the convenience of the iron mines near Boot.

All this activity has now passed into the realm of industrial archaeology, but slate quarrying remains very much a viable industry. The remains of small, early quarries may still be seen in many parts where the Borrowdale Volcanics outcrop. The demand for slate did not make large scale quarrying worth while until cheap and easy transport in the nineteenth century enabled it to be taken to distant places. Before this, and the Honister quarries were certainly in operation before 1750, work had been principally to meet local needs. Work continues at Honister today, as on Kirkstone, at Elterwater and round Coniston. Much of the stone is now used for ornamental purposes, such as cladding buildings, rather than for slates. Sensitive persons are apt to quail at the huge gashes in the mountain sides, but along with farming and forestry, the quarries constitute an essential part of the economic base of life in the Lake District.

Flora and Fauna

Since the Lake District National Park comprises a wide range of habitats, there is a correspondingly wide variety of both flora and fauna. Nevertheless, the sheer weight of public use in recent years has had a noticeable effect in reducing the size and number of places where certain flowers and animals are to be found. The same consequence has followed from farmers draining some of their land more efficiently, or replacing the old flowery hay meadows by a monoculture of nutritious but unexciting grass.

Centuries of heavy rainfall and overgrazing have combined to impoverish the scanty soil at the highest mountain levels. The most interesting plants grow on the few ledges inaccessible to sheep, or where a spring emerges; and the Borrowdale volcanic mountains are richer than the Skiddaw slate ones, inasmuch as their rocky ledges are at least moderately base-rich. In these places many flowers may be found in their season – such as Roseroot or Yellow Mountain Saxifrage. Dr D A Ratcliffe in a paper presented to the Botanical Society of the British Isles (1960) listed fifty-seven species on

the north-east and east faces of Helvellyn between 790 and 850 m (2,600 and 2,800 ft). The rarest plants, like Mountain Avens and Moss Campion, grow on the dry ledges where they can draw nourishment from freshly crumbled and therefore unleached rock. Few of the walkers who tramp over Helvellyn any summer's day will be likely to be aware of these plants, which owe their survival to their inaccessibility. More obvious on the stony wastes is the Parsley Fern. Two other plants which contribute to give a typically Lake District 'feel' to the high screes are the Mountain Fern and the Alpine Lady's Mantle with its silvery leaves and tiny pale green flowers.

Nor is there much bird or animal life on the mountain tops. A few pairs of Dotterel still breed. Snow Buntings are occasional winter visitors. Ravens and Peregrines may also be seen at the highest summits, although their nesting crags are seldom to be found above 2,000 ft. Of the two, the Raven is the more obvious, mainly by reason of its characteristic call. Mountain walks are seldom unaccompanied by its genial croak. In recent years the Golden Eagle has returned as a nesting bird, to add majesty to the scene by its presence. Of small birds, the Meadow Pipit and the Wheatear are the commonest representatives at these highest levels.

The lower fells and moorlands provide a less bleak and windy habitat, but not a much richer one. On the poorer soil of the Skiddaw slate country there is still, especially to the north – 'back o' Skidda' – a considerable amount of heather moor. On the Borrowdale Volcanic fell lands, the better drained soil is usually covered with Bracken Fern up to the

A church in the Vale of Newlands near Derwent Water

1,000 ft contour. Elsewhere, long over-grazing has created a cover of Mat-grass, most clearly distinguishable by its washed-out appearance in winter and of very little value as pasture. Where drainage has not taken place, as in basins, a peaty soil has developed; the wettest of these areas are known as mosses.

In former years Bracken was used extensively as floor covering, for bedding stock during the winter – a certain amount is still cut for the latter purpose – and for burning into ash, rich in potash to be made into soap for the fulling mills. However, during the twentieth century the invasive fronds have spread far beyond the area justifiable by economic criteria, and, picturesque as they are to the visitor, the land which they infest is totally valueless. No creature will eat them, and tree seedlings cannot grow in their stultifying shade. The Mat-grass which dominates the scene between 300 and 600 m (1,000 and 2,000 ft) is scarcely more sympathetic. The moors round Devoke Water are a good example of this impoverished landscape; its characteristic flowers are Speedwell, Milkwort and Tormentil, shining amid the monotonous grasses. The interested seeker may

also discover each of the common types of Club-moss – Stag's-horn, Fir-tree and Alpine.

The richest places at this level are the wet flushes by the tiny moorland becks. Here the Butterwort grows in springtime, the Grass of Parnassus in high summer. Sundew and Bog Pimpernel grow with the *Sphagnum* moss; and, possibly, Purging Flax where the ground becomes a little drier. In the larger boggy areas the yellow spikes of Bog Asphodel are conspicuous in early summer; shrubs typical of these places are Cranberry and Bog Rosemary. Where the ground is slightly less boggy, the familiar white Cotton-grass grows abundantly. In the rocky ravines of the larger becks the trees – Rowan, Holly, Ash, Oak, Birch – are a reminder of the fact that in their natural state the Lake District fells would be covered almost to the highest summits by deciduous woodland.

Birds of the moors include the lordly Buzzard, the Kestrel and (where heather grows) the Merlin among raptors; the Cuckoo where a tree or two remains; the Ring Ouzel in stony places; Wheatears, Meadow Pipits and Wrens. The Curlew and the Snipe nest here, as does the Sandpiper by the lonely tarns. The mammal most closely associated with the moorland is the Fox. No day in the winter is likely to pass without two or three of the fell packs

Little Langdale Tarn, with a farm and slate quarries in the background

strung in full cry across the screes or the open moor, with the hunt followers straining their eyes from some suitably strategic vantage point. Less romantic than the 'sandy-whiskered gentleman', but quite common, is the Adder.

The lower level woodlands and the forestry plantations together form the habitat for the greatest variety of animals. The Fox may have taken over a rabbit hole or a Badger sett as his earth; the former occupants will not be far to seek. Red Squirrels are still fairly abundant – at any rate, chasing each other noisily round a tree trunk, they are less inconspicuous than the nocturnal Badger, or the shy Pine Marten, or even the stealthy little Stoats and Weasels. But it is the Red Deer that most visitors hope to glimpse; in High Furness, parties of stags or hinds may sometimes be seen in such busy areas as the neighbourhood of Tarn Hows. The smaller Roe Deer is a very elusive creature, but is thinly scattered throughout the Lake District woodlands.

A springtime walk in these places is more likely to be rewarded by the sound and sight of the woodland birds, perhaps Wood Warblers or Chiffchaffs; at this time of the year one may also glimpse Flycatchers, Pied or Spotted, and Redstarts. In recent years Nuthatches have established themselves more securely. Jays and Green Woodpeckers can often be heard, if not seen. These birds, and many others, such as the shadowy Woodcock, live in the mixed deciduous woods. The Spruce and Pine plantations have favoured certain small species. The ones most likely to be seen by the patient watcher are Tree Creepers, Coal Tits and tiny Goldcrests; Crossbills are said to be less rare than formerly.

The floors of the oak- and mixed woods (which include Hazel, Ash, Birch and Alder) are much more interesting than those of the coniferous forest. In spring the Lesser Celandine, the Wood Anemone and the slender Earthnut grow, Daffodil, Primrose and Wild Strawberry. Greater Stitchwort, Bluebell and Foxglove follow, and Golden Rod, with many others, depending on the season, the nature of the soil and the density of the tree cover. The Borrowdale woods represent a particularly fine example of this type of habitat, for they are uniquely rich in England in the abundance of their ferns, mosses, liverworts and lichens. Above the Vale of Newlands nearby, the high Keskadale oak-woods may be a fragment of the original forest cover. In High Furness there are considerable remains of the old coppice woods, mainly Hazel and Oak, as well as more than the average amount of 'amenity' woodland, planted anything up to two hundred years ago to diversify and beautify the larger estates. Here, too, the Wild Cherries are conspicuous in springtime, and in winter the dark masses of the Yew trees enrich the bareness of the landscape.

Then, in the extreme south of the park are the limestone woods of Yewbarrow, Whitbarrow and Underbarrow Scar. Ash forms a larger element in these woods, and the Small-leaved Lime grows here, near to its northernmost limit. The strongly-smelling Ramsons is one of the commonest wild flowers, but in some places Daffodils are even more numerous than on the sites made famous by Wordsworth. Rareties include Lily-of-the-valley and three varieties of Helleborine – Broad, Dark-red and Long-leaved. Some unusual butterflies, Scotch Argus and Brown Argus, are to be seen in this limestone country, since their caterpillars feed on plants only to be found here. Near the top of the scars the trees thin out to reveal a bare 'pavement', deeply fissured by crevices often filled with ferns and flowers. Looking down from these heights into the adjoining valleys, that of the Lyth, for example, in spring, the walker cannot fail to be moved by the white profusion of blossom in the Damson orchards.

The hedgerows and pastures of the cultivated dales each

Tilberthwaite and Wetherlam seen from the road at Tarn Hows

Tony Warburton, Warden of Eskmeals Nature Reserve, with Ambrose, an Eagle Owl chick

have their own characteristic flora and fauna. Bird Cherry is still abundant along the remoter lanes; in a few damp meadows the Globe Flower flourishes. In June the wild roses illuminate the darkening foliage of the hedges; and everywhere the yellow Welsh Poppy is to be seen throughout the summer. Although mechanization has speeded the processes, hay-making may well be in progress as late as August at the dale heads, due to the practice of giving the sheep an early bite when the grass first begins to grow, and the unpredictable rainfall.

Certain birds and animals are more noticeable in the dales than elsewhere. The canny Chaffinches assemble at the car parks, knowing they will be fed. Almost any bridge has its attendant Dipper on the stones or in the water below. The stone walls form an ideal home for Pied Wagtails. In villages like Coniston where there is an abundance of heavy late nineteenth-century stone building, the Swifts scream through the streets, and bats come out at night. Darkness also brings the hunting owl, betrayed by its ghostly cries; and the homecoming villager sometimes finds a Hedgehog shuffling along his garden path. Hares live in the fields, and may occasionally raid the cottage gardens during the coldest winters.

The lakes themselves are a source of endless interest to the naturalist. Relatively, there are not many flowers or mammals. In marshy places by the margins the yellow Flag Iris makes a brave show, and in the water the lilac-coloured Water Lobelia is widely distributed, as, in sheltered places, is the Water Lily. The Otter may still live in the national park; the visitor is far more likely to glimpse one of the rapidly expanding population of escaped American Mink.

More attractive and numerous are the wild birds. The Planning Board claims that over seventy species breed round the margin of Bassenthwaite Lake, which it has owned since 1979. Characteristic birds here are the Redshank, paddling along the shore, the dignified Great Crested Grebe, the perky little black and white Tufted Duck which vanishes into the water as you look at it, and the more discreet Goldeneye. The fisherman on the quiet middle reaches of Coniston Water will usually see a Cormorant or two, purposefully heading up or down the lake, a raggy Heron flapping untidily to fresh fishing grounds, and squadrons of Mallard. On the tarns up to about the 300 m (1,000 ft) contour, there will usually be a number of resident Coots or Moorhens; these birds take a winter holiday on one of the larger, milder lakes such as Windermere. Swans, occasionally Whooper or Bewick's as well as Mute, have maintained their long association with the area – Elterwater, in fact, means 'Swan lake'.

Some of the ducks, and undoubtedly the Cormorants, are there for the sake of the fish. The game fish include Salmon, both Sea and Brown Trout, Char, Schelly and Vendace, some of a very local distribution. Coarse fish to attract the angler are Pike, Perch, Roach, Rudd and Eel. Salmon are not plentiful on account of widespread disease during the 1970s, but a few are said to run still through Ennerdale and Coniston Waters, for example. The most usual range of fish consists of Trout and Char, Pike and Perch. All of these are numerous in Windermere, Coniston and Thirlmere; and in Buttermere and Crummock Water of the smaller lakes. Char in particular have long been regarded as a great delicacy – in the seventeenth century Sir Daniel Fleming referred to them most appreciatively. They resemble Trout, but have a more delicate flavour. The principal home of the Schelly is Ullswater, and Bassenthwaite is the only lake where the Vendace is to be found. These two whitefish species are smaller than Trout. In Esthwaite Water there are quantities of Rudd and Roach; but the most widely distributed of the coarse fish are Pike and Perch. Tons of Perch were taken from Windermere

Trail hounds and their handlers, waiting for the start, near Grasmere

in the 1940s as a contribution to the nation's food supply, and now the individual fish tend to be several times larger than they used to be fifty years ago. Catching eels is a specialized business, but the traps at the outfalls of some of the tiny tributary becks testify to the fact that the skill has not been entirely lost.

The coastal section of the national park constitutes yet another type of habitat, and includes the important Eskmeals Nature Reserve, managed by the Cumbria Trust for Nature Conservation. Most of this coastline is remote and sandy, backed by low crumbly cliffs or sand dunes. Its most famous inhabitants are the Natterjack Toads, but they are not the only ones. There is a gullery at Ravenglass; Ringed Plovers nest regularly. Butterflies dance about in the summer time, some of them rare, such as the Fritillaries, Pearl-bordered and Dark-green. The plant life is abundant, too, and includes the yellow Horned Poppy, the Creeping Thistle and the majestic Sea Holly.

Conservation and Recreation

The combination of such a range of attractive habitats with the proximity of millions of human visitors inevitably creates tensions. Unrestricted access and free-for-all development would rapidly destroy those qualities which make the Lake District unique, yet it would be impossible, even if it were desirable, to convert the area into a playground entombed in a museum. Two locally-based voluntary organizations contribute a great deal of informed opinion and sheer hard work to the task of ensuring that development respects the character of the area, and does not needlessly destroy its beauty – the Friends of the Lake District and the Cumbria Trust for Nature Conservation. The Trust, in fact, owns or leases several nature reserves within the national park, where, by its

positive management policies, it ensures that vulnerable habitats and rare species are able to survive. Three national organizations also have a large interest in the Lake District – the National Trust, the Nature Conservancy Council and the Forestry Commission.

In the past the Forestry Commission was often regarded as a destructive agency. Although some of its early planting was unimaginative and insensitive, more recent work has taken account of the appearance of the plantations, and has included a greater number of broad-leaved trees. The Commission's work at Grizedale, indeed, has been entirely constructive. The old oakwoods are managed as hardwood forest; the softwood plantations have been related to the underlying soil and the contours of the land, and carried out in such a way as to preserve the area as a habitat for deer. Numerous forest walks have been laid out and waymarked for visitors, for whose benefit also wild life observation platforms have been constructed. The site of the former Grizedale Hall is a car park, a campsite occupies the area below the garden terraces, and the estate buildings house a museum, a wildlife centre and a theatre.

The Nature Conservancy Council manages national nature reserves in the Lake District as part of its countrywide responsibilities. One of these, North Fen, Esthwaite, where reeds are still building out into the lake, is of unusual scientific interest in the plant and animal communities which it supports. Another, Roudsea Wood and Mosses, by Greenodd sands, includes both Carboniferous Limestone and Silurian rock formations, as well as adjacent mossland. Conservation management here aims to re-establish uneven-aged high forest over the wooded area, and to prevent the mosses from drying out. Land management decisions are relatively straightforward where the Nature Conservancy Council has sole control over a site; elsewhere it can proceed only by persuasion. Landlords have agreed to act in ways which will further conservation objectives – perhaps by maintaining a traditional flowery hay meadow, or planting a stand of broad-leaved trees. In addition, the Conservancy has designated numbers of sites of special scientific interest in the park. These include the Borrowdale oakwoods and the rock ledges of Helvellyn and Fairfield.

By its management policies the National Trust likewise contributes a great deal to the positive conservation of the Lake District. As owner of many hill farms, including those at such spectacular and vulnerable dale head sites as Brotherilkeld in Eskdale and Cockley Beck in Dunnerdale, the Trust goes to a lot of trouble and expense to ensure that its properties are well maintained in a style which matches their situation. In return, the Trust expects, and receives, a high standard of farming practice from its tenants. As well as these often marginal agricultural properties large areas of the highest ground in the national park – from Scafell round to Great Gable and Kirkfell, and Bowfell and the Langdale Pikes – are owned or leased by the Trust.

The most important conservation agency is the Lake District Special Planning Board. In the words of its own publicity leaflet, 'As well as the tasks imposed by the National Parks Act – preservation of beauty and promotion of enjoyment – the Board has a third duty to look after the welfare of the people who live and work inside the National Park'. It is not always easy to reconcile these duties, and sometimes the Board has to come down firmly on one side or

Wastwater, deepest of the lakes at 258 ft, and the Screes

the other where interests conflict. Thus it has followed a policy of establishing speed limits on all the major lakes except Windermere; and very detailed guidelines have been prepared on the vexed question of the circumstances in which barn conversions will be allowed.

The board impinges on the general public most clearly in the work of its specialist agencies. Through the Youth and Schools Liaison Service it is endeavouring to educate a new generation to the responsibilities of using a national park, in terms of safety rules on lake and mountain as well as consideration for residents and other holidaymakers. This service operates principally through its numerous publications and the courses for instructors which are organized. The full-time Rangers with their teams of Voluntary Warden helpers really do range the fells and dales throughout the year. Their tasks are multifarious – helping walkers who are in difficulties, clearing litter by the sackful, helping the Royal Society for the Protection of Birds to protect Peregrine Falcon eyries, patrolling the lake to ensure that the by-laws are being observed. Thirdly, there is the Upland Management Service, which was pioneered in the Lake District. Management staff, working on a very small budget, have done a great deal to smooth relationships between farmer and walker, and to make life easier for both. Examples of this work in 1981–2 were improvements to bridleways in Borrowdale, including the construction of bridges, and a new riverside footpath in Grasmere village. The Upland Management Trail in Great Langdale demonstrates in a practical way the concepts behind this work. The visitor is able to see, as he walks from Dungeon Ghyll into Mickleden, how walls have been repaired, drains improved, trees planted, eroded paths rebuilt, and a new footpath created by agreement with the farmer, which has had the effect of reducing damage to his walls and haycrop by straying walkers.

In its Visitor Centre at Brockhole (Britain's first National Park Centre), between Windermere and Ambleside, the Planning Board attempts to set out the scope and objectives of its work. It incidentally provides a whole range of activities for the benefit of holidaymakers. Some of these are fairly strenuous, like the regular guided 'Troutbeck Trot', a three to five mile scenic jog. Others are gentler, maybe tours of Brockhole's magnificent gardens, sloping down to the Windermere shore. Others again are informative, lectures or slide-shows, not forgetting the children, for whose interest there are many special programmes.

However, individually-planned outdoor activities are the principal form which recreation takes in the Lake District, and walking remains easily the most popular. Much of the upland is common land; there are many clearly signposted low-level footpaths. These circumstances make the national park ideal walking country. The fitter and more adventurous make for the high fells, where the rock faces on

many of the Borrowdale Volcanic mountains also give the opportunity for rock climbing. Paths to the popular summits like Helvellyn or Coniston Old Man have become broad eroded scars, and roped queues are apt to form by the Napes Needle on Great Gable, but it is never difficult to find quieter and equally rewarding places, even at the height of the holiday season. Particularly in winter, climbing or even fell walking can be exceedingly hazardous on account of the severity of weather conditions. As an alternative to mountain walking, especially if there are young children in the party, the miles of sandy shore north and south of Silecroft are firm, clean and usually empty.

Since snow cover is not reliable, skiing is an occasional recreation only. One of the most popular venues is the top of Kirkstone pass, where the Planning Board has provided car parking space, and the near presence of a friendly inn adds to the attractions. Orienteering is less dependent on the vagaries of the weather, and in recent years has increased in popularity, as has pony trekking.

The lakes provide their own range of recreational activities; as on the fells, always tempered by hazard. Many people like to swim, but, for example, Coniston Water suddenly becomes very deep within a few yards of much of its shoreline, and Wastwater is cold as well as deep. A more sedentary sport is fishing, which is permitted on most of the lakes. Local inquiries should always be made on the subject of licences. Sailing is easy on Ullswater, Derwentwater, Windermere and Coniston where regular pleasure boat services operate during the season. The smallest-scale service is also the most picturesque one, that provided on Coniston Water by the National Trust's rebuilt 'Gondola'. Bassenthwaite lake, along with the ones listed above, is open to rowing boats, canoes, dinghies and wind surfboards. Each lake has its own rules and regulations about moorings and launching. On Bassenthwaite, as an illustration, arrangements are under the control of the Bassenthwaite Sailing Club which uses the area at the foot of the lake, and the Planning Board, which owns the lake. Only on Windermere does power boating, with its attendant throng of water skiers, take place. Plans are currently afoot under the aegis of the Planning Board to give the public access to the shores of Thirlmere, and to permit quiet forms of sailing.

At a less purely physical level, the Lake District provides ideal conditions for pursuing outdoor hobbies such as photography, bird watching or industrial archaeology. Two important sites connected with the iron industry, the Stony Hazel forge, Rusland, and the Duddon Bridge furnace, are under the care of the Planning Board, with a view to their ultimately being opened to the public. Hundreds of thousands of people each year visit the various houses or gardens in or just outside the National Park, which have historical or literary associations.

Of the former, the best known are Muncaster Castle, near Ravenglass; Lingholm, south of Keswick; Hutton-in-the-Forest, north of Skiddaw; Lowther and Dalemain in the north-eastern quarter; Holker in the south, near Cartmel, where the old priory church is worth the trouble of a long pilgrimage to see; and Levens Hall and Sizergh castle quite close to each other, off the A6 road south of Kendal. Visits to the 'literary' houses alone would fill a week's crowded itinerary. Wordsworth more than anyone else shaped our vision of Lakeland, so it is fitting that there should be houses where he lived at Cockermouth, Hawkshead, Grasmere (where a splendid museum has now been established next to Dove

Cottage) and Rydal. Ruskin's home for thirty years, Brantwood, is on the east side of Coniston Water; Tennyson had considerable associations with Mirehouse, on the east side of Bassenthwaite; Hill Top at Sawrey has become a national shrine to Beatrix Potter's immortal characters.

The Lake District, then, is a place where people live and work, and also one to which they come to re-create themselves. On one of the tiny diamond panes in the south window of Wasdale church is an etching of the Napes Needle, with the words, 'I will lift up mine eyes unto the hills whence cometh my strength'.

Walkers in the Vale of Newlands, returning from the Borrowdale fells

Hikers, sleeping in on a fine morning at Whistling Green, Duddon Valley

Useful Addresses

Lake District Special Planning Board HQ: Busher Walk, Kendal

Lake District National Park Centre: Brockhole, Windermere

Nature Conservancy Council: North-west Regional Office, Blackwell, Windermere

The National Trust: North-west Regional Office, Rothay Holme, Ambleside

Cumbria Trust for Nature Conservation: Church Street, Ambleside

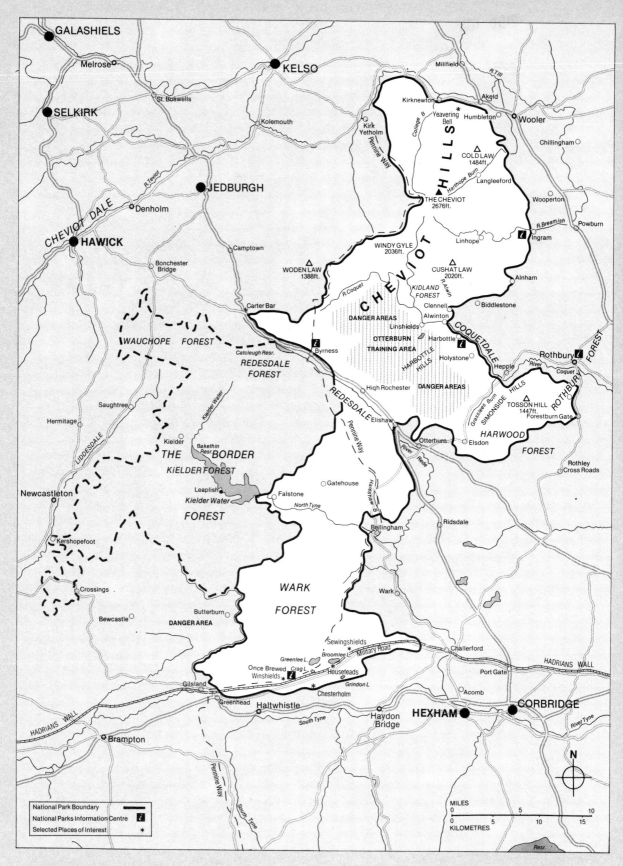

NORTHUMBERLAND NATIONAL PARK

Geoffrey Wright

Northumberland

THE NORTHUMBERLAND NATIONAL PARK was designated in 1955 and covers 1,031 square km (398 square miles) of mainly open upland country in England's most northerly county. Extending from the Roman Wall area in the south as far as the Scottish Border along the crests of the Cheviot Hills over forty miles away, it embraces many diverse types of landscape and scenery, which fall naturally into five distinct regions. In the north are the Cheviot Hills themselves, forming the largest of these regions, and extending southwards to the Coquet valley. Coquetdale itself, and the eastward-curving arc of the Simonside Hills, form the second region, while further south the softer, more pastoral valleys of the Rede and North Tyne form the third and fourth regions. Finally, along the park's southern edge, the area of the Roman Wall comprises a stretch of country whose historical background makes it unique in Britain.

Much of the park area is moorland and hill-country of sombre colouring and smooth lines, with birches and heather and out-cropping crags. Valleys and dales contain few villages, but many stone-built farms with their green meadow pastures and shelter-belts of trees. Beyond the Tyne gap moors rise steadily, their even slopes repeatedly broken by north-facing escarpments, the land gradually becoming higher towards its Cheviot climax.

Geology and Landscape

The rocks which make up the solid geology of the park are of two types formed during two distinct periods of time. The older group comprising the Cheviot Hills are of Old Red Sandstone age, made up of volcanic and associated rocks brought to the surface about 300 million years ago. Lying around them is the younger group of sedimentary rocks, a series of crumpled layers dipping and tilting away from the Cheviot dome and forming a broad concentric vale round its eastern and southern flank, its smoothness broken by occasional sandstone outcrops which are important landscape features on the south of the Coquet valley.

The Cheviot Hills are made of igneous rocks, formed under intense heat deep down inside the earth. Violent volcanic explosions, probably centred on a crater west of

Cheviot itself, brought huge masses of molten debris to the surface, scattering it as a thick deposit of agglomerate, upon which successive lava flows emanating from many craters, accumulated to thousands of feet in thickness. These lava flows eventually solidified, only to be partially re-melted with more masses of molten rock forced to the surface by great subterranean pressures a long time after the original volcanic activity had subsided. This new mixture, rich in silica, is granite, its upper face lying some distance below the old lava surface. Subsequent smaller-scale movements resulted in the formation of vertical sheets of molten rock, two to one hundred feet thick, known as dykes. These were intruded into the granite, spreading radially in the southern part of the Cheviots.

Eventually, after millions of years, weathering gradually eroded vast amounts of surface lava down to its granite stock, together with the dykes, and this hard, grey Cheviot granite forms the main mass of these northern hills. One well-known exposure of it can be seen by Linhope Spout, on the Linhope Burn at the head of the Breamish valley. Where dykes cross streams, their hardness has left them as outcrops, while at Biddlestone the conspicuous hillside scars mark where the red, fine-grained rock of the dykes has been quarried for road stone.

Subsequent erosion on the Cheviots brought down huge quantities of boulders and pebbles to the shore-line which surrounded the hills, spreading them out into deposits which eventually consolidated into conglomerates. On top of these, finer deposits of sand and mud were slowly laid down on the sea-bed, with alternating conditions of clear water in which various forms of marine life flourished. These lime-bearing organisms resulted in layers of limestone being formed, alternating with the sandstones and shales, a succession of strata known as the Cementstones, the oldest of the Northumbrian Carboniferous rocks, nicely exposed in the gorge of the Coquet above Alwinton.

Above the Cementstones, and therefore younger than them, are hundreds of feet of Fell Sandstones, created as a huge delta of a river which drained mountain ranges to the north and west. Subsequent geological events repeated what had gone before, with the addition of periods of growth of vegetation in swampy areas, resulting first in the formation of peat which later became compressed into coal. Thus, with the 1,200 m (4,000 ft) of successive layers of sandstones, shales and limestones thin coal seams occur, the most workable being in the Scremerston Coal group.

Earth movements which followed Carboniferous times, concentrated in the Cheviot area, brought the Carboniferous rocks above the older lava flows and tilted the latter outwards. Faults developed into which dykes of molten basalt or dolerite were forced, and sometimes this magma intruded horizontally between layers of sedimentary strata, as sills, of which the Great Whin Sill extending from Greenhead in the south-west to Bamburgh and the Farne Islands is the most distinctive and famous. Its average thickness is about 30 m (100 ft), although in places it exceeds 60 m (200 ft), and because it is hard, its resistance to erosion has resulted in its playing an important role in creating dramatic scenic effects across Northumberland.

Within the past million years England was almost completely and repeatedly covered by vast ice-sheets, the last time being about 12,000 years ago. Broader landscape features survived, but changes in relief and surface detail did occur. The Cheviot Hills were sufficiently high and extensive to build up an ice-cap and hence create a centre of ice accumulation, but the rest of the park area was largely covered by ice sheets streaming eastwards from the hills to the west in northern Cumbria and southern Scotland. Scouring the land and tearing debris from its surface, these ice sheets – flowing as glaciers in valleys – deposited debris as

Hadrian's Wall near Housesteads, following the Whin Sill escarpment

boulder-clay to a thickness of thirty feet, subsequently creating a landscape of quite low relief. The main river valleys were smoothed, and as the ice sheets gradually receded moraines and melt-water channels were formed.

On the northern and eastern flanks of the Cheviots are many examples of deep channels, sometimes at high level, cutting across hill spurs between neighbouring streams, and frequently 'dry'. Monday Clough above Humbleton, near Wooler is a spectacular example, while a few miles south, at Powburn, the A697 follows such a channel cut through the Fell Sandstone ridge. Another feature of boulder-clay deposits is the result of stagnant ice-sheets trapped by land relief and slowly decaying *in situ*, forming hummocky ground of sands and gravels. Kettle moraine ground such as this occurs west of the A697 near Wooperton.

At the southern end of the park the characteristic profile of the Whin Sill escarpment has been sharply emphasized as a result of erosion by southward-moving ice. The ice scooped out hollows in the soft shales before riding over the much harder rocks, well demonstrated in the westwards view from Hotbank Farm on the Roman Wall, where Crag Lough fills such a hollow. Sewingshields and Winshields, east and west of Crag Lough respectively, are two further vantage points from which this glacial feature can be observed.

Man in the Park

As the ice retreated and the climate improved to allow the growth of trees and forests in warm, damp conditions, small groups of Mesolithic hunters and fishermen reached Northumberland from the eastern flanks of the Pennines further south. There is no evidence that they penetrated the park area, but between 3000 BC and 2000 BC Neolithic immigrants, bringing some knowledge of arable and pastoral farming, filtered to the eastern edges of the park, settling in the central and lower parts of valleys. Later, the Beaker-folk from Rhineland and the Low Countries reached the east coast and worked their way inland along river valleys. A stone burial-cist lying in the heather at Lordenshaw on Garleigh Moor, south of Rothbury, and other open cists above Happy Valley south of Wooler date from this period. Burial-mounds or cairns of Early Bronze Age date suggest that the Simonside Hills were favoured by settlers, while the enigmatic 'cup-and-ring' markings, probably of about 1500 BC, also occur along the Fell Sandstone arc stretching north-eastwards from Simonside. On the east slope of the Lordenshaw hillfort are a number of these marked rocks.

Over the next thousand years successive immigrants from the continent, bringing a Celtic way of life and an iron-working culture, gradually infiltrated the existing Bronze Age population. Many settlements of this pre-Roman Iron Age culture exist in the park area. Revealed by crop-marks or excavation these took the form of groups of timber-built round houses grouped within protective fences or palisades, usually on upland sites. On the ground it is hard to differentiate between 'camp', 'enclosure', 'settlement', or 'hillfort', but the Ordnance Survey use 'hillfort' whenever justified by the siting of such earthworks on hills.

The greatest concentration is in the Cheviot area, where the largest hillfort, on Yeavering Bell west of Wooler contained at least 130 hut sites within an area of thirteen acres enclosed, unusually, by a good stone wall. Most settlements, however, were much smaller – rarely more than an acre – and can be identified on hills above most valleys along the northern and eastern fringes of the Cheviots, down to Coquetdale and the Simonside Hills, the numbers diminishing in Redesdale and North Tynedale. A journey up the Breamish valley above Ingram shows a characteristic proliferation of settlements on hill-spurs above each side of the river, culminating with the evocative survival at Greaves Ash, above Linhope, at the end of the road. Forty huts in two groups are enclosed within outer walls containing many huge boulders. Iron Age hillforts and enclosures were occupied before, during, and following the centuries of Roman domination, and it is written Roman sources which provide evidence of the Celtic way of life.

The Northumberland National Park has the distinction of possessing one of the most impressive monuments of European antiquity. Striding across the crest of the Whin Sill the Roman Wall still evokes an impression of imperial power. The Roman conquest did not reach the Tyne until 79–80 AD, and its garrisoning was based on an east–west route, the Stanegate, between terminal forts at Corbridge and Carlisle. The line of this Roman road forms, for many miles the southern boundary of the park, and includes the intermediate fort at Chesterholm (*Vindolanda*). The wall itself was started about 120 AD, by the Emperor Hadrian, as a raised, fortified patrol route, a physical barrier to withstand and trap attackers from the north. At intervals along it were forts, Housesteads (*Vercovivium*) being the most outstanding one within the park area, once housing 1,000 men. Today, the most spectacular remains of the wall are between Sewingshields in the east and Gilsland, just across the Cumbrian border, eighteen miles away. Between the main forts were mile castles and turrets, of which many sites survive. Easy access to the wall is from the 'Military road', B6318, which follows it closely from Chollerford to Gilsland. Near the National Park Information Centre at Once Brewed, between Housesteads and Cawfields, the Steel Rigg carpark is a convenient base from which to explore particularly fine stretches of the wall.

North of the wall the national park has three forts on Dere Street, the Roman road now followed by the A68, from Corbridge northwards to the Scottish border, but the most dramatic of Roman encampments must surely have been that at Chew Green, on the Border itself, 425 m (1,400 ft) up in the Cheviots, and accessible only to walkers following the Pennine Way beyond High Rochester, in Redesdale, or by a track leading from the head of the Coquet. Skylark song and sheep voices are the only sounds breaking the solitude above the enormous, grass-covered ground-plan of two adjacent rectangular camps.

In the fifth century, following the departure of the Romans, Northumberland's scanty population reverted to its pastoral life. The area of the park remained very much a waste, with native Britons occupying defensive hillforts. Sixth and seventh-century Anglian settlement rarely penetrated into the upland valleys, but gradually Northumbria emerged as a strong independent Kingdom by the eighth century. The park area continued to be economically very poor, much of it debatable land fought over by Scots and the Vikings who had settled in the north during the ninth century; but by the end of the tenth century an earldom of Northumbria had been established with a northern frontier, the first Anglo-Scottish one, running roughly along the Tweed valley to Yetholm and then along the Cheviot ridge. The park area lay within this earldom which continued through the Middle Ages to retain features of an independent kingdom, divided into modest baronies, and remarkably unaffected by the Conquest. The Norman family of de Umfraville held the Liberty of Redesdale (including upper Coquetdale) from 1100 to the fourteenth century, building as their first headquarters the motte-and-bailey castle at Elsdon, and later the castle at Harbottle, both guarding routes into Scotland. Of the Liberty of Tynedale only part of the North Tyne valley comes within the park area, with its old headquarters at Wark Castle just outside the boundary.

For centuries before the Conquest grazing stock had cleared scrub and vegetation from Northumbrian hillsides. Herds of cattle moved regularly between seasonal grazing lands. Almost all the hills between Coquet and the Border were grazed by sheep owned by Cistercian monks of Newminster, near Morpeth, yet between about 1150 and 1300 adventurous settlers continued to colonize some of the remotest areas, virgin land was cleared and ploughed, and even the moorlands of Rothbury Forest and the slopes of Simonside were cultivated for the first time. Population growth and increasing prosperity resulted in the churches at Bellingham and Elsdon being built – the only notable ones in the park area. By far the most outstanding structures are the peles and bastles which date from the time of the Scottish wars, between 1296, when Edward I declared war on Scotland, and the Act of Union of 1603.

Edward also instituted the system of control by Wardens of the Marches, with the English side of the Border a military zone divided into two, later three, Marches, with

off the tenants, contributed to this – Clennell and Biddlestone both being thus affected. Many villages in upper Coquetdale were deserted, but the old ridge-and-furrow pattern of their fields survives as a shadowy reminder, illustrated to perfection on the grassy hillsides above Alwinton.

One outcome of the Act of Union was a revival of the old drove roads through the Cheviots, and into Tynedale and Redesdale, and these saw their heyday during the eighteenth-century droving trade which brought thousands of Scottish cattle southwards. Many of the tracks converge, and where this occurs there is likely to be a frontier village, of which Elsdon is the ideal example, with a large village green (the only one in the park area), which served as a grassy market-place, with drovers' inns, a pound, and a church occupying an island site. This, like other churches in the Cheviot area such as Alnham, Alwinton and Holystone, has a characteristic open bell-turret on its west gable wall. Elsewhere in the park the very few churches have small western towers, which, like their windows, are later additions.

Domestic buildings, from the simple one-storey cottages to the larger farms and manor houses, are of stone, usually with slate roofs. Along the southern and eastern edges of the Cheviots hamlets are formed round four-square late Georgian farmhouses with a cluster of farm buildings and cottages nearby, built for the farm labourers. Stone walls, usually of the late eighteenth century, divide upland fields, while hedgerows do the job in the valleys. Circular enclosures, dry-stone walled, called 'stells', are a feature of Cheviot valleys, and were used for impounding sheep.

Farming is by far the chief form of livelihood in the park, and since three-quarters of the area is rough grazing, mainly on land above 305 m (1,000 ft), sheep-breeding predominates, and there may be as many as a quarter of a million sheep on summer grazings. On the 'white' land (ie Cheviot grasslands) is the Cheviot breed native to the Border country, while the hardier Scotch Blackface is likely to be seen on the 'black' land of the Simonside moors. Cattle are more likely to be suckler than dairy herds.

A number of farms, leased from the Ministry of Defence, occupy the military ranges in the Otterburn Training Area. This covers about one-fifth of the national park, between Redesdale and the Coquet valley, and is the Army's principal training area in the north of England. Live firing takes place on up to 300 days each year, but none during the critical period of spring lambing. Public access is severely restricted, and there is a comprehensive warning system. One possible benefit from the military occupation is that the area of rough grazing it covers has not been afforested.

Wark Forest, in the southern part of the park, forms part of the Border Forest Park which abuts the western park boundary as far as the Scottish Border. Rothbury Forest covers part of the Simonside Hills, and some private

almost the whole of the present park area coming into the Middle March administered from Harbottle Castle. For three centuries, apart from the occasional larger battles, conflict took the form of skirmishes, but most of the fighting was about small scale raids aimed at stealing cattle and horses, with most raiding by Scots simply because England was richer, with more worth looting.

To protect themselves, their property and their stock during the few hours which such raids would last, families occupying isolated homesteads in vulnerable areas such as the upper valleys of the North Tyne, Rede and Coquet built towers, pele-houses and bastles. These are a response to physical and historic factors unique in Britain, and their differences are largely of social degree. Towers, or small castles, were the homes of greater landowners, pele-houses of lesser gentry, and bastles more in the nature of fortified additions to farms. Good examples of bastles survive at Gatehouse, above Bellingham, and Akeld, north-west of Wooler. Vicars' peles at Elsdon and Alnham, though modified, are still lived in, but many towers and peles have been incorporated into larger, later structures, or are hidden in farm buildings. When the crowns of England and Scotland were united in 1603 the age of Border fighting ended, the age of peace began, and on the windy uplands sheep could safely graze.

Years of strife had led to a steady depopulation of the Borders and the dispersal of monastic lands to lay landowners, many of whom emparked their estates, thus driving afforestation now darkens some lower slopes above Cheviot valleys. Tourism has affected the Rothbury area, and of course, the southern section of the park, by the Roman Wall, much more than in the remoter country of Cheviot.

Flora and Fauna

In the post-glacial period which followed the retreat of the ice-sheets from Northumberland slowly improving climatic conditions allowed a tundra vegetation to develop. Moss, grass and sedge started to colonize the land, followed by low-growing shrubs, and investigations of peat borings suggest that by about 5000 BC open Birch forest with some Pine was established on higher ground. By 2000 BC there was some decline in this vegetation, and on hillsides Oak, Elm, Ash, Rowan and Hazel were growing, Lime made its appearance and Alder became increasingly common in the valleys.

From prehistoric times man's activities gradually depleted woodland from drier and better-drained sites. This process of deforestation accelerated through Iron Age times to a climax during the period of Anglian settlement between 450 and 950 AD. Woods were cleared for homesteads, farming and fuel, and although woodland grazing by livestock prevented natural regeneration, it favoured the growth of grasses at the expense of other herbs, or, on poorer soils the development of heather moor. Extension of monastic grazing-lands during the mediaeval period resulted in the replacement of much remaining woodland by moorland, so that only those woods on steep valley slopes, difficult for sheep to graze, managed to survive.

Thus, over much of the park area heather moor, grass moor and areas of peat replaced the former mixed deciduous woodland. But over the past 200 years in particular man has modified these habitats, largely through animal husbandry. The first Ordnance Survey maps of the area of about 1860 show deciduous woodland confined to valley slopes, with small, regularly-shaped coniferous belts already appearing on open moorland in the Roman Wall area. By the 1930s the Forestry Commission plantations had begun to darken some of the uplands of Redesdale and the North Tyne. Most of the planting has been carried out during and since the 1950s particularly on the Simonside Hills, in Kidland Forest above Alwinton, and in the basin of the Threestone Burn above Wooler. Today, almost one-fifth of the Park area is woodland of one sort or another, well above the national average of eight per cent, but most of it is of commercial, non-native, coniferous species grown as a timber crop.

Allied to the diverse natural beauty of the park is the richness and variety of its wild life. Within the landscape zones already referred to, it is convenient to identify four broad wild life habitats, best described in terms of their vegetation, and these are moorland, wetland, woodland and

Dry-stone sheep pen in Coquetdale, the heart of the Cheviots

Clipping sheep at Langleeford Farm in the Harthope valley

improved farmland, and within each of these various sub-divisions exist.

Moorlands comprise the upland regions of the park and form the largest habitat, covering about seventy per cent of its area. Of this, the montane grasslands of the Cheviots and on the military range are the major component. With their wide, uninterrupted, often dramatic views and their sense of isolation and remoteness they represent the nearest approach to 'wilderness' in the park. All are grazed by sheep, whose selective feeding is a controlling influence on their vegetation. Rough grazing extends almost to the Cheviot summits, but on the highest ground this gives way to peat which forms a large area of blanket-bog which is now eroding quite quickly. On the peat hags which can dry out during the summer heathers and Cloudberry grow, but where damper conditions obtain these favour Crowberry, Bilberry, Cotton-Grass and Deer Sedge. To the north-west of Cheviot's bleak plateau the headwaters of the College Burn flow down rocky ravines, and in the Bizzle, Henhole and Dunsdale corries conditions are suitable for an arctic-alpine flora which includes Starry and Mossy Saxifrages, Alpine Willow-herb and Hairy Stonecrop.

Below the zone of blanket-bog the steeper, well-drained slopes of the Cheviot support extensive swards of nutritious Bent and Fescue grasses, brightened in late spring and summer by Milkwort, Tormentil and Heath Bedstraw. Stands of Bilberry sometimes hide from view the delicate little Dwarf Cornel in one of its rare English locations. Where soils are more than about nine inches deep Bracken Fern has invaded the hillsides to a height of 518 m (1,700 ft), probably as a result of sheep having replaced cattle whose heavier tread inhibited Bracken growth.

The montane grasslands are the places to see various birds of prey, including the Peregrine Falcon and the smaller but swifter Merlin, while the faint 'mew' of the high-circling Buzzard is an appropriate counterpoint to the Raven's croak above the lonely uplands. No call is more evocative of hill country than the Curlew's bubbling, liquid crescendo, and few are more plaintive than the Golden Plover's pipe. Probably the most distinctively-coloured of the smaller birds is the Ring-Ouzel, resembling a blackbird with a white crescent across its breast, and noisily pugnacious in territorial defence.

Rock outcrops on some valley slopes weather to produce a rich brown soil which accumulates on rocky ledges, encouraging the growth of tall herb communities. Bluebell, Woodruff, Foxglove, Wood Cranesbill, Golden Rod and Burnet Saxifrage commonly inhabit such sites, and where soils are damper Marsh Hawksbeard and Water Avens occur. In marshy places flushed by base-rich spring waters such as the meadows above Uswayford, Purple and Spotted Orchids, the distinctive yellow Globe Flower, Melancholy Thistle and beautiful Grass of Parnassus are rewards for careful observers.

The lower slopes of steep valley sides retain relict woodland areas of Birch, Hazel, Alder, Oak and Ash, their delicate greens of late spring showing a harmonious contrast to the russets of old Bracken. Grazing stock limits natural regeneration, but characteristic plant communities within these woods include Wood Sorrel, Primrose, Bluebell, Golden Saxifrage, Meadow Sweet, Foxglove and many ferns. Undoubtedly one of the memorable sights in June is the blaze of colour created by the Western Gorse, particularly in the College valley and to a lesser extent in the Harthope, Breamish and Coquet valleys. Locally known as 'whin', a word of Scandinavian origin, it formerly covered vast areas of land now farmed, and clearing it was one of the greatest problems of eighteenth-century agricultural improvers. Before then it was cultivated, used for thatching, hedgerows, yellow dye and even cattle fodder. Sheep still graze it in the absence of anything better, and this produces a close-cropped low bush.

In broad, boulder-strewn flat valley floors, where Cheviot rivers and burns flow in frequent wide, shallow reaches, over gravel beds, aquatic habitats provide their own delights, with Meadow Cranesbill in Coquetdale showing unusually wide colour variations. In the quiet upper reaches of some rivers and burns Monkey Flower has become well established.

So far as bird life is concerned, riverside and valley habitats, together with deciduous woodlands, ensure a good range of species. Dippers bob and curtsey on midstream rocks, rarely more than a pair to half-a-mile of stream; Pied and Grey Wagtails frisk and scamper, Common Sandpipers are inconspicuous against the rocks and pebbles but the Oyster-catcher's red bill makes this graceful bird easy to identify. The lazily-flapping Heron is not commonly seen, and does not now breed in Cheviot country, but Redstarts may be expected in the valley woodlands.

Where the Fell Sandstone predominates, as on the Simonside and Harbottle Hills, and between the North Tyne and the Rede, the resultant acid, sandy soils are ideally suited to heather moorland. The difference between this and the grass moorland of Cheviot country is vividly displayed on opposite sides of the Coquet valley above Rothbury. Heather moor occupies a zone between 305 and 420 m (1,000 and 1,400 ft), dominated by heathers and Bilberry which impart a visual uniformity most spectacularly apparent during August when the moors show a pink and purple mantle. The composition of such moorland largely depends on moor burning, ideally done every eight to fifteen years to encourage a regular supply of young heather shoots so important for sheep and grouse. Good management also produces a dense stand of heather, with remarkably little other plant life except a ground-cover of mosses and lichens, although shortly after a burning, areas of Cross-leaved Heath occur locally. On the margins of the moorland a Bent-Fescue vegetation establishes itself, while in damp areas around moorland flushes Bog Myrtle is abundant, characterised by its grey-green leaves which, when crushed, emit a delicate fragrance. Purple Moor-grass and Eared Willow are other plants of these wet places.

A large area of the Harbottle Moors is designated a site of special scientific interest, within which about 160 hectares (400 acres) around and including Harbottle Crags are managed as a nature reserve by the Northumberland Wildlife Trust. This is to safeguard the Fell Sandstone outcrops from afforestation and to preserve an important area of heather moor. A public footpath crosses the reserve to the Drake Stone and Harbottle Lake.

The Harbottle Moors show interesting variations from the heather-dominated Simonside Hills, in having numerous examples of very wet bogs of the basin mire types. These basin mires have a hummock-and-hollow surface appearance dominated by Bog Moss (*Sphagnum*), with abundant stands of Bog Myrtle. Associated with these, and often growing by streams draining from bogs, colourful plants compensate for the apparently uninteresting scene, among them being the yellow Bog Asphodel, pale pink Bog Rosemary and the insectivorous Sundew. Common Cotton-grass, Hare's-tail Cotton-grass and Cross-leaved Heath can also be expected.

The main areas of bog within the park are west of the North Tyne, identifiable on the Ordnance Survey Map as islands of white in the extensive 'sea' of Forestry Commission green. Most of them are situated between 230–305 m (750 and 1,000 ft) contours, with raised blanket bog predominating, although valley bogs are developed where water draining from acidic rocks stagnates in a depression and keeps the soil perpetually wet. In Northumberland these are usually called 'mosses', and the most outstanding ones are in an area known as Irthinghead Mires in Wark Forest at the extreme west of the park, very remote from any roads. The Nature Conservancy Council considers some of these to merit the status of sites of special scientific interest, one of which, Coom Rigg Moss, is the only national nature reserve in the park. Haininghead Moss, Hummel Knowe Moss, Gowany Knowe Moss and The Lakes are all Northumberland Wildlife Trust Nature Reserves leased from the Forestry Commission, and because of the delicate balance of their plant communities access to these reserves is necessarily controlled by a system of written permits.

Heather moorland is the natural home of Grouse, but Curlew, Golden Plover and Kestrels are also likely to be seen. The Short-eared Owl, a wide-winged daylight owl with a characteristic 'drunken-sailor' flight across moorland, is a regular breeding-species although its numbers fluctuate, while of the smaller birds the insignificant little Meadow Pipit seems to have the widest habitat range, while the attractive summer-visiting Wheatears never seem to venture far from stone walls and other useful perching-places.

Woodland areas can be considered under two headings, broadleaved and coniferous. Relict woodlands are all of deciduous trees and are limited in extent, being generally confined to steep-sided ravines and rock-screes in the Cheviot area, together with some lower slopes in valleys both there and on the hills of the Fell Sandstone ridge. The richness and variety of what survives is largely dependent on the extent to which such woodlands have been managed and the amount of pressure through grazing stock preventing natural regeneration.

The valley of the Grasslees Burn which separates the main Simonside range from the Harbottle Hills to the west contains the best old woodland in the area and includes a rare surviving semi-natural Alder wood. Other smaller examples occur in Cheviot valleys, but most relict woodlands are dominated by Birch, sometimes associated with Ash, Hazel, Oak and Rowan, especially in the valleys of the College and Harthope Burns. The only road between Redesdale and the Coquet valley, from Elsdon to Hepple, affords splendid views of the Grasslees Burn and Billsmoor woodlands, tawny-gold in their autumn colourings, and designated a site of special scientific interest.

Two woodlands near Holystone are managed as nature reserves by the Northumberland Wildlife Trust, with public access along waymarked paths. Holystone North Wood is a rare Northumbrian example of a semi-natural, upland acid Sessile Oak wood probably planted on moorland during the eighteenth century. Many of its trees are twisted and multi-stemmed, suggesting former coppicing with the better ones removed. Birch, Rowan and Holly are also present, together with much Bracken in the lower part. Although the field-layer has few species, Chickweed Wintergreen occurs, and there is a variety of mosses.

About a mile away Holystone Burn Wood covers the floor and slopes of a sheltered valley with a wide range of woodland, upland and moorland vegetation. The valley floor is the best park location for Juniper scrub, while Oak and Birch are abundant. A rich field-layer of woodland and wood-edge plants includes Lesser Twayblade in the Bog Myrtle–Purple Moor-grass flushes, and on the upper slopes a species-rich heather moor contains Petty Whin, with a luxuriant carpet of heath mosses and *Sphagnum*.

Relict woodlands such as these, with their abundance of dead or decaying trees and branches, with loose bark and holes, offer a variety of nesting sites for birds and niches for small invertebrates. Woodcock may be seen in its 'roding' flight along woodland rides, owl-like against the dusk, and Green Woodpeckers may be heard drilling old wood or piercing the quiet with their alarm call. Pied Flycatchers may be seen in spring, and the colourful Redstart approves of the availability of nesting-holes. Willow Warblers, Wood Warblers and Chiffchaffs are more likely to be heard than seen among fresh green woodland glades.

Coniferous woodlands were planted during the late eighteenth and nineteenth centuries as shelter belts and a timber source. Small in scale they were composed mainly of Scots Pine, European Larch and Silver Fir. Since 1919 and the establishment of the Forestry Commission large areas of coniferous plantations have changed Northumbrian uplands, most of it within the Border Forest Park, but some within the area now covered by the national park. The main forests in the park are Wark, Redesdale, Harwood, Rothbury and Kidland, whilst new planting has occurred at Uswayford, Hosedenhope and Threestoneburn in the Cheviot hills, with smaller forests in the College valley and at Carshope and Stewartshields on the military range.

Although Spruce predominates, covering about seventy-one per cent of the planted area, with Pine at twenty-two per cent, individual forests show differences in species-composition. Spruce is very important in Wark and Redesdale Forests, but much less so in Harwood, Kidland and Rothbury Forests where sheltered sites and better-drained soils allow more Pine to be grown.

While young plantations encourage some bird species such as Kestrel, Short-eared Owl and Meadow Pipit, this is usually at the expense of moorland birds of prey, and a close-canopied mature forest allows very little ground flora to develop. However, Roe Deer are common among the great conifer stands, elusive, graceful and most likely to be seen feeding in open glades in early morning. Roe Deer are so small that, even if they break from the woods on to the moors beyond, the deep growth of heathers will hide them. Red Squirrels are not yet competing with the Grey Squirrel in Northumberland, so their rust-toned daintiness may still be appreciated.

Although the Redesdale and North Tyne section of the park is predominantly moorland, with a mixture of rough

Summer sunshine and a gentle walk in the Cheviots

grazing and heather moor, some land has been improved and scattered farmsteads are more prominent. The valleys themselves are fairly sheltered and fertile, but whereas Redesdale is broad, straight and open, the North Tyne flows in a more winding course, often with heavily wooded banks, in a more varied landscape, giving way on its west to the Border Forest Park. Open areas of 'haughland' in the valley bottom contrast with afforestation beyond. Hawthorn hedgerows or stone walls enclose the fields, with small belts of woodland giving extra tree cover. The wildlife of such areas is noticeably richer than that around Elsdon, where post and wire fencing prevails. The normal field and hedgerow birds can be expected, but perhaps it is the sight of the erratic, wheeling Lapwing which symbolizes the nature of these open farmlands, beyond hedgerows gay with spring flowers, and white-frothed with May to herald the arrival of summer.

At the southern edge of the park the appeal of the Roman Wall area is one dominated by history. Nevertheless, geology and topography have given it unique landscape character, while in its central section the glacial lakes or loughs are additional distinctive features. Broomlee, Crag and Greenlee Loughs north of the Wall, and Grindon Lough to its south, on the boundary, are the most important

stretches of open water in the national park, although much smaller loughs are to be found on Simonside and Harbottle Hills. Since their formation all of the loughs have been gradually evolving through the various stages of reed swamp and fen to raised bog, a succession well illustrated at Crag Lough. This starts with open water plant communities, and by the time a raised bog or Willow carr is reached, with a resultant build-up of organic matter above water-level, some *Sphagnum* species are established, and given adequate rainfall acid bog develops on top of the fen peat. The Willow carr formed on the drier fen is a notable characteristic of these Roman Wall loughs and includes Common Sallow (the familiar 'pussy' Willow), and Bay Willow, differentiated by its browner-grey bark finely fissured by narrow orange-buff cracks.

Ornithologically the loughs are very attractive to many species of waterfowl and waders, both as breeding sites and feeding and resting places. Whooper Swans, with their long, straight necks and yellow-based bills, are regular winter visitors to all the Roman Wall loughs, while among the ducks to be seen are Teal, Wigeon, Shoveler and the most colourful and distinctive Goosander. Grindon Lough, the smallest and shallowest of the four natural lakes, is a Northumberland Wildlife Trust nature reserve, situated close to the metalled road which follows the line of the Stanegate, from which its abundant bird life can readily be viewed. Pedestrian access to the lake requires special permission, however. One of the great satisfactions of Roman Wall country is that of looking down from the crests of the crags to watch the aerobatics of the wind-tossed flight of Jackdaws which nest on rocky ledges, contrasted with the graceful, predatory hoverings of the occasional Kestrel. The talus slopes below the crags, apparently uninteresting at a distance, support their own vegetation – Fir Club-Moss, Parsley Fern, and, on the limestone beneath the Whin Sill, Common Rockrose. On stabilized screes and rock ledges heathers and Bilberry are abundant, and the sombre tones of grey-brown rock are brightened by Rosebay Willow Herb.

Recreation in the Park

Although the Northumberland National Park is relatively remote from the main centres of population, about four million people live within two hours' driving time of its boundaries, and most areas of the park are within fifty miles of the Tyne–Wear conurbation. As a result it is very popular with casual day visitors, particularly at weekends, as well as proving attractive to holidaymakers staying for longer periods. However the lack of sizeable settlements and the absence of accommodation facilities within the park area, apart from farmhouses, results in most visitors staying in the villages and towns on the edge of the park such as Wooler,

Rothbury, Otterburn, Bellingham, Haltwhistle and Hexham. There are four youth hostels in or adjacent to the park, at Once Brewed, Acomb, Bellingham and Wooler, and the popularity of the Roman Wall area is underlined by the fact that the number of overnight stays at Once Brewed, very near the wall, is more than double that at any of the others. Camping and caravanning facilities are very limited and most are situated on the periphery of the park, mainly in the South Tyne valley.

Most visitors tend to follow some informal recreational activity, such as touring by car, finding an attractive location for car-parking, perhaps near water that provides added interest and offers a safe place for children to play, or as a starting-point for a short walk from the car to an archaeological or historic site, or an outstanding natural feature. In upland areas the valleys of the College Burn, Harthope, Breamish, Alwin and Coquet are especially popular, having quick-flowing, shallow, clean rivers, with haughland areas adjoining – though not always available – for informal parking and picnicking. The Breamish valley has the added advantage of an information centre and toilet facilities. Other information centres exist during the season at Rothbury, Byrness and Once Brewed, while that at Harbottle is open at weekends and Bank Holidays from late May to early September.

Waterfalls and viewpoints have a special appeal for many visitors, being focal points for short walks. The Simonside Crags above Rothbury, Harbottle Crags further up the Coquet, and the Holystone Woods, are deservedly popular, and Forestry Commission leaflets give useful details for exploring these areas. Hareshaw Linn and Linhope Spout are two waterfalls which merit short, scenic walks from Bellingham and the head of the Breamish valley respectively, whilst many tracks in the Forestry Commission plantations have been waymarked to provide sheltered forest trails of various lengths. Generally, however, the dispersed settlement pattern and the prevalence of farmland in the North Tyne valley and lower Redesdale has resulted in there being few field and riverside paths.

During the summer months 'Discovery Walks' with a national park warden or voluntary warden and 'Walks with a Specialist' are arranged from various convenient starting-points. They are informal and informative, cover up to five miles and last about three hours each, though some evening ones are naturally of shorter length and duration.

Since the Northumberland National Park contains such a wealth of archaeological and historic sites such as native British settlements, Roman fortifications and settlements, castles, peles, bastles and churches, some of regional significance, others of international importance, these attract the attention of a large number of visitors. It is worth pointing out that the finest stretches of the wall cross the southern edge of the park area and are easily accessible from the Military Road, B6318, but can be explored closely only on foot.

The national park contains some of Britain's finest hill-walking country, with the Cheviots and Simonside Hills outstanding. Historic tracks, ancient drove roads and other rights-of-way in the Cheviots give them a special appeal for the seekers of solitude who can penetrate by remote valleys to the Border ridge and beyond into Scotland. The Pennine Way itself does this, and almost a quarter of its whole length of 400 km (250 miles) is through the park. Indeed, the scenic contrasts between the stretch along the Roman Wall and the climactic conquest of Cheviot's windy summit could hardly be greater. In between are sections through the forests and across the moorlands between the North Tyne and Redesdale. Although the Simonside and Harbottle Hills rarely exceed 420 m (1,400 ft) their open views and rocky outcrops contribute to a feeling of much greater height.

Rock-climbing is mostly confined to three areas in the park – Crag Lough and Peel Crags below the Roman Wall, Simonside and Ravenshaugh near Rothbury, and the outcropping granite at Henhole and Bizzle at the head of the College valley. The Whin Sill and Fell Sandstone faces offer good quality climbing on excellent rock, and all three areas are in regular use throughout the year. Skiing, which is obviously dependent on suitable weather conditions, is possible on the Simonside Hills if there is sufficient depth of snow, but in a good year the north-facing slopes of Cheviot, though remote, are particularly rewarding, though more difficult of access than the valley slopes above Langleeford. No permanent facilities have been developed anywhere in the park.

The open moorlands and forests in the area are very well suited to horse-riding and pony-trekking; there are three centres in the North Tyne valley and another adjoining Kidland Forest. Stables at Wooler, Rothbury, Hexham and Kirk Yetholm, on the edge of the park, arrange treks. In addition to the forest rides and tracks the North Tyne

A runner follows the Roman Wall near the Whin Sill Crags

and upper Coquet valleys have many miles of splendid bridlepaths.

Forest and moorland landscapes provide ideal terrain for the orienteering enthusiast as well as for motor rallies, and the annual RAC Rally, as well as other regional ones, regularly use forest tracks in Wark Forest. These rallies are governed by regulations adopted by the RAC. Touring cyclists may also enjoy using some of the many unclassified roads and tracks in the forests and uplands of the park where there is little conflict with the motorist.

Water-sports enthusiasts will find their needs adequately provided for at Kielder Water, situated just beyond the park boundary in the upper part of the North Tyne valley west of Bellingham. This huge new reservoir in its forest setting is being developed for recreation and tourism. Boat-launching facilities, canoeing, dinghy-sailing and boat hire operate from the main base at Leaplish on the southern shore, but at the present time power-boating is not permitted. Worm and fly-fishing are available from bank or boat on the main reservoir, while Bakethin, at the head of the lake, is available for fly-fishing only.

Within the park sailing is limited to Greenlee Lough, north of the wall, but this is restricted to members of the Westwater Lakes Society which has converted the nearby Bonnyrigg Hall into a club-house with facilities for overnight accommodation. Canoeing, mainly on the North Tyne, is restricted to members of the two or three local clubs affiliated to the British Canoe Union.

The upper reaches of the Tyne and Coquet are within the national park, while part of the Tweed river system also falls within the boundary, but because these are mainly headwaters, their potential for angling is limited. Streams and river tributaries are valuable as spawning-grounds for Salmon, Sea Trout and Brown Trout. However, sections of certain rivers do offer some fishing, mainly on the Coquet between Rothbury and Alwinton, the North Tyne between Falstone and Bellingham, and the lower part of the Rede just before it joins the North Tyne, and these reaches are usually let to angling clubs or breweries who own public houses and small hotels in the area, and from which day permits may be obtained.

The College Burn flowing from its source near the summit of The Cheviot

Useful Addresses

National Park Headquarters: Eastburn, South Park, Hexham NE46 1BS

National Park Information Centres (Open daily from 10 a.m. to 6 p.m. during the season):
    Ingram (Cheviot Hills)
    Rothbury (Coquetdale & Simonside Hills)
    Byrness (Upper Redesdale)
    Once Brewed (Hadrian's Wall)
    Harbottle Centre (Upper Coquetdale) (weekends and B. Hols. only)

National Trust (Regional Office): Scots Gap, Morpeth, Northumberland NE61 4EG

Northumbria Wildlife Trust: The Hancock Museum, Newcastle-upon-Tyne

The North York Moors looking west from Wheeldale Moor

Derek Statham

North York Moors

THE UPLAND block of country in North-East Yorkshire known as the North York Moors has a unique character, despite superficial resemblances to other British uplands. It is the only national park on the eastern seaboard and experiences a drier, more continental type of climate than the other parks. Furthermore, it is the only truly upland area of Britain formed out of the younger sedimentary rocks which cover much of the lowland plain of England.

The park covers an area of 1,438 square km (553 square miles) and is roughly oval in shape with its main axis from east to west. The boundaries are well defined topographically in spite of the relatively low altitude which nowhere exceeds 454 metres (1,490 ft) OD. The North Sea marks the eastern boundary with a coastline of high, rugged cliffs. The northern and western boundaries follow the steep escarpment edge of the Cleveland and Hambleton Hills respectively. Only the southern fringe lacks a sharp topographical feature, the boundary meandering along the back slope of the Tabular Hills between Helmsley and Scarborough.

The upland nature of the park is emphasized by the flat, fertile lowlands which surround it. To the north is the Cleveland Plain consisting of good quality farmland threaded by the Teesside industrial towns, including the largest complex of chemical plant in Europe. There is no more dramatic view in the park than the lights of Teesside and its industries from the top of Carlton Bank at night. By day, the startling contrast between heavy industry and remote moorland within a distance of a few miles is one of the more unusual environmental experiences available to the visitor in this part of England.

The rich agricultural Vales of York and Mowbray lie to the west and the flat, formerly lake covered, Vale of Pickering lies to the south. A small ridge of land, the Howardian Hills, runs south from the park and separates the Vales of York and Pickering.

The origin of the name of the park is not known but is comparatively recent. Historically, the central and northern moorlands were known by the more romantic name of Blackamore, an apt description of the heather moors for much of the year. The landscapes are many and varied, offering an unusual mixture of environments for the enjoyment of the visitor. They range from windswept heather moorland to lush, broadleaved woodlands and include high cliffs, sandy coves, extensive coniferous woodlands, dale farming country and rich arable land. The wide horizons of moorland are the most enduring impression of this park.

Geology and Topography

The park is classic territory for the geologist. The simple relationship of the surface topography to the underlying rocks coupled with the large number of exposures, especially along the coast, attracted the attention of early geologists. Some of the original interpretation of British sedimentary rocks was carried out in the area by William Smith of Scarborough, often styled the 'Father of English Geology', and his colleagues.

The rocks of the North York Moors are almost entirely of Jurassic age and were laid down in seas, river estuaries and deltas. They consist of limestones, sandstones, gritstones, shales and clays but include mineral deposits such as ironstone, alum and coal. Underlying the Jurassic rocks are older rocks of the Triassic and Permian periods containing valuable minerals which, with the aid of modern technology, are now being exploited at great depths. They include potash which is mined at Boulby on the edge of the park, and small pockets of natural gas and petroleum.

Overlying the Jurassic rocks was originally a great thickness of rocks of more recent origin, particularly of chalk. These have been worn away over a long period of time to expose the Jurassic strata. The area was gradually uplifted some seventy million years ago so that the rock strata dip gently southwards with the older rocks to the north.

Topographically, the park is essentially an uplifted plateau containing a sequence of steps or scarps, mostly north facing. Thus, the limestones and gritstones of the Tabular Hills rise gently out of the Vale of Pickering to fall away abruptly in a line of steep hills between Helmsley and Scarborough. This line is broken in many places by south flowing streams and the result is a characteristic headland known locally as a 'nab end'. The string of villages along this scarp each has its 'surprise view', this being the sudden falling away of the land after a very gradual, often imperceptible, climb from the Vale of Pickering. The views are framed by the horizon of the central moorlands and for visitors travelling north, mark the beginning of the moors. The Tabular Hills derive their name from the flat, table-like nature of their summits separated by steep-sided valleys.

The Hambleton Hills with their impressive west facing scarp are a continuation of the limestones and gritstones of the Tabular Hills. Both these areas contain good quality agricultural land on the plateaux, with woodland on the valley slopes.

The Cleveland Hills on the northern edge of the park terminate in another steep scarp overlooking the soft rocks forming the Cleveland plain. The rocks of the Cleveland Hills and of much of the central moorlands consist in the main of hard sandstones with some gritstones and limestones. They weather to produce thin and largely infertile soils. In the dales, softer clays and shales are exposed and these same strata occur on the lower reaches of the escarpments and along the cliffs of the coast. It is widely assumed that the cliff-like nature of the Cleveland Hills has given rise to their name.

Wade's Causeway, the Roman road from Wheeldale towards Stape

Within the rocks of the Cleveland Hills are bands containing ironstone which, for much of the nineteenth century and the early part of the present century, were extensively mined as the raw material for the Cleveland iron and steel industry. There is an offshoot of the main iron-bearing beds in Rosedale which was exploited in a short, but intensive, boom in the late nineteenth century. Although vast quantities of iron ore were mined, the park is remarkably free from mining eyesores and dereliction. The last iron ore mine closed in 1964 but production had dwindled to a tiny fraction of the peak output by the 1920s. Thus was brought to an end a mining industry which began in prehistoric times and flourished in various places throughout the park for over 2,000 years.

Other minerals of importance which were mined in the past include alum, which is used in paper making, and jet, a fossilized wood deposit popular as a material for ornaments. These deposits occur widely and were exploited in a series of small quarries along the seams where they outcrop. The line of quarries and their waste can be clearly traced along the Cleveland Hills and in places along the sea cliffs.

Many of the hard rocks have been quarried for building and associated uses; some limestone on the southern edge is still quarried today for road stone and industrial uses. For a time in the eighteenth and nineteenth centuries, the massive sandstones near to Whitby were extensively quarried for use outside the area; Covent Garden Market, Waterloo Bridge and the Houses of Parliament are some of the better known buildings constructed in Whitby stone, as well as notable local buildings such as Whitby Abbey. One hard rock of particular value as road stone was actually mined near Goathland. This is the igneous, or volcanic whinstone, the only outcropping rock of non-Jurassic age in the park. It occurs in a narrow dyke running from Great Ayton in the north to near Ravenscar on the coast and forms a high sill in many places.

The basic drainage pattern of the moorland plateau was established in its present form a considerable time ago. Most of the streams run north–south from the main moorland divide. The one main exception is the Esk Valley with its east–west alignment. It is possible that this is a remnant of a former river which rose in the Pennines and flowed to the North Sea across the park before the area was uplifted.

Many of the details of the present surface drainage, and some striking topographical features, are the result of recent glaciation. During the last glacial epoch, the high moorlands were not covered by ice which lapped in great sheets around them. In the later phase, ice-dammed lakes were formed which overflowed to scour deep channels as the water escaped at the lowest point. Thus a glacial lake in Eskdale overspilled southwards to a much larger lake in the Vale of Pickering when North Sea ice cut off its natural drainage

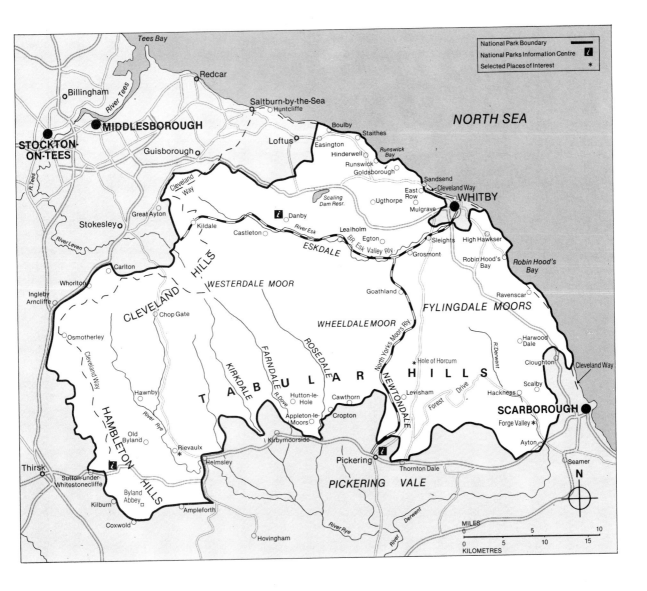

eastwards. The result is the classic overspill gorge of Newtondale. The vertical sides of this deep gorge are testimony to
the power of water escaping in large quantities.

The other main effect of glaciation was to deposit a
variety of sands, gravels and clays over the area. The coastal
plain in particular was covered with a thick sheet of boulder
clay which explains why it contains good farmland in marked
contrast to the nearby moorlands at similar elevations. From
a purely scenic point of view, the result is a somewhat tame
edge to the park and only at Ravenscar does the moorland
sweep to the coast.

Man in the Park

There is probably no area in Britain that is richer in
archaeological remains than the North York Moors and,
furthermore, the area has attracted a large number of
researchers over the years. The result is an impressive body

of evidence about man's presence and activities, though
inevitably there are still some gaps in our knowledge.

The earliest occupation can be traced back to the
Palaeolithic period, or Early Stone-Age, around 10,000
years BC and shortly after the end of the last Ice-Age. There
is evidence, mainly in the form of flint heads, that the southern part of the park was used by hunting groups, possibly in
food forays from a base further to the south. The activities of
these groups became more widespread in the succeeding
Mesolithic, or Middle Stone-Age, and as the climate continued to improve, so it appears the population expanded and
the area was permanently settled. Recent research has
revealed that even at this very early stage, around 5000 to
6000 BC, there were attempts to manage the environment by
burning to create a type of forest cover optimal for grazing
animals such as Elk, Deer and Aurochs. It is thought that the
social development of the tribes based on hunting and gathering reached its peak at this time before the introduction of

agriculture in the succeeding Neolithic, or New Stone-Age, around 3500 BC.

The introduction of agriculture marks a major turning point in the settlement and land use of the moors, and of much of the rest of Britain. It is not known how the new techniques were established but the rapidity of their adoption and the enormous social and economic changes which must have accompanied them strongly suggest that there was an influx of new settlers from continental Europe. Within a short time, mixed farming with arable cropping and livestock rearing was established in the more fertile areas, mainly on the Tabular and Hambleton Hills. In comparison, the higher moorlands which were exploited by the earlier hunter/gatherer cultures appear to have been only lightly settled and utilized.

The remains of the Neolithic period consist of long barrows containing burial chambers, of which there are some twenty in the park, stone axe heads, crude pottery fragments and flint implement heads. They are found mainly in the Tabular and Hambleton Hills. There are also some remains of rudimentary field enclosures.

The second main cultural revolution was the introduction of metal tools in bronze which ushered in the Bronze Age, around 1750 BC. There are extensive remains from this period indicating a widespread and probably relatively dense agricultural settlement. The long barrow type of burial chamber was superseded by the smaller round barrow of which large numbers remain; over 200 have been excavated. Considerable numbers of artefacts, including bronze axes and daggers, food vessels and other pottery, have been recovered from this period. Sufficient evidence has been produced for archaeologists to postulate the main components of the Bronze Age society. It is likely that there were no large settlements and no chieftains or hierarchically ranked communities. Rather the evidence points to a widespread, small scale settlement of self-sufficient groups who controlled a variety of habitats, usually including fertile dale country, hill pasture, woodland and stream catchments. The watersheds between the dales often marked the territorial boundaries and many modern parish boundaries follow these today.

Another development of importance to the present landscape occurred at this time. The effect of grazing and cultivation on the thin soils of the sandstone moors very quickly led to soil exhaustion and the leaching of nutrients, resulting in acidification and establishment of heathers and

The glaciated valley of Eskdale

related plants. This process, known as podsolization, probably began as early as the Mesolithic period when deliberate burning was carried out but it was in the Bronze Age that it spread on a large scale. It is to all intents and purposes an irreversible process and represents a major environmental degradation as a result of human intervention.

The end of the Bronze Age, around 600 BC, produced another landscape feature of the moors. For a time, large linear earthworks were constructed in several places, particularly in the limestone areas in the south and west. The largest and best preserved are the Cleave Dykes in the Hambleton Hills, and the Levisham and Scamridge Dykes in the Tabular Hills, though there are many smaller examples elsewhere. Although they may have been territorial boundaries, their precise function is not clear, particularly as the quantities of earth moving involved in the parallel dykes were immense. Their construction indicates wealthy communities, however, bent on conserving their territories. They are also probably evidence of a ranked society, disciplined to organize labour on a large scale.

The introduction of iron-making around 600 BC marks another threshold in the development of British society. Until recently, it was thought it had little impact on the moors and the Bronze Age cultures continued with little change until the Romans came. It is now clear that this was not the case and remains of Iron Age houses and field patterns, iron smelting works and defence sites such as hill forts, have been discovered, all indicating a powerful, well-organized society. The Roman occupation did little to alter the native social and economic settlement pattern but imposed on it a stable, military rule. Most of the park was in the military zone of the Roman occupation and only the southern area was settled and colonized by the conquerors. There are several important remains including a well preserved example of a Roman road on Wheeldale Moor, a fort on Lease Rigg near Grosmont, and a unique group of military practice camps at Cawthorn, near Pickering. Towards the end of the Roman occupation, around 400 AD, a number of signal stations were established along the coast, including sites at Ravenscar, Huntcliffe and Goldsborough, to give early warning of raids by Saxon invaders from the continent.

During the succeeding centuries, the so-called Dark Ages, the area was subjected to waves of raiders from the continent, some of whom settled in the park. It is a crucial period in the history of British land use as by the early Mediaeval period, most of the present pattern of settlement and roads, civil boundaries and many field boundaries had been established. There are very few remains of the Teutonic settlers, despite their influence in determining the nature of the present landscape. Most place names are Old English or Norse and an important landscape inheritance from this period is the moorland cross, of which there are about forty

in the park. Their precise origin is unknown but it is possible that they were erected for both religious and utilitarian purposes, as they usually stand on a boundary or old route. They have fascinating names such as Ralph, Ana, Redman, Fat Betty, Stump, Lilla and Brown Howe. Ralph Cross appears on the emblem of the national park.

During the Mediaeval period, from the eleventh to the fourteenth centuries AD, the population of the area grew, although ravaged by the Black Death plagues in the late fourteenth century. The open field system of farming flourished in the south of the park but the prime agricultural managers of this period were the monastic foundations, particularly of Rievaulx, and they pioneered large scale sheep farming in the moors. The area boasts a number of fine castles and abbeys from this and earlier periods including Whitby, Rievaulx and Byland abbeys, and Mulgrave and Helmsley castles.

In the succeeding centuries, the population continued to grow steadily but the economy of the area based on agriculture and mining did not change materially until the later part of the nineteenth century when the resorts along the coast and a few inland places became popular. The main development was the building of the railways of which now only two remain; the British Rail Esk Valley Line to Whitby and the privately-owned line through Newtondale, constructed in 1836 by George Stephenson. The latter is a spectacular route through remote valleys and gorges where there are no roads and the antiquity of the line makes it of considerable interest to the student of industrial history.

The development of the motor-car and of mass recreation in recent years goes hand in hand with the considerable landscape changes which have taken place. These include the planting of large areas of conifers on the lower moorlands, particularly in the south and the steady reclamation of moorland for improved agriculture. Since 1950, some 155 square km (60 square miles) of moorland have been taken for forestry or agriculture and the moorland has shrunk at the rate of nearly one per cent per annum.

Although the recent technological changes in agriculture have affected the park, their environmental impact has not been as great as in the nearby lowland areas. There has been some building development around the farms and a general intensification of land management with the ploughing of old pastures, re-seeding, drainage of wet areas and some removal of trees and hedges. These developments have been on a small scale, however, because of the nature of hill sheep farming and cattle rearing with its low input/low output system. Of greater consequence has been the marked reduction in employment in farming which means fewer hands to attend to the upkeep of the land; hedge and woodland management, heather-burning, maintenance of stone walls, stiles and gates have all suffered as a result. One of the

The ruins of Rievaulx Abbey in Ryedale, founded in 1132

primary purposes of national park management programmes is to redress this balance so that, although the inevitable changes in farm practice mean landscape and ecological change, the traditional beauty and character are retained. It is an interesting reflection to note that the impact of the major developments of the past fifty years on the landscape is probably much less than the transformation which occurred with the introduction of agriculture around 3500 BC.

Flora and Fauna

Although it has an abundance and great variety of wildlife, the park contains few nationally known habitat sites. It is in many ways a transitional zone between highland and lowland Britain. Thus some species have their southern and some their northern limits here. Included in the former are Dwarf Cornel, a rare plant with its southernmost station in the Hole of Horcum and the Few-Flowered Sedge found with another rare plant, Bog Rosemary, on Fylingdales Moor. Plants reaching their northernmost limits include the Stemless Thistle and Stinking Hellebore.

Apart from the geographical position, other major influences on the wildlife habitats are the climate and soil conditions. The climate is generally dry and cool. Occasional incursions of cold air from the North Sea bring biting cold winds with snow showers in winter and cool misty conditions, often accompanied by sea mist or 'roak', in spring and summer. Throughout the greater part of the year, however, in the predominantly westerly conditions, the park enjoys a

favourable climate with dry, clear weather. Rainfall is generally around 760 mm (30 inches) with the high moors receiving more than 1,000 mm (39 inches) and the coastal area less than 660 mm (26 inches).

Soil conditions vary considerably over the area. The typical moorland soil is a shallow, acid peat over sandstone or gritstone but there are many variations. Podsols are widespread on the moors, often with an impenetrable layer or 'pan' at 150–400 mm (6–16 inches) below the surface. They act as major constraints to plant growth unless ploughed and drained. In the valleys and throughout the coastal plain and Tabular and Hambleton Hills, 'brown-earths', slightly acidic but fertile soils, predominate but there are some stony red soils, known as rendzinas, on the limestone hills. Blanket peat and other deep peat deposits are not widespread but there is a substantial area of peat across the main watershed, especially on the high moors between Rosedale Head and Wheeldale.

An understanding of the present pattern of wildlife habitats is impossible without a knowledge of the ecological history of the area. Fortunately, there is now a substantial body of information, much of it obtained by the techniques of pollen analysis and radio-carbon dating, though the interpretation of stratified remains of plants and animals has also helped.

A convenient starting point for the ecological history of the area is the end of the last Ice Age, about 16,000 years ago. The higher moors were free of ice during this last glaciation and as the climate became warmer, the initial vegetation appears to have been of a very open and rapidly changing nature. Grass-heath communities developed, dominated by grasses, sedges and dwarf shrubs, such as Crowberry, Juniper, Willow and Dwarf Birch. Later, stands of Tree Birch developed and around 8000 BC, there began a marked climatic improvement resulting in forest trees spreading into the park. At first, Birch and Hazel were the main colonizers but Scots Pine followed and eventually Oak, Elm, Lime and Alder. Trees appear to have colonized some areas more rapidly than others and parts of the high sandstone moorland were probably only lightly wooded.

Animal remains of this period include Reindeer, Red Deer, Aurochs and Wild Horse, with Wild Pig and Roe Deer becoming more common later as the forests spread. The presence of these large mammals was a major factor in the subsistence of the Mesolithic tribes of the time who relied on them for their food supply.

Eventually, forests covered the greater part of the area as the climate became somewhat warmer and drier than at present. Nevertheless, blanket peat began to form at this time in shallow basins; some researchers believe its growth was initiated by human interference with the vegetation, principally by burning to remove the forest cover.

At around 4500 BC the climate reached its so called post-glacial optimum, warmer than the present but becoming increasingly wetter as the spread of Alder and Ash demonstrate. The mixed deciduous forest of this time is usually regarded as the natural climax vegetation of the post-glacial period in which we now live, sometimes called the Flandrian interglacial. Of particular interest is the evidence for rich brown-earth soils over the majority of the areas, even over the acid sandstones where poor podsolic soils now predominate.

Perhaps the most exciting discovery of recent research, however, is the realization that the hunter/gatherer population of this period manipulated the environment by burning to such an extent that, by the end of the Mesolithic, there must have been a mosaic of open woodland and regenerating scrub communities with semi-permanent areas of open ground, bog and heathland. Acidification of the soils on the central moors probably began in a few places at this time and, combined with increased loss of organic matter by erosion after the fires, represents the first phase of a long and increasingly severe process of ecological impoverishment.

With the introduction of domesticated livestock grazing around 3500 BC, the areas of forest diminished, particularly on the plateaus of the Tabular Hills. The migration into the area of the Bronze Age peoples brought major clearance of the forests to make room for both cereal cultivation and pasturalism. Heath and bog communities expanded on the plateaux with the onset of podsolization but some woodland remained on steep slopes and in the wetter dales and surrounding lowlands.

At the end of the Bronze Age and beginning of the Iron Age, around 600 BC, the climate deteriorated becoming cooler and wetter. Over parts of the area, particularly on the central moorlands, further forest clearances took place and moorland plants became widespread and dominant. It is likely that the moorland landscape of today emerged at this time although deforestation, particularly in the dales, continued into Mediaeval times.

The Mediaeval monastic farmers not only developed sheep walks on the moors but cleared the daleside woodlands for charcoal for their iron bloomeries. Apart from the enclosures of the seventeenth and eighteenth centuries, the economic management of the area since the Middle Ages led to few changes in its effect on wildlife habitats until recently, when there has been a substantial reduction in the area of moorland through afforestation and agricultural improvement. The loss of large areas of semi-natural vegetation is regrettable but the creation of a new habitat, the coniferous forests, has added variety to the wildlife.

The present distribution of flora and fauna can best be considered in the context of the principal habitats. These are the open moors, the sea cliffs, the coniferous plantations, the few remaining broadleaved woodlands and the enclosed farming country.

Open moorland currently occupies about 500 square km (192 square miles) or approaching thirty-five per cent of the area of the park. The dominant plant is Common Heather or Ling which often occurs as the only species but usually is accompanied by other acid-heath plants such as Crowberry and Bilberry, together with other heaths such as Cross-leaved Heather and Bell Heather. Rushes, Cotton-grass and Bracken Fern are also common plants of the moors. There are two main types of moorland; the dry, heather-dominated upland heath which covers the greater part of the area and the wetter moorland on deep peat where there is a greater admixture of plants including Cotton-grass and rushes, together with *Sphagnum* moss and occasional rarer plants and mosses. Bracken, until recently a plant of the moor margins and slopes, has spread on to the plateau moor in the past few decades.

The moors are managed for sheep and Red Grouse, the latter being restricted to the British Isles. Under intensive management, the grouse population can be increased to many times its natural numbers. The method of management consists mainly of burning in a twelve to fifteen year rotation to create small patches of half a hectare of heather at varying ages, accompanied by strong culling of vermin, crows, foxes, stoats and, until very recently, hawks and other predators. The object is to maintain ideal breeding and feeding territories but the main effect of grouse management is the

Sheep being herded on the village green at Hutton-le-Hole

Robin Hood's Bay, a striking village and a beautiful bay

creation of almost a monoculture of heathers over large areas. The drainage of the small areas of wet bog by 'gripping', or open ditch drainage, further depletes the variety of wildlife.

A long term moorland management programme under the direction of the national park staff is being implemented with the moorland owners to prevent further degradation and enhance the nutrient status of some of the fire-damaged areas. These now cover about 8,000 hectares (20,000 acres) since the disastrous fires of the summer of 1976 when numerous small and several very large fires burned off not only the vegetation, but also the peat in some areas, exposing the bare rock. These severely damaged areas take many years to recover.

The fauna of the moors is a very restricted one. There is a small insect population including the Northern Eggar moth which is found in heather and the Green Hairstreak and Common Heath butterflies. Animals include Fox, Rabbit, Hare, Adder, Common Lizard and, interestingly, large populations of Wood Mice, even on the high moors. Typical moorland birds, apart from the Red Grouse, include Curlew, Golden Plover, Lapwing, Wheatear, Ring Ouzel and Merlin. The latter is a small bird of prey which is restricted to moorland and is declining nationally. The North York Moors may well be one of its last strongholds in England.

The coastal flora is not particularly distinguished by maritime species, mainly because of the lack of salt marsh and sand dunes. The cliffs are steep and frequently unstable with much slipping, particularly on the boulder clay. Consequently, the most common plants are grasses, Coltsfoot and Field Horsetail, but Sea Rocket, Sea Beet and other more common plants such as Wild Thyme, Birdsfoot Trefoil and Sea Plantain also occur.

The cliffs are the breeding sites of sea birds and the wooded cloughs or 'wykes' running into the sea contain a rich habitat for other birds. Cliff-nesting birds include Fulmar, Kittiwake, Cormorant and Herring Gull and there are numerous other species visiting the coast for part of the year or merely passing through on migration.

The clothing of large areas of moorland and dale sides with conifers has often been deplored by conservationists. The number of species found in these areas is small and the trees themselves are usually exotic species, the most common being Sitka Spruce, Contorta and Lodgepole Pine, Douglas Fir and European Larch. Nevertheless, as the forests mature, with thinning and replanting taking place, the variety of wildlife is increasing. Both Roe and Fallow Deer populations have expanded considerably, particularly the former, and there are some Red Deer and Muntjac. Foxes and Badgers have taken advantage of the increased cover and there have been some interesting additions including a rare bird, the seed-eating Crossbill. The Nightjar, a nationally uncommon and declining species, seems to be holding its own and even expanding in the forests.

In marked contrast to the conifer plantations, the native broadleaved woodlands are rich in both numbers and variety of species. The woods on the dale sides in the limestone areas are particularly noteworthy and the park's only National Nature Reserve in Forge Valley near to Scarborough consists of mature oak/ash woodland over a fertile calcareous soil. Besides Oak, Elm (now being rapidly removed by Dutch Elm disease), Lime, Ash and Alder occur, with other small trees such as Bird Cherry, Rowan, Field Maple and Holly. The herb layer is especially rich, with some rare plants including Lily-of-the-Valley, which grows in profusion in Kirkdale, Herb Christopher, Herb Paris, Bird's nest Orchid and Columbine. These occur with a great variety of more common plants, ferns, mosses and fungi.

The famous Farndale daffodils, now protected by the National Trust

Although the limestone dales of the Rye and Derwent possess perhaps the finest examples in the park, the many smaller woodlands based on the sandstones, shales and clays in the dales further north are significant reserves of wildlife. The Sessile Oak is the dominant tree in such woods but Birch and Scots Pine are common. The field and herb layers tend to be much poorer in these woods and they are prone to invasion by Bracken and, regrettably, by sheep from the moorland grazings above.

The agricultural area of the park contains much of value and interest. The wet meadows of the limestone belt are particularly rich in species including Globe Flower, Bird's-eye Primrose, Marsh Helleborine, and other orchids. The dry limestone pastures have decreased in area quite considerably and action is needed to protect the few remaining sites. In some of the more fertile areas of the limestone country, the most valuable remaining wildlife refuges are the road verges where a rich flora can still be found, including Primrose, Cowslip, Oxslip and a variety of orchids and violets. Agricultural improvement involving drainage and ploughing has destroyed many valuable sites and much care and vigilance is needed to safeguard the remaining resources.

A striking feature in April is the extensive area of riverside daffodils in Farndale. There are several local legends as to the origin of these plants, some suggesting that the Romans introduced them, others, the Mediaeval monks. The Daffodil is, however, native to the area. Quite why it grows in such profusion in Farndale along the banks of the River Dove and its tributaries is not clear. Daffodils are found in other dales nearby but nowhere in such large concentrations. The flowering of the Farndale plants attracts visitors in their thousands and special traffic and wardening arrangements have to be made to accommodate them. For some time now, it has been an offence to pick the flowering

plants and the whole of the dale was designated a Local Nature Reserve in 1955.

Conservation in the Park

The park is undergoing a rapid change in its landscape and wildlife habitats. The combination of a dry climate, flat plateau surfaces and increasingly sophisticated agricultural and forestry techniques creates a considerable potential for improved agriculture and forestry. There are three problems of a particularly pressing and urgent nature.

The first and the most important in national park terms is the future of the moorland, the largest stretch of heather moorland in England. Its area has fluctuated over the centuries, tending to decrease in periods of high farming, such as the years of the Napoleonic wars when large areas were brought under cultivation, only to increase as the marginal areas were abandoned in periods of recession. Nevertheless, there has been a marked reduction in the area of moorland in the present century and if present trends were to continue, it would disappear completely in the next. This is unlikely for a number of reasons, not the least of which is the very strong aesthetic attraction of the heather moors. Nevertheless with the present techniques, it would be possible to afforest successfully approximately eighty-five per cent of the remaining area of moorland and to improve at least twenty-five per cent for agricultural purposes. The threats to the remaining moors are very real, therefore. Factors which mitigate against moorland conversion include the existence of commoners' rights, currently over about half of the moorland area, the value of grouse moors and the inherently infertile and degraded state of some of the central moors. In fact, the latter problem is probably the greatest threat to the maintenance of moorland in the long term. Apart from the

The Hole of Horcum, a great natural hollow in Levisham Moor

degradation and desolation of the areas damaged by fire, there is growing evidence that the cycle of burning and grazing has depleted the moorland soils over wide areas to such an extent that a threshold has been reached beyond which they can only become healthy and productive with considerable effort and expenditure.

A second major problem concerns the future management of the many small broadleaved woodlands – a problem shared with most other national parks and, indeed, the rest of the country. There is little economic incentive to manage these woods properly, despite increased rates of grant from the Forestry Commission in recent years. A woodland management scheme has been established by the Park Authority to encourage better management and some woods have been purchased or leased by conservation bodies including the Park Committee, the National Trust and the Yorkshire Naturalists' Trust.

The third problem concerns the management of enclosed agricultural land. Drainage, ploughing, removal of hedges, trees and stone walls, the vastly increased use of chemical fertilizers, herbicides and pesticides have all diminished the rich variety of wildlife and landscape. Fortunately, there is a tradition of conservation amongst the farmers which augurs well for the future. The main issue at present concerns the resolution of conflicts with conservation objectives when farm improvements are contemplated. The machinery for resolving these conflicts under the provisions of the recent Wildlife and Countryside Act is clumsy and bureaucratic and appears to be unpopular with both the farmers and the conservationists. Given these ineffective

official procedures, it is likely that local negotiations and cooperation will bring better results. The conservation of the park will thus depend to a large extent on the good sense and taste of the Yorkshire farmer.

Recreation

The natural attractions of the park and its proximity to urban areas ensure that it is well used for many forms of outdoor recreation. Furthermore, it is well placed to receive visitors from further afield, being readily accessible on the principal road system. Surveys have revealed that, in a typical year, the park is visited by over ten million day visitors. In the main, such visitors come from the nearby towns, particularly from Cleveland. Holidaymakers visiting the park mostly stay in resorts just outside.

Perhaps more than most, the North York Moors Park has the physical potential to absorb a large number of visitors without appearing crowded. It has a good network of roads, many of which cross open country where there is ample opportunity for informal parking and picnicking. In addition, there are many areas of forest open for public enjoyment. For the visitors on foot or on horseback, there are some 1,770 km (1,100 miles) of public rights of way and numerous quiet lanes and byeways. Congestion is confined to a few popular beauty spots, particularly in the attractive villages, and along the coast. Over the years, car-parking space has been well provided and the accent now is on developing small scale facilities to relieve local problems and to provide access to a greater variety of scenic and recreational attractions. It is also a cardinal principle of national park policy to protect the qualities of quietness and solitude found in the remoter dales and moorlands.

The motorist and touring visitor can appreciate the varied landscapes to an unusual degree because the ridge top route followed by the majority of the main roads allows many panoramic views over the moors. There are fewer country roads in the new forest areas but these have been

Quoits, a favourite local game, being played at Egton Bridge, Eskdale

opened up by the Forestry Commission who have provided forest drives laid out specifically for recreation with car-parks, picnic areas, toilets, nature trails and information facilities.

Visiting the coast is not so easy. There are few access points and these can become crowded in summer. The old fishing villages of Staithes and Robin Hood's Bay draw large numbers of visitors who have to be prepared for steep climbs on foot if they are to appreciate the local attractions.

The park is fortunate in possessing two railways still functioning. The British Rail Esk Valley Line is a magnificent scenic railway which follows closely the valley of the Esk, crossing and re-crossing the river many times. Visitors can leave the train at several stations in the valley and enjoy the many waymarked walks, some led by guides, to return on a train later in the day. Danby Lodge, the National Park Visitor Centre, is a short distance from one of the stations: in the centre there is a wealth of information about the park with a wide range of services for the visitor. The privately-owned North York Moors Historic Railway runs from Grosmont, where it connects with the Esk Valley Line, to Pickering, 29 km (18 miles) to the south. It is one of the world's oldest railways, with a fascinating engineering history. Passengers can alight at several intermediate stations, including a platform in a particularly remote and beautiful section of the Newtondale gorge where there is a series of waymarked walks laid out specifically for them.

The park is excellent walking country. The easy access to the moors and the predominantly dry, springy turf make it a particular attraction for the long distance walker. There are some sixteen regionally and nationally known routes and more are being designed every year over the network of public paths. The official long distance route is the Cleveland Way. This walk follows the boundaries of the park, including the coast, and covers a distance of 150 km (93 miles). The best known route is the famous Lyke Wake Walk which crosses the park from east to west along the main moorland watershed for some 67 km (42 miles). The walk has become so popular, mainly because of its competitive and social connotations, that severe erosion has developed in the central section where it traverses deep peat. A publicity campaign has been organized by the National Park Authority with the aim of reducing the usage so that remedial measures can be undertaken. There are numerous other delightful and shorter walks and details can be obtained from the National Park Information Centres in the area. One significant difference from other parks is the lack of formal access areas on the open moors. The reason for this is the tradition of public access to the moors, an inheritance which is carefully fostered by both the Park Authority and the landowners and farmers. The Park Ranger Service is the crucial catalyst in this situation and the fact that many local people give up their time to become voluntary rangers is also an important factor.

In addition to the popular informal activities of sight-seeing and walking, a whole host of specialist recreational activities is pursued. Pony-trekking and horse-riding are popular activities over the many bridleways, as might be expected in a horse-loving Yorkshire. There are two gliding clubs and the growing sport of hang-gliding is practised from a few suitable localities, including the Hole of Horcum which is suffering from overuse. Rock-climbing is possible in several places but the park does not possess the rock edges and faces needed for the advanced practitioner. The forest areas are widely used for the modern sports of orienteering and car rallying: motor-cycle scrambling and the new sport of trail riding are also popular. These sports tend to cause conflicts with visitors and residents seeking peace and solitude on the moors. Sailing is possible on the Scaling Dam Reservoir and off the coast and there are large marinas just outside the park at Whitby and Scarborough.

For the field sport enthusiast, the park has much to offer. The grouse moors are internationally known and therefore grouse shooting is very expensive, but there are many opportunities for rough shooting in the dales and woodlands where pheasant, partridge, duck, hares and rabbits are taken. Hunting of foxes and hares is well established over the whole of the park. There are several good fishing rivers and reservoirs including the famous Esk Salmon runs and excellent fishing for Trout and Grayling in the Rye, Derwent and some of the smaller rivers.

With such a rich variety of recreational resources, it is not surprising that the North York Moors National Park is so well used. But, by and large, the balance between recreation and conservation is an acceptable one. It is easy to exaggerate the problems and there is no doubt that the area admirably fulfils the specification of a national park as laid down in the 1949 Act.

Useful Addresses

North York Moors National Park Dept: The Old Vicarage, Bondgate, Helmsley, York YO6 5BP

Danby Lodge National Park Visitor Centre: Lodge Lane, Danby, Whitby YO21 2NB

National Trust Information Centre: Ravenscar, Scarborough, North Yorkshire

Yorkshire Naturalists' Trust: 20 Castlegate, York

Cleveland Nature Conservation Trust: 38 Victoria Rd, Hartlepool, Cleveland TS26 8BL

The Winnats Pass near Castleton in the Peak District

Roy Christian

Peak District

PEAK NATIONAL PARK

ESIGNATED IN April 1951, the Peak District National Park is the oldest of Britain's ten Parks. Its 1,404 square km (542 square miles) of diverse scenery – often wild to the point of desolation but always beautiful – at the southern tip of the Pennines extend into six counties: Derbyshire, Staffordshire, Cheshire, Greater Manchester, South Yorkshire and West Yorkshire. This largely explains why, instead of being administered by a county council committee, it has its own administration, the Peak Park Joint Planning Board, which includes representatives from the six counties. This autonomy is a valuable safeguard against severe external pressures, for while only 38,000 people live within the park about seventeen million – nearly one-third of the population of the United Kingdom – have their homes within fifty miles of its boundaries. Its western edge overlooks the sprawling conurbation of Greater Manchester; twenty miles away on its eastern fringe the city centre of Sheffield is within walking distance. The northern tip stands above the Oldham–Huddersfield road linking the traditional cotton towns of Lancashire with the woollen towns of Yorkshire. Nottingham, Derby and the Potteries all lie within twenty miles of the southern boundary.

From Meltham Moor in the north the park extends southward for nearly forty miles to Fenny Bentley. Its western tip at Pott Shrigley, overlooking the Cheshire Plain, is twenty-four miles from the eastern edge near Owler Bar. The park's roughly oval outline has been distorted by the deliberate exclusion of certain areas which were already marred by industrialism (mainly limestone quarrying), the most conspicuous being a long, narrow peninsula biting deeply in from New Mills in the west to encircle Buxton. A less noticeable incision in the south-east excludes Matlock.

The name 'Peak' is misleading for an area in which few hills have pointed summits, but it derives in fact from the people who lived there around the seventh century. They were called simply Pecsaetans, 'hill dwellers'. The hills over which they roamed rarely exceed 610 m (2,000 ft) or fall below 244 m (800 ft). Central southern Peakland, southward from the Hope Valley, is basically a grassy plateau through which the rivers have cut deep, narrow, winding trenches

that are the famous Derbyshire Dales. On three sides of the plateau is a horseshoe of higher, wilder country which extends northward to the park boundary as a moorland plateau. The two distinctive areas are often called the Low Peak and the High Peak, but the Ordnance Survey draws a clearer distinction in calling them the White Peak and the Dark Peak after the colour of the dominant rocks.

Geology and Landscape

To know the Peak Park you need to know something of those rocks; 'the stone', as Sir John Betjeman put it; 'stone of such variety, colour and quality as is found nowhere else in England'.

Carboniferous Limestone and Millstone Grit with subordinate shales are the most important rock formations. The Carboniferous Limestone came first, laid down over 300 million years ago from the shells and bodies of minute organisms and from decaying stone-lilies under a shallow sea – sometimes clear, sometimes muddy – that then extended over the whole of what is now Peakland. The calcareous remains of myriads of tiny creatures fossilized to form limestone. In time reefs built up to form an irregular chain around a lagoon some twenty miles long and ten miles wide whose bed was composed of crinoid – sea-lilies – coral and shell-sand. This lagoon is now the central limestone area of the park; the reefs around its fringes – in the Castleton area and the distinctive conical hills of the upper-Dove valley – are rich in fossils. Beyond the reefs lay deeper water into which was washed mud from rivers farther north to become the Edale Shales. Later, coarser sediments – grit and gravel – were carried down from the same direction to form sandbanks which eventually became the massive hard rock we call Millstone Grit. Spasmodically during this gradual process, small submarine volcanoes erupted, throwing out lava which solidified to become the local toadstone. Blocked vents of extinct volcanoes have been identified at Grange Mill and Calton Hill.

Occasionally the land rose above the water. Seeds and spores driven by water and wind settled and germinated in a warm, moist climate to form tropical forest. Gradually the

A school party visiting Padley Chapel, near Grindleford Bridge

Erosion and a slight sinking of the land continued after folding ceased. Debris from distant mountains added to existing lowland piles, burying all Peakland under waste. It remained covered throughout the Mesozoic Era of about 120 million years, during the later part of which most of Britain lay under a clear, warm sea. When it finally re-emerged, the streams of water pouring off the Derbyshire Dome helped to wear away the younger rocks and expose again – and even cut into – the Carboniferous rocks, following courses they had cut through younger rocks and ignoring the folds of older rocks below. This superimposed drainage system accounts for the wide variety of scenery found in the river valleys.

When the streams started cutting through Cretaceous rocks the Peak outline was already formed; only the detailed carving remained. In this the Great Ice Age played a much less significant part than in Snowdonia or the Lake District. Although ice from the north-west penetrated the valley of the Derwent as far south as Matlock, and may have changed the river's course, its chief effect on the scenery can be seen in the north-west, where there are moraines in the Goyt Valley at Taxal and in the Todd Valley near Whaley Bridge. The mysterious trench called the Roosdyche, running from the Goyt Valley to Eccles Pike, is now attributed to glaciation rather than man, but the main effect of the arctic conditions was to intensify the action of more normal agents of erosion on valley slopes.

The work of such denuding agents as rain-water and frost can be seen most dramatically in Dovedale, where by vertical erosion the Dove has cut down from its peneplain (*pene*=almost) through successive layers of younger rocks to carve itself a trench in the limestone. As the river winds through the deep ravine it reveals round each bend a fresh picture of the effects of weathering. Massive monoliths like Ilam Rock and Tissington Spires are the remnants of spurs that projected into the gorge until frost, attacking from both sides of the spurs, worked its way along the main joints to detach them. Rain-water containing dissolved carbon dioxide then dissolved the corners and edges to produce pinnacles that often rise sheer from the water. Fan-shaped screes at the base of the cliffs – 'slitherbanks' locally – have been formed by melting snow filling vertical cracks or joints and near-horizontal bedding planes, and then, as ice, expanding, prising out lumps of limestone from the cliff-face. Cliffside caves, like Dove Holes and Reynard's Cave are the result of tributary streams dissolving themselves underground courses which were drained dry when the Dove itself deepened its channel below their level. Reynard's Cave has a splendid detached doorway, a natural limestone arch twelve metres (forty feet) high and five and a half metres wide.

Streams that disappear underground are fairly common on the limestone. Manifold, Bradford and Lathkill all flow below ground for considerable distances in all but the wettest

debris of plants became peat which was buried under mud and clay when the land was again submerged. The resultant pressure and the chemical reaction that followed changed the peat into coal and the mud above it into shale. This sequence of events, repeated several times, resulted in the building up of a series of grit layers interspersed with shales and occasional coal seams.

Great pressure on the earth's crust then crumpled the Carboniferous rocks into a series of folds. One broad fold running north and south – 'like an irregular and elongated dome' as Patrick Monkhouse put it – is known today as the Derbyshire Dome. In cross-section it resembles a wave about to break; its eastern side gradually rises to a crest from which it falls sharply on the west and is broken by faults or rock-fractures. When the crests of the folds were thrust upwards they were attacked by frost and rain which removed the accumulations of clays, shales, fine sandstone and coal seams – collectively known as the Coal Measures – to deposit their debris in the lowlands, leaving the Millstone Grits exposed to these abrasive forces. Being harder, they withstood them better. Only in the south of the area were the grits so worn away as to expose the limestone core. Farther north and on each side the gritstone cover remained. One may think of the Derbyshire Dome – in a simplified form – in terms of an ageing man's balding head when viewed from the front, with the flesh (Carboniferous Limestone) exposed from brow to crown and then hidden under hair (Millstone Grit) from there and at the sides.

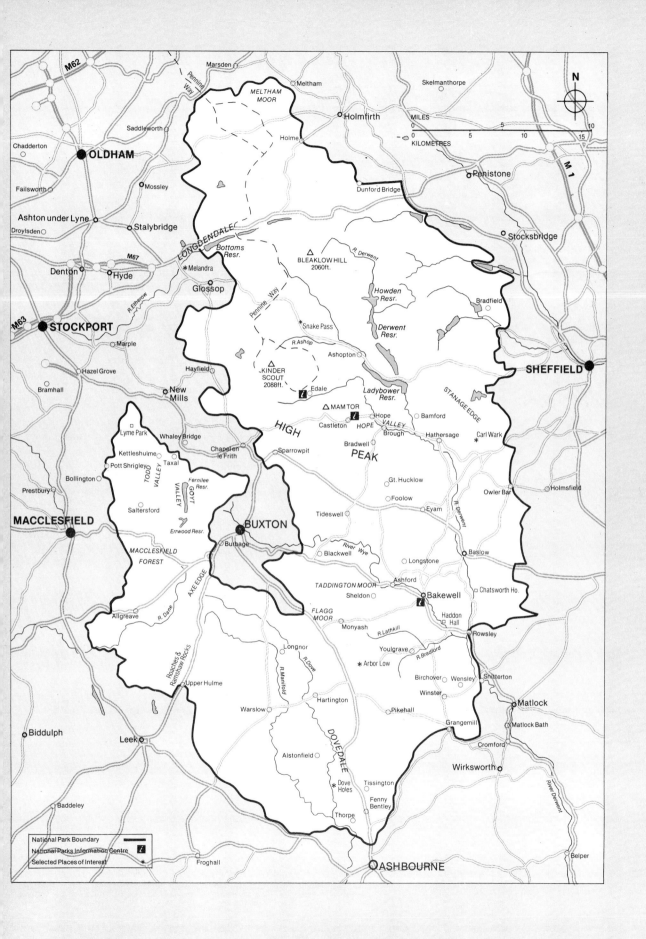

seasons, having descended down cracks and joints in the rock until reaching the water table. The water then follows a subterranean course, dissolving away the limestone on either side of its paths. The level of the water table rises or falls according to the wetness of the season and may eventually dissolve the roof of the cave which it has carved out. This then becomes a new dale which may be dry for part of the year. Most of the numerous caves occur on the margins of the limestone area where streams flow down from the higher gritstone on to highly soluble reef limestone, as in the Castleton–Bradwell area. Westward, in the Winnats–Sparrow-

Monkey Flowers by the River Dove in Dovedale, a favourite haunt of Izaak Walton

pit area, streams running off the shale or grit beds have passed underground through the system of joints or fissures in the limestone, forming swallow holes, whose points of entry have been enlarged over a long period into inverted cone shapes.

In finding the most convenient routes off the gritstone the rivers take widely divergent courses. The Derwent, rising on the eastern side of Bleaklow, flows south-eastward to the Trent, but the Etherow, from a source only slightly north, takes a westerly course to become a constituent stream of the Mersey with the Dane and Goyt which have followed widely different routes from adjacent sources on Axe Edge, close to those of Dove and Manifold which ultimately join the Trent.

Those high northern moorlands, on which Derwent and Etherow rise, convey a sense of exhilaration that comes only in wild places, but they could become monotonous were it not for the endless variety of cloughs; narrow, steep-sided ravines carved out by streams fed by a vast underground reservoir to which rainwater has penetrated through several hundred feet of gritstone. East of the Derwent the western limit of the moorland is defined by a series of gritstone scarps – known locally as 'edges' – which run for miles above the valley as an almost continuous high wall of rock stretching to the park's southern limit. On the western margin of the Dome sharp north-to-south folds crossed by minor ones trending west to east have produced a more varied scenery of ridges and valleys, but there is no more impressive gritstone scenery within the park than the rocky face of the ridge formed by the Roaches and Ramshaw Rocks whose face has been carved into strange shapes by the action of wind, rain and frost.

Man in the Park

Man came to the region before the end of the Ice Age, but the evidence he left in limestone caves is so fragmentary as to suggest that the Palaeolithic (Old Stone Age) hunter was a mere fleeting visitor seeking temporary shelter while pursuing the reindeer. Mesolithic (Middle Stone Age) man also came rarely, but left behind evidence of an early industry. A rock-shelter above the Wye revealed 588 man-made implements of flint and chert, the majority shaped from local materials.

The earliest settlers – the first to make tentative changes to the landscape – were Neolithic (New Stone Age) farmers who arrived about 3000 BC from the west, probably from North Wales, to settle mainly on the limestone uplands, where eight of their chambered barrows have been found, including Five Wells, on Taddington Moor, at 427 m (1,400 ft) the highest sited megalithic tomb in Britain. From bones, flint and pottery found in these tombs and in caves, one can visualize groups of pastoralists herding livestock in woodland clearings on light, well-drained soil close to emerging springs, and through the grazing of their sheep and goats beginning the woodland clearance that continued until coke and coal replaced charcoal for lead smelting and lime burning in the eighteenth century.

On these limestone uplands lie the majority of the numerous round barrows of the Late Neolithic and Bronze Age periods, though the gritstone summit of Stanton Moor has more than seventy barrow and stone circle sites. From that period, about 2000–1500 BC, comes the most spectacular, most atmospheric of all the park's prehistoric monuments; the Arbor Low stone circle, commanding the limestone plateau from an isolated, wind-swept hillock at 375 m (1,230 ft). Whether its forty recumbent stones on their ditch-enclosed grassy platform within a surrounding fifty feet mound were ever upright is as much a mystery as the purpose of the site and its link with Gib Hill, the largest round barrow, 300 yards southward.

Similar uncertainty surrounds the purpose, even the date of most of a dozen Iron Age forts. The largest, on the summit of Mam Tor above the Hope Valley, has been dated around 500 BC, roughly the time when iron was first used, belatedly, in the area. But Carl Wark, on a splendid defensive site on Hathersage Moor, may be 1,000 years later, after the departure of the Romans, who worked the lead locally but left little trace on the face of the park, whose harsh climate and wild terrain discouraged settlement. Small forts at Brough (*Navio*) and Melandra, just outside the park, guarded an east–west road, now known as Doctor's Gate. From Brough another road (Batham Gate) ran to Buxton (*Aquae Arnemetiae*), where two Roman baths were excavated in the seventeenth and eighteenth centuries and later destroyed. A road leading south-eastward towards Little Chester (*Derventio*), has been traced intermittently, but much remains undiscovered about the Roman communications network.

Almost two centuries passed after the Romans left before Anglian settlers from the Mercian lowlands moved into the hills late in the sixth century. A few place-names – Wensley, 'Woden's Glade'; Friden, 'Frig's Valley' – suggest pagan Anglian settlements. Christianity followed from its first Mercian centre at Repton a century later. Various preaching crosses have survived, the most complete being now in the churchyards at Eyam and Bakewell. Both date from the eighth century and were found on the moors. No Anglo-Saxon church fabric survives except a few fragments at Bakewell, where a vast pre-Norman church was planned on the site of an earlier church but never completed.

Anglo-Saxon place names – Ashford, Ashopton, Birchover – suggest a wooded landscape. The scarcity of Danish place-names – Thorpe and Kettleshulme being rare exceptions – hint at freedom from Viking or Scandinavian invasion. When the Domesday Book was compiled the pattern of settlement in the park that we know today was already established. A few sites have since been deserted because of changes in farming, the extension of parklands, or, in our time, the construction of the Ladybower Reservoir, the largest of more than fifty reservoirs that have drowned agricultural land in the valleys. But the vast majority of the present villages were mentioned, though most within the 180 square miles of the Royal Forest of the Peak were described as 'waste'. These were only settled – or re-settled – during the Middle Ages as the edges of this tract of wild country were nibbled away until it ceased officially to be a royal hunting forest in 1674.

Peakland parishes tend to be much larger than the average of about 1,000 hectares (2,560 acres) for lowland Midland parishes. Hope parish embraced two-thirds of the Forest and even at the end of the nineteenth century it still covered 15,500 hectares (38,400 acres) – of mostly empty grouse moor – for 2,000 inhabitants. Hartington, stretching sixteen miles from north to south, was divided into four quarters, still named on modern maps as Upper, Middle, Nether and Town Quarters. Its population was – and is – about 400.

The villages, occupying a fraction of their parish, sprang up where water and level ground coincided. Names like Bakewell, Bradwell and Tideswell, all on permeable limestone, are significant. Typical limestone villages stretch out lengthways along narrow shelves of level ground, as at Wensley and Youlgrave, or on a valley floor alongside a stream as at Tideswell. Nucleated villages around a green occur exceptionally at Monyash, Hartington, Foolow and Tissington, each with a mere, or pond, by the green. The Dales are usually too narrow for settlement. On the gritstone and shale, where water is more plentiful, settlement is more dispersed, with south-facing sites favoured in the northern valleys.

Villages are built of locally quarried stone, though, even in limestone areas, features like lintels and quoins are often of gritstone. Many buildings survive from the late seventeenth century 'Great Rebuilding', with local stone slate roofs and mullioned windows, but as in the Cotswolds the vernacular style has retained a unity that makes dating difficult. This is particularly true of the small but charming manor houses. New fashions came late to the remote Peak and such typical 'Elizabethan' houses as Eyam, Hartington and Snitterton Halls date in fact from the seventeenth century.

Collectively, the churches are less noteworthy than the houses, but there are fine buildings at Bakewell, Hartington, Youlgrave and Alstonfield, among others. The most unusual church is the little early-Georgian Jenkin Chapel at Saltersford. The most impressive is the massive, grand and dignified

Stone walls enclose the ancient lane running behind Tideswell Church

parish church of Tideswell, rich in monuments and carvings and surmounted by a splendid eight-pinnacled tower. Built over a fifty year period in the fourteenth century – with a break because of the Black Death – at a time when the small market town was a booming wool and lead centre, it owes its preservation to a decline in prosperity that precluded changes to the fabric.

Sheep and lead were the basis of the economy before the nineteenth century. Religious houses as distant as Dunstable Priory in Bedfordshire and Basingwerk Abbey in Flint had great sheep runs on the high ground. Many of the monastic granges from which these ranches were managed remain, much modernized, characteristically sheltering in a fold of the hills. Beyond the farmstead, the land is criss-crossed by a network of mortarless stone walls, dating mainly from late eighteenth century enclosures, though some survive from earlier piecemeal enclosure. Sometimes a single strip was enclosed, which explains the long, narrow fields round some upland villages, though in remote areas gavelkind (inheritance by all sons in equal portions) may have been practised. The open-field system, though not universal, was widespread, but not necessarily with a three-field rotation; Sheldon had a single open-field, and there is evidence of two and four-field systems.

Sheep-rearing continues today, especially in the Dark Peak, where the traditional speckle-faced, hornless Derbyshire Gritstone breed may now be equalled in number by the smaller but equally hardy Swaledale. Heavier, more fastidious Cluns and Kerry Hills are numerous on lower ground. But in the White Peak, sheep may be outnumbered by beef cattle which have recently increased at the expense of dairy herds. Away from the gritstone tops, farms tend to be mixed and holdings small, although the holders of less than seventy-five acres, whose ancestors combined farming with lead mining to earn a living, are disappearing very rapidly, along with the field-barns, and the artificial meres so necessary on permeable limestone until the advent of piped water in the last half century. Farmhouse holidays and caravan camps – carefully controlled by the Park Board – provide useful cash-crops for enterprising farmers, while some barns are being converted, experimentally, into 'stone tents' to provide basic, low-cost accommodation for tourists.

If, as the Park Structure Plan says, 'farming activity has created most of the scenery of the Peak District', lead-mining has contributed countless mine-shafts, spoil-heaps, lines of trees planted to keep cattle off polluted ground and the occasional crumbling engine-house. Less obtrusive among riverside foliage are the mouths of soughs, drainage channels bored at enormous cost to rid the mines of their major enemy, water. Lead-mining continued almost to World War II, but as a major industry it perished nearly a century earlier. Its spoil-heaps have been reworked in this century for the fluorspar that the miners rejected. Three-quarters of Britain's fluorspar, used in the chemical, ceramic and steel industries, comes from a small area on the eastern side of the limestone uplands, mostly now from mines which damage the landscape less than past open-cast workings which have scarred the profile of Longstone Edge.

The extraction of such other minerals as barytes – used in underwater oil-drilling – calcite and chert, even of gritstone – so heavily in demand for nineteenth century railway buildings – has done far less damage to the landscape than limestone quarrying, which before the recession, was consuming land at a weekly rate equivalent to the area of a football pitch and the height of a two-storey house. While the industry creates much-needed employment and carves out some exciting rock scenery, this loss of land, the attendant mess and the generation of heavy lorry traffic impose severe strains on an area which otherwise scenically is the sort of Paradise that it was to eighteenth century visitors.

Flora and Fauna

The first point to be made about the natural history is that the park is a transitional area between highland and lowland Britain. For many species it coincides with their southern or northern limit. W H Hudson made this point earlier in the century when he visited the Peak District, 'just to spend a few weeks during the breeding season with half a dozen birds, all familiar enough to most ornithologists, but which are not found, at all events not all together, nearer to London than the Derbyshire hills!' So he went off to Axe Edge 'on the gritstone formation, harsh and desolate in aspect, but covered with a dense growth of heather, bilberry and coarse grasses – a habitation of birds'.

Before looking at those birds, it is necessary to make a second point; that the covering of those gritstone moors has changed greatly since the Ice Age, as modern techniques of pollen analysis have shown. After the last snow in sheltered hollows had melted, Pine, later Alder, and even Oak, gained a foothold and eventually became dominant. Probably because the climate became wetter after about 6000 BC, *Sphagnum* bogs developed and peat started to accumulate at heights over 366 m (1,200 ft). As bog displaced the tree cover a peat blanket formed, gradually evolving a drainage pattern as bog bursts occurred on the margins of raised bogs to weaken the peat's stability. Forest vegetation, however, survived at lower levels where the climate was less severe and steep slopes prevented waterlogging. Here, pollen counts reveal a decline of the Elm around 3000 BC, caused partly by a slight change to drier conditions and partly by Neolithic man's first attempt at woodland clearance, and, as there is an accompanying increase in grass pollen, at agriculture. The amount of tree pollen in the peat declines steadily from this time, and the presence of charcoal around 1300 AD suggests the use of burning in man's attack on the wilderness then, an attack which was only just beginning on the higher Kinder and Bleaklow plateaux where there is no marked drop in the tree pollen count until after 1100 AD.

Great changes have taken place in the last two centuries. The most dramatic is the replacement of *Sphagnum* moss by tussocks of Cotton-grass above deep bog and eroding peat on the flat wet plateau summit. Strictly speaking a sedge, which explains its fecundity on poorly drained land, the fluffy white Cotton-grass brings a lightness to the moors in early summer which is lacking for the greater part of the year. The masses of downy whiteness may account for such names as Featherbed Moss and White Path Moss. Beneath this surface mat of Cotton-grass the peat consists mainly of *Sphagnum* remains, but very few patches of true *Sphagnum* bog have survived and consequently such plants as Cranberry, Round-leaved Sundew and Bog Rosemary have become very rare indeed. One rich growth of Cranberry flourishes on Goldsitch Moss below the West Moors along with Bog Asphodel but, oddly, the sundews which normally thrive in similar conditions are missing. Above 460 m (1,500 ft), especially where the peat has eroded, patches of Cloudberry survive in its most southerly habitat.

Several factors may have influenced the change from *Sphagnum* to Cotton-grass. A slight reduction in precipitation – still over 1,524 mm (60 inches) annually, compared with 890–1,016 mm (35–40 inches) in the White Peak, with snow falling on an average of seventy days – and the eighteenth century drainage schemes may have played some part, as have sheep grazing and trampling. The main factor has probably been atmospheric pollution since the beginning of the Industrial Revolution, much of it borne by the prevailing westerly winds from industrial Lancashire and north Cheshire but some from the South Yorkshire coal and steel area, as well as from lime kilns and quarries closer to hand. The rarity of lichen, acutely sensitive to atmospheric pollution, supports this theory as does the noticeable recovery of plant life on the East Moors since Sheffield has become smokeless.

The policy of burning, at first to aid sheep grazing and, since the mid-nineteenth century, as a contribution to grouse moor management, has helped to destroy the lichen and to encourage heathers to become the dominant cover on the gentle, well-drained western and northern slopes of Kinder and Bleaklow and in the Upper Derwent Valley up to about 460 m (1,500 ft), above which Cotton-grass takes over. Moor-burning produces a patchwork effect. Within each patch all the heather plants develop at about the same rate and many of the plants formerly associated with the heather tend

Raking hay near Little Hucklow

to be excluded. This would account for the disappearance within the last century of species of Club-moss, and the presence of Bearberry – here almost at its southern limit – Twayblade, one of the least conspicuous of larger orchids and Chickweed Wintergreen only in a few places where burning is rare.

The third type of vegetation mentioned by Hudson is dominated by Bilberry, which is less widespread than either Cotton-grass or heathers. Sharing with heathers a preference for drier conditions, it thrives best on moderate gradients with a thinner layer of peat. Below the Kinder plateau it forms an almost continuous fringe and at lower levels it shares the ground with the heathers. With heathers and Mat-grass it helps to cover the summit of Bleaklow, from which the peat cover has vanished. Tracts of Bilberry, and Cowberry, are found on the East Moors, an area otherwise dominated by heathers, and both plants produced vastly more fruit here than on the wetter areas of Kinder and Bleaklow. Bilberry also grows luxuriantly in well-drained patches of woodland on steep-sided rocky slopes of cloughs and below the gritstone 'edges' in places inaccessible to sheep.

It is due to this inaccessibility that the remnants of the oak and birch forests that once cloaked the gritstone hills survive, the gnarled, stumpy trees rooted in leaf-mould and decaying grit between the boulders. The most extensive is Padley Wood, on the gritstone slopes above the Upper Derwent Valley, which may be a survival of the natural oakwood that once covered the Burbage Valley and beyond. Although too rough and rocky for regular grazing, it has been penetrated by occasional wandering sheep, preventing regeneration of the Oaks. Almost half the survivors are between 100 and 300 years old, and Birches which regenerate freely are becoming the predominant trees, though Alders flourish on the damper, lower slopes and there are occasional Rowans. In the shade of the trees, large heaps of twigs and leaf midribs cover the nests of the northern type of Wood Ant, *Formica rufa*, which is not found further to the south-east. The older trees provide nesting sites for the Green and Great Spotted Woodpecker, Tree Creeper and that rare summer visitor the Pied Flycatcher, a bird which used to breed only in the north and west of Britain but now seems to be extending its range southwards.

Nowadays, coniferous woodlands, planted by the Forestry Commission, Park Board, water authorities and some private owners, cover a greater acreage than broadleaved varieties. The ancient Macclesfield Forest in the west of the park, surprisingly ignored in the Domesday Book, although it must already have existed, has re-emerged under a coat of softwood trees. Slightly to the north east, a new Goyt Forest has been born, and there are similar recent arrivals on valley slopes elsewhere, particularly around the

A cottage in the Hope Valley, between Bamford and Castleton

reservoirs. Scots Pine covers about half the area under softwood timber, but there is much Lodgepole Pine and Sitka Spruce around the Derwent reservoirs. In the wild valleys of the Ashop and Alport, around the Snake Pass, Japanese Larch has done well. These newer coniferous woodlands seem to retain their resident birds for some time, but once they have gone it may be many years before new species arrive. More mature woodlands, especially when they contain a smattering of deciduous trees, as in parts of the Derwent valley, attract the Woodcock, Sparrowhawk, Tawny and Long-eared Owl in addition to Tree Creeper and Great Spotted Woodpecker. The newer plantations, lacking much ground vegetation have little attraction for ground insects

Mergansers have been reported from the Goyt ones, where such rare visitors as Puffin and Leach's Petrel have been observed. Otherwise Moorhens, a few pairs of Mallard and Common Sandpipers, fewer Teal are the regular residents, though Gannet and Red-throated Divers have been among occasional visitors.

The gritstone moorland offers much more to ornithologists. That is the place to hear the cry of the Curlew, the Golden Plover with its characteristic 'peep-eep' and the rasping warning notes of the Red Grouse defending its territory. That is where Hudson went to find 'the bird life peculiar to the district – grouse, curlew, golden plover, snipe and summer snipe, water and ring-ousel'. In winter the Red Grouse – in fact brown with black wings – may have the hilltops to himself, appropriately perhaps for a bird which has greatly influenced the history and appearance of the moors. It attracted wealthy Victorian sportsmen whose gamekeepers deterred sheep and ramblers while encouraging the growth of heathers and Bilberry. The grouse feeds mainly on close-cropped youngish heather – of five or six years' growth – but for nesting longer heather of around twelve years is preferred, which contributes to the patchy appearance of the moors.

Gamekeepers drove out most predators, but Sparrowhawks, equally unpopular with shepherds and farmers, survived in small numbers and may be found on the slopes of such valleys as Longdendale, Woodlands and Edale, as well as in more remote cloughs where Merlin have their habitat. Kestrels are fairly common, unlike the diurnal Short-eared Owls, which began to breed again on the moors in the war years when gamekeepers tended to be engaged elsewhere, but have declined again since. They depend on a good supply of small mammals, especially the Short-tailed Voles which have increased in number since the reduction of the predator population. Gamekeepers persecuted even possible predators like the Raven. Once fairly widespread in the High Peak, as place-names like Raven's Tor and Raven's Nest testify, they were driven out in the second half of the last century and are now very rare visitors. Of other birds, the Black Grouse breeds in small numbers and sightings have been reported of cocks performing their peculiar courtship dances, known as 'leks'. Golden Plover and Snipe, both mentioned by Hudson, maintain their numbers. The less numerous Dunlin nest on the highest, soggiest moors. In recent years there has been a marked increase in numbers of Twite, that attractive member of the finch family, but the most common of all moorland birds is possibly the Meadow Pipit.

Many species of birds are common to all areas of the park, among them the Dipper, whose 'dip dip' call and dipping action from some island boulder is as likely to be encountered on the limestone dales as in rivers of the Dark

other than a small number of moths whose larvae feed on pine needles.

The newer reservoirs, similarly, have so far attracted little wildlife. The eighteenth century Combs Reservoir, a mile outside the park, attracts more birds than any inside, partly perhaps because it has gently sloping banks and comparative freedom from acidity. The six mid-nineteenth century Longdendale reservoirs, the three in the Upper Derwent Valley and two in the Goyt Valley, all built in the twentieth century, repel birds because of their elevation, high retaining walls, lack of suitable shore vegetation and depth and acidity of the water. But Blackheaded gulls have recently bred in the Longdendale reservoirs, and breeding

A group of young ramblers follow the leader in Dovedale

Peak. That used to be equally true of the Ring-Ouzel, but more intensive farming on the limestone seems to be forcing him almost exclusively on to the gritstone.

If the birds of the gritstone are more distinguished, those of the limestone are more numerous and varied, except on the central upland plateau, which is almost treeless apart from shelter-belts, mainly of Sycamore and Beech, around farmsteads and occasional groves. Skylarks and Lapwings are the characteristic birds of this open country which must have lost its tree-cover by the mid-sixteenth century when William Camden wrote of 'grassy hills and vales which feed abundance of cattle and great stocks of sheep very securely'. When the woodlands went, the deep, brown plateau soil became subject to leaching, and small patches of heath remain in places to attract the birds of the gritstone country. Elsewhere, the bedrock has a deep protective covering of insoluble debris from the weathering of the limestone, and dust brought in by cold northerly winds in glacial times. Consequently, farming can be successfully carried on at over 300 m (1,000 ft), although, paradoxically, the soil tends to be lime-deficient.

The lower slopes of the valleys of the mid-Derwent and Wye are beautifully wooded, mainly as result of planting by Georgian landowners. Successive Dukes of Devonshire have planted many thousands of trees on their estates since the early eighteenth century. The fifth Duke of Rutland planted

Hang gliding off Mam Tor on a hot and hazy day

extensively along the Wye Valley in the early nineteenth century, and other landowners followed these examples. These woods, and the ash woods on the thinner soil of the dale slopes, support many of the commoner woodland birds, particularly the Chaffinch and Willow Warbler, with a recent marked increase in Nuthatch. House Martins often nest in crags above the dales and Herons have been known to nest in some of the larger areas of woodland. Little Grebe, Mallard and Moorhen nest in the dales, while Tufted Duck and Coot may be found where the water flows slowly. Pied and Grey Wagtails share rocks with Dippers in their search for insects. Kingfishers are by no means rare. Kestrels, Jackdaws, Little Owls and Wheatears inhabit the dry dales.

If the birds of the dales are unexceptional, there is ample compensation in the richness of the plant life. To mention more than a small selection would be too space-consuming. It may suffice to glance at the Derbyshire Dales Nature Reserve, established in 1972 as the first national nature reserve in the park. It now extends into five of the dales. The largest section, in Lathkill Dale comprises mainly ash and elm woodland; in the other dales are limestone outcrop and screes, scrub and grassland. The reserve offers some of the best examples of woodland, grassland and scrub on Carboniferous Limestone in Britain. Beneath the canopy of trees

in Lathkill Dale the astonishing variety of shrubs includes Mezereon, whose fragrant pink flowers are rarely seen now in early spring in the calcareous woods of southern England, and only in the Peak on about half a dozen sites. There are also Wild Privet, Guelder Rose and Dogwood, Bird Cherry, Rock Whitebeam, and Purging Buckthorn. The herbaceous plants are no less impressive: Dog's Mercury, which carpets the woods on limestone screes in summer, Wood Sanicle, the white-flowered Enchanter's Nightshade – which is unrelated to other nightshades – Solomon's Seal and Herb Robert are among them. Monk's Dale's quite different but equally varied selection includes that rare Derbyshire native the Spring Cinquefoil, the Nottingham Catchfly, which flourishes more widely on south-facing limestone screes in the park than anywhere else in Britain, and, in one place only, Herb Paris, a strange plant whose sole greenish flower surmounts a whorl of four leaves.

The Derbyshire Naturalists' Trust and similar neighbouring bodies administer around two dozen nature reserves in the park. Many of them are in disused limestone quarries, where orchids flourish particularly well and kestrels breed on the rock faces. Plant life is equally vigorous on lead-mine

The local custom of well-dressing is here performed at the Town Well, Tissington

*The Duke and Duchess of Devonshire with the
magnificent west front of Chatsworth*

spoil heaps. Where the lead content is high, Spring Sandwort (locally known as Leadwort) grows among the Sheep's Fescue on its most southerly sites in Britain. Where the ore is prevalent the mounds are made more colourful by blue and yellow Mountain Pansies, purple Thyme, blue Germander Speedwell and, rarest of all, the Alpine Pennycress, which grows nowhere else on the mainland of Great Britain. Silica sand-pits are now among the few sites in the park that support the uncommon Stagshorn Club moss, relative of the ferns. Even the ugly lagoons of slurry from the fluorspar workings attract concentrations of gulls and migrant water birds. The Derbyshire Naturalists' Trust has carried out several rescue transplants, with the cooperation of the firms concerned, from sites threatened by industry. Colonies of the rare Red Helleborine, Bee Orchid and Stagshorn Clubmoss have been saved in this way.

Signs of an increase in the butterfly population must be linked to a noticeable advance of scrub in the dales in recent years. The Dark Green Fritillary and the Peacock butterfly seem to have re-established themselves after long absences, and the Small Pearl-bordered Fritillary was seen in the Via Gellia in the 1970s for the first time for seventy years.

One of the most interesting resident mammals is the Mountain Hare which feeds on heathers and Cotton-grass on the peat moors. A native in pre-historic times, it disappeared from the area around 4000 BC and was reintroduced from the Scottish Highlands a century ago. In summer it is distinguishable from the more common Brown Hare because its fur has a slight grey-blue tinge that gives it the alternative name of Blue Hare. In mid-winter the fur turns almost completely white, as does that of the Stoat – less common in the park than the Weasel – in exceptionally hard winters. A few Red Squirrels may still survive in coniferous woodlands and Badgers are fairly numerous in the dales.

Visitors to Chatsworth will probably be rewarded with a distant view of Fallow Deer, and another herd roams Stanton Park. A Red Deer herd has inhabited Lyme Park since 1300. But the most unusual animals in the park are the Wallabies which survive after escaping from a private zoo half a century ago. After a series of mild winters their numbers increased to about forty, but the severe winter of 1981–2 is thought to have reduced them.

Recreation

The Peak Park is a paradise for walkers, and walking is easily the most popular form of recreation. For people who want to see the high moors or the dales it is a necessity, for these areas are inaccessible to motorists. Walking in the Kinder Scout and Bleaklow area, including the southernmost – and arguably the hardest – thirty miles of the Pennine Way from Edale, is only for those fully equipped in every sense. The weather up there can change with dramatic suddenness, and a peat bog in mist and sleet is no place for a walker in city shoes and without a compass. Less ambitious walkers will find pleasant, safe and level walking in attractive surrounds on the Tissington, High Peak and Sett Valley Trails along the tracks of former railways. The Monsal Trail (opened in 1982) along the old main Midland Railway line through the Peak will prove equally popular when the Park Board have the funds to lay a more even surface than the present limestone chippings. Before the last war the Staffordshire County Council established the first of all these ex-railway tracks through the Manifold Valley which provides a walk almost as exciting as through neighbouring Dove Dale on a path less badly eroded by the trampling of too many feet. Weekdays out of season are the best times for tramping the Dales.

The park provides some of the best rock-climbing in England. The gritstone 'edges', in particular, have proved excellent training faces for Everest climbers. Those who prefer the added spice of climbing underground find the numerous subterranean cave-systems and pot-holes in the park much to their liking, and constantly add to the store of knowledge about this fascinating and often watery underworld.

Going almost literally to the other extreme, gliding can be watched every weekend in the year from the viewing enclosure on the ninety-acre flying field of the Derbyshire and Lancashire Gliding Club at Great Hucklow, where the World Gliding Championships were held in 1954. A series of five-day holiday courses for those wishing to sample the sport are held during the summer, course members being accommodated in the clubhouse, where full board is provided. Hang-gliding is a newer variation practised from Stanage Edge and elsewhere in the High Peak.

In an average Peakland winter, Edale becomes a winter sports centre for the valley slopes are considered to provide the best ski-ing in the park. Good ice-climbing practice can be obtained locally in the gullies of Kinder Scout and Bleaklow in suitable weather.

Pony-trekking has become increasingly popular, and there is a corresponding growth in the number of centres, sometimes combined with farmhouse holidays. Most of the trails already mentioned are open to riders and cyclists – who can hire cycles from several centres, mostly adjacent to the trails.

The park has some of the country's best trout streams, as readers of *The Compleat Angler* will recall. Much of the

fishing in them is private, but riparian hotels usually have stretches reserved for residents. Fly-fishing on the Ladybower Reservoir is permissible with a permit obtainable from the Severn–Trent Fishery Office at Bamford.

Dinghy sailing clubs operate on Errwood Reservoir in the Goyt Valley and Bottoms Reservoir in Longdendale.

A celebrated pack of harriers, the High Peak, hunt the long-legged Mountain Hare two days a week in the season over land mainly above 300 m (1,000 ft), and hold a point-to-point meeting on Flagg Moor each Easter Tuesday.

For people wishing to learn more about the countryside, and the park in particular, courses are held in the Peak Park Study Centre, Losehill Hall, a nineteenth century mansion at Castleton. The courses vary in subject, length and intensity, but many are suitable for the great majority of people who just come for recreation and sightseeing. Such visitors will find much to admire in the villages and the only small market town, Bakewell, with two mediaeval bridges across the Wye and an interesting Old House Museum. Many will visit the four caves at Castleton and another at nearby Bradwell. Any time between Ascension Day and early September they will come across, in some village or other, the custom of dressing the wells with pictures, usually Biblical, made from natural objects from gardens, lanes and woods, a custom which has survived almost uniquely in the Peak where the water vanishes quickly through the limestone and the springs once made all the difference between life and death. Above all, they will visit the great houses: Haddon Hall, 'the most romantic of all manor houses', which has undergone no major alterations since the Dukes of Rutland made Belvoir their main seat from 1700; Chatsworth, the most magnificent 'Palace of the Peak' of the guide book writers, and Lyme Hall, in the extreme north-west, part-Elizabethan, part-Palladian by Giacomo Leoni, in its extensive parkland. There is indeed much to see and do in this Peak National Park of infinite variety.

Useful Addresses

The Peak Park Joint Planning Board: National Park Office, Aldern House, Baslow Rd, Bakewell, Derbyshire

The Peak Park Study Centre: Losehill Hall, Castleton, Derbyshire

Derbyshire Naturalists' Trust: Estate Office, Twyford, Barrow-on-Trent, Derby

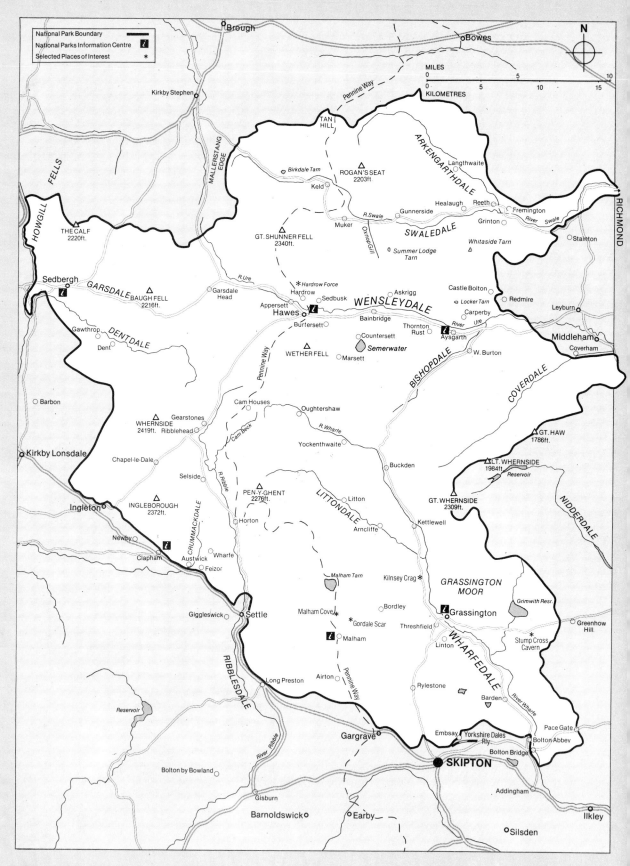

Legend:
- National Park Boundary
- National Parks Information Centre *i*
- Selected Places of Interest *

MILES
0 5 10 15
KILOMETRES
0 5 10

N

Brough
Bowes
RICHMOND

Kirkby Stephen

MALLERSTANG EDGE

TAN HILL

ARKENGARTHDALE
Langthwaite

Birkdale Tarn
ROGAN'S SEAT 2203ft.
Keld

HOWGILL FELLS

THE CALF 2220ft.

GT. SHUNNER FELL 2340ft.
Muker
R. Swale
Oxnop Gill
Gunnerside
Healaugh
Reeth
Fremington
Grinton
River Swale
Stainton
SWALEDALE

Sedbergh *i*

GARSDALE
BAUGH FELL 2216ft.
Garsdale Head
R. Ure
*Hardraw Force *
Hardraw
Sedbusk
Appersett
Hawes *i*
Burtersett
Bainbridge
Askrigg
Summer Lodge Tarn
Whitaside Tarn
Castle Bolton
Locker Tarn
Carperby
Thornton Rust
Aysgarth *i*
River Ure
Redmire
Leyburn
Middleham
Coverham

WENSLEYDALE

Gawthrop
DENTDALE
Dent

Countersett
Semerwater
Marsett
WETHER FELL
W. Burton

BISHOPDALE

COVERDALE

Barbon

Cam Houses
Oughtershaw
R. Wharfe
Yockenthwaite
GT. HAW 1786ft.

WHERNSIDE 2419ft.
Gearstones
Ribblehead
Cam Beck

LT. WHERNSIDE 1984ft.
Reservoir

Kirkby Lonsdale

Chapel-le-Dale
Selside
R. Ribble
Buckden
GT. WHERNSIDE 2309ft.

Ingleton
INGLEBOROUGH 2372ft.
PEN-Y-GHENT 2276ft.
Horton
Litton
Arncliffe
Kettlewell
LITTONDALE

NIDDERDALE

Newby *i*
Clapham
Austwick
Wharfe
Feizor

CRUMMACKDALE

Malham Tarn
Kilnsey Crag *
GRASSINGTON MOOR
Grimwith Resr.

Giggleswick
Settle

Malham Cove *
* Gordale Scar
Bordley
Grassington *i*
Threshfield
Stump Cross Cavern *
Greenhow Hill.

Malham *i*
Linton

WHARFEDALE

Long Preston
Airton
Pennine Way
Rylestone
Barden
River Wharfe
Pace Gate
Bolton Abbey
Embsay
Yorkshire Dales Rly
Bolton Bridge

Gargrave

RIBBLESDALE

Reservoir

River Ribble

SKIPTON

Bolton by Bowland

Addingham

Gisburn

Barnoldswick
Earby
Silsden
Ilkley

YORKSHIRE DALES NATIONAL PARK

Geoffrey Wright

Yorkshire Dales

Yorkshire Dales National Park

ESIGNATED IN 1954 the Yorkshire Dales National Park is one of five in the north of England. Sitting comfortably astride the Pennines it covers 1,761 square km (680 square miles) of hills and dales with the A65 forming its convenient southern boundary between Skipton and Ingleton. To the north it shares a boundary first with Cumbria, and, for a few miles east of Tan Hill, with Durham, while on the west Yorkshire's old boundary represents the limit of the park, although Sedbergh, Dentdale, Garsdale and the southern section of the Howgill Fells, all formerly in the West Riding but now in Cumbria, remain for planning purposes within the Dales National Park. The eastern boundary has been drawn to exclude the market towns of the lower dales, the 'military' moorlands near Richmond, and the Nidderdale watershed – being sacrosanct gathering-grounds for Leeds and Bradford reservoirs.

The Yorkshire Dales are accurately named, 'dale' being a Norse word for valley. Although there are over fifty dales in the park it is a handful of major ones which form the main landscape themes. Swaledale is narrow, grand and tinged with the melancholy of old industries; Wensleydale is green and broad, generous with trees; Wharfedale is wild at its head, sylvan lower down, and always lovely. Ribblesdale and Malhamdale embrace the Craven crescent where the bones of landscape are near the surface, and limestone cliffs and scars gleam in the sunlight. Dentdale is intimate, charming; Garsdale a deep trough carrying a main road westwards through the Pennines.

A score of fells top the 610 m (2,000 ft) contour, of which Yorkshire's 'Three Peaks' are best-known, their names and heights engraved on hearts and boots of generations of climbers – Whernside 736 m (2,419 ft), Ingleborough 723 m (2,372 ft), and Penyghent 694 m (2,273 ft). These and other high fells in the Dales Park form some of England's last wilderness areas, where there is solitude but never loneliness, and winds sough through grass and heather, or buffet against rocky outcrops.

Geology and Landscape

The geology of the Yorkshire Dales is not too complex for the layman to understand. The principal rocks of the Pen-nines belong to the Carboniferous System laid down as sediments in seas, swamps, and river deltas between 250 and 300 million years ago, on a foundation of older Silurian rocks, mainly slates, exposed occasionally in the area between Malham Tarn and Ribblesdale. South-west of Dent, Barbondale separates the Craven limestones to the east from the Silurian rocks to the west, where these form the smoothly rounded summits of the Howgill Fells above Sedbergh.

When the ancient seas covered the north of England the seabed was uneven, with troughs and basins, and when the Carboniferous Age deposits, carried by broad rivers from mountain ranges to the north, started to settle, they did so in the more northern troughs, leaving clearer seas to the south, over what is now Craven. There the pure, fine-grained Great Scar Limestone was slowly deposited, reaching a thickness of 1,525 m (5,000 ft). It is this limestone which dominates the scenery from Wharfedale westwards to Ribblesdale. Kilnsey Crag is a massive outthrust of Great Scar Limestone in the

A modern approach to rounding up sheep on Horton Moor, Ribblesdale

middle section of Wharfedale, the most famous natural landmark in the valley above Grassington. A few miles to the west Gordale Scar and Malham Cove represent the limestone's southern bravura appearance. Indeed, Malham itself is the obvious centre from which to explore and appreciate the unique delights of naked white limestone. Malham Cove is a great, curved inland cliff, almost 275 m (300 yds) across and nearly 91 m (300 ft) high, obviously the remains of an old waterfall which has gradually been cut back. Above the Cove is a remarkable limestone pavement, jointed and fissured as a result of water action.

The Great Scar Limestone outcrops above Settle at Attermire Scar, and at other places in Ribblesdale. Its upper surface forms a platform at about 366 m (1,200 ft), on which Ingleborough stands, and dips gradually northwards through the Dales, so that by the time Wensleydale is

Characteristic stone barns and dry-stone walls in Swaledale

reached it lies beneath the valley floor, and actually forms the terraces over which flows the River Ure at Aysgarth Falls. The Great Scar Limestone plays no part in Swaledale's scenery.

Above it, and therefore younger, is the Yoredale Series, a sequence of rock strata about 366 m (1,200 ft) thick, comprising limestones, shales, sandstones, and thin coals intermixed in a particular order, and varying only slightly. Each repeated unit sequence is called a cyclothem, and in Wensleydale – from whose old name the Series is called – there are as many as eight cyclothems from the valley-floor to the tops of the fells. It is these strata sequences which are primarily responsible for the characteristic terraced scenery of Wensleydale and Wharfedale. The limestones tend to weather into long horizontal scars, outcropping as vertical cliffs along the valley sides, as above Askrigg and Carperby in Wensleydale, and around Kettlewell in Wharfedale. Above the limestones the shales, being softer, are eroded to leave upper surfaces of the limestones flat; above these again, but usually hidden beneath the scree and debris of the next limestone, is the sandstone layer. It is these sandstones which have yielded the building stones, flagstones and roofing-slates for most of the dales buildings. None of the strata is particularly thick, most of the limestones being between 6–9 m (20–30 ft).

The Yoredales create waterfalls, especially in upper Wensleydale, where becks, tumbling down fellsides into the main valley, have carved steep-sided, wooded gorges, with falls formed at almost each cyclothem. Hardrow Force, near Hawes, and Whitfield and Mill Gill Forces, near Askrigg, are typical examples. In Swaledale, similar, though lesser, waterfalls have been created, particularly around Keld. The Yoredales, dipping northwards like the Great Scar Limestone, are lower in Swaledale, and above them lies the Millstone Grit, which forms the base rock of the vast fells and Cotton-grass moors stretching northwards beyond Arkengarthdale to Stainmore and the Tees. Sombre gritstone moors also form high land between the various dales, traversed by wild, narrow roads reaching 520 m (1,700 ft) between Swaledale and Wensleydale, and 580 m (1,900 ft) between Hawes and Upper Wharfedale. The three peaks themselves are capped with Millstone Grit, which has weathered to a plateau above the highest strata of the Yoredales.

Above the Yoredales, but below the Millstone Grit, thin seams of coal occur. Some of these, above Garsdale, Dentdale and around the head of Swaledale and Arkengarthdale, were worked for centuries, the last worked pit near Tan Hill finally ceasing in the 1930s.

Rocks form the bones of landscape. Bones fracture, and it is major geological fractures called 'faults', which have resulted in some easily-identified landscape features in the Yorkshire Dales. In a 'fault', a rock-slip causes strata on one

The well-preserved ruins of Castle Bolton overlooking Wensleydale

side to be displaced vertically by as much as several hundred feet. The major landslip is the Craven Fault, running along the edge of Giggleswick Scar, through Ingleton and Settle to Malham, crossing into Wharfedale at Grassington and Nidderdale at Pateley Bridge, with a marked displacement of strata to its west and south. Geologically, the effect is one of having tilted the whole area of the dales slightly from west to east, and even less from south to north. Later earth movements have caused further uplift, so that the strata rise to a slight dome around Ingleborough.

The rock ingredients are basically the same throughout the Yorkshire Dales. It is in their proportions, successions and details that differences occur, creating the distinctive individuality of each main dale, so that the dales are variations on a noble theme.

The Ice Age

During the Ice Age, which ended about 10,000 BC, caps of snow and ice blanketed the hills of northern England, and in the Yorkshire Dales only the higher summits above 650 m (2,100 ft) remained above the ice. From the high Pennines glaciers flowed outwards, following existing valleys. They smoothed the shoulders of the hills, scouring the landscape and carrying away rock debris and soil. Softer strata were eroded most – in Wharfedale and Wensleydale the shales were removed, exposing the now-familiar limestone scars along the hillsides. V-shaped valleys were rounded to their present U-shape, and sometimes, as at Kilnsey Crag, glacial erosion caused undercutting of the limestone.

Glaciers carried rocks away from their original positions and, when the ice melted, dumped them elsewhere as 'erratics', of which the Norber boulders above Austwick are a classic example. Smaller debris carried by glaciers, and called boulder-clay, is spread over most of the Dales, being thickest in the lower valleys and the Craven lowlands – where drumlins are also commonest – well seen in upper Ribblesdale above Horton. Moraines were formed during glacier retreat when more ice was melted from the front of a glacier than was added at its rear. Large moraines cross most valleys, resembling low embankments, and after the Ice Age these acted as dams to impound lakes which gradually filled up with alluvium. Eventually, overflow channels drained the lakes, but it is these old lake-areas that are the first to flood after heavy rains, and their swampy character determined the siting of settlements above the floor-plains. Moraine edges, tucked against hillsides, offered well-drained gravel sites for villages as well as routes for roads up the dales.

Many tarns have been made where glaciers scooped out boulder-clay lined hollows or left small moraines which dammed streams. Malham Tarn, on impervious Silurian slate, is held by a morainic dam at its southern edge, and Semerwater is a perfect glacial lake whose outflowing River Bain has cut a channel through glacial debris in its short course to Bainbridge. Rare Pennine examples of glacial cwms occur at Combe Scar in Dentdale, and Cautley Crags, on the Howgills, near Sedbergh – two impressive natural amphitheatres of near-vertical crags.

The Ice Age had a profound effect on the soils of the Yorkshire Dales which, after the removal of rock-debris, have been directly formed from the underlying rocks. In the Craven area the Great Scar Limestone yields a thin, calcareous soil; in the area of the Yoredale Series – Wharfedale, Wensleydale (and their tributary dales) and part of Swaledale – the soils are naturally more mixed, while the Millstone Grit uplands have sandy acid soils. Limestone soils are light, well-drained and, being rich in calcium, suit a large variety of plants; in the Yoredales, vegetation is zoned according to the strata, producing a very rich variety of plant life; sandy and gritstone soils are heavy and lacking in humus at high levels, gritty and porous on lower moorlands. When mixed with shale-based clays they yield workable loams.

Much of the area of the Dales lies above 183 m (600 ft), and at this height it is not until mid-April that the mean temperature reaches 6° C, the point at which plant growth commences. The growing season lasts for only 6–7 months, so that careful planning by farmers is necessary to take fullest possible advantage of this limited time. No crops are cultivated on the uplands; oats cannot easily be ripened above 305 m (1,000 ft) – the maximum height on south-facing slopes at which hay is grown for winter feed. On north-facing slopes this is usually thirty to sixty metres (100–200 ft) lower.

Man in the Dales

As the climate slowly became milder and damper after the Ice Age vegetation followed the retreating ice, and, in turn, animals and occasional hunting tribes. About 5000 BC the tree-line, as now, was about 520 m (1,700 ft), below which Birch, Hazel, Pine, Oak, Elm, Willow and Alder clothed the hillsides.

The remarkable limestone pavement above the great curve of Malham Cove

By 3000 BC there was some New Stone Age settlement on the lower slopes, and over a thousand years later early Bronze Age settlers have left us several 'henge' sites in the park, the two best being at Castle Dykes, Aysgarth and Yarnbury, above Grassington. Stone circles of Middle Bronze Age date have been identified at Appletreewick, Bordley, Embsay and Yockenthwaite, all in the Wharfedale area, and above Carperby in Wensleydale.

The Celts reached the northern Pennines about 100 BC, and, mingling with existing tribes called Brigantes they established an Iron Age culture. Ingleborough's proud summit claims the only Iron Age hill-fort of the Dales, and its fifteen-acre plateau enclosed by a wall 915 m (3,000 ft) long contained nineteen circles. Other hut circles and irregular field patterns of Iron Age times emphasize how the well-drained limestone areas of Craven country were favoured by these early farmers.

The Romans left few impressions on the Dales landscape, although they did exploit lead mines at Greenhow Hill and in Arkengarthdale. In Wensleydale a large drumlin at Bainbridge formed an ideal site for the Roman fort of *Virosidum*, garrisoned almost continually from 80 AD to the end of the occupation more than three centuries later. It was linked to Lancaster by a road, which can still be followed (mainly on foot), crossing the fells south-west of Bainbridge, by Wether Fell and Oughtershaw Side, dropping into the Ribble valley above Gearstones, where it joins the B6255 to Chapel-le-Dale and the minor road along the west of the Greta to Ingleton.

The present settlement pattern of the Yorkshire Dales is largely the result of successive waves of colonization by Angles, Danes and Norsemen from the seventh century to the early eleventh century. Anglians and Danes moved up the Pennine valleys from the east, evidenced by the '-ley', '-ham', and '-ton' place-name elements. Following later, Danish settlers in-filled between existing villages, '-by' and '-thorpe' elements providing clues. Early in the tenth century Norse settlers colonized the upper dales, moving across the Pennines from their Irish Sea footholds. In Arkengarth-dale they reached Langthwaite, in Swaledale, Gunnerside; they settled in Wensleydale above Askrigg, and in the upper part of Wharfedale above Buckden. They colonized Gars-dale, Dentdale, and upper Ribblesdale, and brought with them their own system of pastoral farming, of spring and autumn grazing in the valleys, moving to hill pastures during summer months. The summer shieling was called a *saetr* – 'pasture with houses' – an element appearing regularly in place-names, especially around Hawes – Appersett, Bur-tersett, Countersett, Marsett. Because Norse farmers and shepherds spent so much time on the uplands, natural land-scape features were important to them, and they have given us those splendidly evocative names so characteristic of the western Pennines and Lakeland – crag, clint, scar, fell, beck, rigg, gill, mere, moss and tarn – names which add their own euphony to the northern map.

Whereas Norse settlement in the upper dales took the form of a series of farms dispersed up fell sides or sheltering in narrow side valleys, Anglian and Danish settlements tended towards nucleated villages with farmsteads and houses grouped round a central area which was probably used for safe keeping of stock overnight or when danger threatened. From this arrangement have probably developed the present village greens which form attractive features at Reeth, Redmire, West Burton, Linton and Arncliffe.

Monastic influence upon the Dales landscape lasted about as long – four centuries – as that of the early colonizers. Cistercian monks bringing great sheep-breeding skills, founded Fountains Abbey in 1132, and Jervaulx Abbey in 1145. Augustinian canons settled at Bolton in Wharfedale, in 1155, and other foundations were established during the twelfth century at Coverham and Easby. These, together with more distant monasteries such as Bridlington, Furness and Salley, owned huge estates which embraced almost the whole of the park area. In addition to large-scale sheep farming the monks exploited the mineral wealth of the Dales, especially lead, and built some of the earliest walls.

Most of the stone walls, however, which are such a feature of the Dales landscape, are the result of Enclosure Awards between 1760 and 1820, giving straight-edged, rect-angular fields of between eight and twelve acres. Much smaller fields, enclosed by older walls, are often seen as village crofts close to a number of villages, such as can be seen at Linton and Thornton Rust. Walls of different dates can readily be identified at Gunnerside, in Swaledale, around Malham, viewed nicely from the top of the Cove, and in much of Wharfedale.

The Dissolution of the Monasteries was followed by a break-up of the former monastic estates. In the centuries since then livestock farming has predominated, following generally the basic pattern of dairying in the meadows and on the lower slopes, with sheep higher up and on the fell tops. Farms of 40–120 hectares (100–300 acres) carry dairy and suckler herds, and sheep flocks may number 300–800 breeding ewes – the higher up the valley the greater is the orientation towards sheep. Grazing on the thousands of acres of upland commons is an important aspect of the farming economy.

Most Dales farms and their associated field barns date from the late seventeenth to the early nineteenth centuries. All are constructed of local stone, mainly sandstone, as are the unpretentious yet quietly dignified houses and cottages in villages and small market towns. The Dales were never rich enough for the building of great mansions, and the park area can claim only one castle, Bolton Castle, in Wensleydale, although the great Norman strongholds at Richmond and Middleham are just on the edge. Two fortified tower-houses, Nappa and Barden, survive, if rather ruinously, from the late fifteenth century.

Old industries, too, have left their legacy of haunting, if melancholy, memorials. The eighteenth and nineteenth-century heydays of lead mining scarred the lonely fells above Swaledale and Arkengarthdale, Grassington Moor, and Greenhow Hill. Remains of old workings, smelt-mills and flues have their own appeal. The railway-age brought to the Dales the most expensively-engineered line in England, the famous Settle–Carlisle, with its burrowing tunnels and soaring viaducts among the wild and windy uplands of Ribble Head and Dentdale.

Farming remains the main occupation in the Dales. Limestone-quarrying, in Ribblesdale and Wharfedale, continues to provide work for relatively few people, but building stone is no longer quarried. Private afforestation is now clothing some hillsides, in upper Wensleydale, upper Wharfedale, Garsdale and Dentdale, but Forestry Commission lands are mainly outside the park. Tourism is an increasingly valuable source of income, and recent years have seen a marked increase in all aspects of this, especially in the field of holiday cottages, bed-and-breakfast accommodation, and the use of camping and caravan sites.

Flora and Fauna

A time-traveller journeying back to the end of the Ice Age, about 10000 BC would find some forms of life in the Dales

The River Wharfe, a famous trout stream, at Langstrothdale Chase

comparable to that of today, for when the glaciers retreated a tundra vegetation started to colonize the land. Moss, grass and sedge were quickly followed by trees, mainly Birch and Willow. As the climate slowly became milder and wetter conditions for plant-growth improved, and soon Hazel and Pine were growing on the fellsides. By 5000 BC Oak, Elm and Alder were established and then, as now, the tree-line was about 520 m (1,700 ft). Above that was bare moorland with its carpet of moss, sedge, heath and coarse grass, below it, thick woodland cover. Fragments of this broad-leaved woodland survive, albeit in an attenuated form, as scar and gill woods, especially in the area of the Yoredale Series of rocks. Elsewhere, man's impact on the Dales environment,

The view from Wether Fell towards the dales around Hawes

largely over the past 1,200 years, has been a mixture of exploitation and control.

The park area offers a wide range of plant and animal habitats, determined largely by soil and climate, the latter largely a product of altitude, in the context of which it is worth pointing out that a rise of seventy-six metres (250 ft) in height is equivalent in terms of climate to a movement northwards of 1 degree of latitude – about seventy miles. Since the high fells are usually at least 305 m (1,000 ft) above their neighbouring valleys, their climatic environment is vastly different from that of lower levels.

Peat covers most of the higher, western and wetter Pennine uplands to a depth of up to ninety metres (thirty feet). Vast areas above 427 m (1,400 ft), visually dark and sombre, dreary and dour to tramp across, are an environment hostile to man. They are a wilderness landscape, recognized and felt in a journey across the tops from one dale to another. Any of the roads out of upper Swaledale show this character, as does that from Hawes to upper Wharfedale over Fleet Moss, at 580 m (1,900 ft), Yorkshire's highest road.

Its name, Moss, is significant. Mosses, many of them named on the OS maps, are characteristic of these high moors. They show a remarkably uniform vegetation, of few plant species, with Cotton-grass dominant, its white, cottony fruiting heads lightening the scene in early summer. The basal sheaths of Cotton-grass are rich in nitrogen and potash, making the plant useful in giving sheep a nutritious early 'bite' in spring. Other plants of the Mosses are related to the wetness – Bog Moss, Cross-leaved Heath and Round-leaved Sundew occurring in the wetter places, while Bell Heather and Ling, Bilberry and Crowberry prosper in drier situations, together with a few rushes, sedges and grasses.

On high summits and ridges above the Cotton-grass plateaux steep slopes are both better-drained and more exposed, and Cotton-grass is no longer dominant. The summits of Whernside, Ingleborough and Penyghent have what may be described as sub-alpine pasture, made up of moor grasses, heathers, Bilberry, Crowberry and various rushes.

Peat is a constant characteristic of the high, west Pennines, and is composed mainly of the remains of Cotton-grass accumulated over thousands of years. Until quite recently it was economically important to dalesfolk as a fuel, both for domestic use and in the smelting of lead-ore. Each village or township had – and still has – the rights to dig peat ('turbary right') on specified areas of its upland commons. Formed under conditions of excessive moisture and absence of oxygen, moorland peat of the Pennines is markedly acid, but its main characteristic is that it absorbs water like a sponge. As such it regulates water-flow through a moss so that becks draining from it rarely dry up, except in conditions of severe drought. When this happens the Cotton-

grass dies and disappears and moorland plants – heathers, Bilberry, Crowberry – gain a foothold, together with a few rushes, grasses and sedges. If drying-out continues, further denudation occurs, peat-banks dry and crumble, peat-hags are formed which are almost devoid of plant life. Lead-mining activities of the seventeenth and eighteenth centuries, and gamekeeping on grouse-moors last century, both contributed to the drying-out of several upland Mosses.

Heather moors themselves occupy the zone below the Cotton-grass moors and above the rough grazing, say, between 300 and 425 m (1,000 and 1,400 ft), although they reach as high as 519 m (1,700 ft) between Swaledale and Wensleydale, falling to 214 m (700 ft) where the long ridges descend as spurs towards the eastern margins above Reeth and Grinton. Over vast areas of such moors heathers are dominant, imparting to the scene a remarkable uniformity of texture and colour, especially in August, when the moors present a majestic mantle of purple and crimson. Bilberry and Crowberry flourish on drier ridges and the edges of moors and rocky escarpments, while Cross-leaved Heather and rushes may be expected in slightly damper patches. Young heather provides a good 'bite' for sheep in early

Aysgarth Falls on the River Ure, where salmon may occasionally be seen

spring when other food is scarce, and to ensure a good supply of fresh shoots careful moor management is necessary, with old heather controlled by burning. If this is overdone, or liming is too heavy or draining too drastic, the ecological balance is disturbed. Mat-grass takes over, which is useless as a sheep food. At lower levels bracken invades the heather, when cattle may be introduced to keep it in check. Grouse also like young heather, but the older plant offers better shelter. Thus, gamekeeper and shepherd share common aims in moor management.

Plant species of the heather moors are few. Along the moorland edge Mat-grass usually dominates the grasses which grow, its pale straw colour from autumn to spring explaining its name. On damper soil it yields to the more attractive Blue moor-grass. Sheep's Fescue, Silver Hair-grass and Common Bent are other grasses of the moorland margins. The yellow Tormentil, delicate blue Milkwort, Spearwort, various Eyebrights, and Knapweed add splashes of colour along the sheep-cropped edges of heather moorland, especially at lower altitudes, but it is the dainty trefoils and vetches, being leguminous, which add to the pasturage value of grassy swards.

Valleys and hillsides of the Millstone Grit country were originally densely wooded, with Willow and Alder in valley

bottoms, damp oakwoods on lower slopes, Birch and Oak on the upper slopes, with Birch scrub on moorland spurs. Three noticeable periods of tree-planting since Anglian settlement have helped to maintain the wooded appearance of the Dales. In the Middle Ages monastic and lay landowners planted Oaks, mainly associated with their deer-parks; possibly the venerable specimens in the Valley of Desolation near Bolton Abbey are survivals from those days. In the eighteenth and nineteenth centuries coverts and woods of mixed deciduous trees were planted as shelter-belts, game preserves, or for beautification of the scene. This century coniferous afforestation, by municipalities in connection with water catchment, by private landowners, and – on the edges of the park – by the Forestry Commission, has darkened many hillsides. Very recently, the National Park Authority has actively encouraged, by grant-aid and management agreements, small-scale planting, mainly of mixed deciduous trees, by private landowners.

The Birch woods which formerly clothed the moors are now represented by the gill woods of the Dales, common in those areas where the Yoredale Series of strata occur, and tributary becks cut their way down steep hillsides, forming sheltered ravines out of range of grazing stock. Sharing the dominant Birch scrub are Mountain-ash, Hawthorn, Holly and Willows, with a ground-flora comprising intruders from the moors, together with common woodland plants such as Primrose, Bluebell, Ramsons and Wood Sorrel. In Swaledale, gill woods can be seen near Healaugh, above Gunnerside, around Keld – all on the north side of the valley, with good examples at Oxnop Gill and by the road to Summer Lodge. Wensleydale's best gill wood extends for over a mile up the hillside north-west of Askrigg, starting as Mill Gill and continuing as Whitfield Gill to about 381 m (1,250 ft), where a few Oaks and Larch add variety to the wooded ravine.

In upper Ribblesdale, east of Ribble Head, and accessible from High Birkwith above Horton, Ling Gill is a fine example of a gill wood, designated a National Nature Reserve. Covering about twelve acres at 305 m (1,000 ft), the steep sides of the wooded limestone ravine have Ash and Hazel as dominant trees, with Hawthorn, Willow, Aspen and Mountain Ash quite common. Among the ground-flora which flourishes under the prevailing, sheltered, moist conditions, are Mountain Everlasting, Globe Flower, Giant Bellflower, Herb Paris, Wood Cranesbill, Melancholy Thistle, and Marsh Hawksbeard, together with many luxuriant ferns.

We have seen how the natural vegetation of the Cotton-grass fells and Millstone Grit moorlands comprises a succession of plant assemblages of simple composition and limited species, resulting in broad masses of colour, tone and texture extending over huge areas of upland. Limestone

country, except for its scar woods, yields a prospect of delicate greys and greens – pearly-grey of bare limestone and the rich greens of good grassland which formerly supported a cover of loose scrub and open woodland reduced and restricted since the twelfth century by the grazing flocks of sheep of monastic and lay landowners.

The main characteristic of limestone country is its immense variety of plants, which includes some of the most delightful of British flowers, which colour the pastures and rocks, the ledges and walls, and even the dark fissures in limestone pavements.

Sheep's Fescue dominates limestone grassland. With Sweet Vernal Grass, Hair Oat and Crested Dog's Tail it has a higher food value than other limestone grasses, False Oat, Quaking-grass and the two Brome-grasses. On limestone pavements, above Malham Cove, on the lower slopes of Ingleborough, around Ribble Head and in Crummackdale, no soil survives, and only mosses and lichens grow on the bare rock. But in the damp, shady fissures – called grykes – soil accumulates, and, safe from summer heat or grazing animals, a woodland-type of flora is found, including Wood Anemone, Dog's Mercury, Wood-sorrel, Ramsons, Herb Robert, Green Spleenwort, Hart's-tongue Fern and Holly Fern.

Colt Park Wood, near Ribble Head, a national nature reserve, is a rare survivor of a tree-covered limestone pavement, one of the best British examples of an aboriginal scar ashwood. Ash is dominant, but Willow, Hazel, Birch, Bird Cherry, Rowan, Alder and Hawthorn also grow directly on the clints, their roots penetrating into the grykes. Astonishingly, over the twenty-one acres covered by Colt Park, the ground-flora totals over 150 species. Occasional islands of peat have been left on some limestone pavements, resulting in the anomaly of lime-hating plants like heathers and Bil-

berry growing close to limestone outcrops such as Churn Milk Hole, on Penyghent, and at Moughton, near Horton-in-Ribblesdale, where Juniper thrives, albeit to a diminishing extent.

Limestone scars and cliffs which characterize the Craven uplands, as well as Wharfedale and Wensleydale, have a rich plant life. Scar woods grow at a height of 214–305 m (700–1,000 ft) above Grassington, Kettlewell and Buckden in Wharfedale, between Arncliffe and Litton in Littondale, and along both sides of Wensleydale between Aysgarth and Bainbridge. Swaledale examples occur near Gunnerside and Keld, and there are smaller scar woods around Chapel-le-Dale, Austwick and Feizor, and one of the best-known to motorists grows above the busy A65 west of Settle, where the road cuts across the foot of Giggleswick Scar. Ash and Hazel are the dominant trees, usually associated with Holly, Bird Cherry and various kinds of Thorn. A woodland flora flourishes, with true rock plants on the bare scars, and sufficient soil depth on ledges to allow grassland plants to survive. The resultant richness is exemplified in Grass Wood, near Grassington, a 600-acre nature reserve of the Yorkshire Wildlife Trust, extending to limestone pavement and consolidated scree. Sycamores, Beech and conifers have been added to the existing Ash woodland, and the flora includes over 400 species.

On higher scars, such as the rocky ledges and cliffs of Ingleborough and Penyghent, where limestone lies just below the Millstone Grit, other plant assemblages occur. Dwarf Willow, Hoary Whitlow-grass, Vernal Sandwort, Yellow Mountain Saxifrage, Purple Saxifrage and Spiked Speedwell share these upland habitats with, unusually, some maritime species such as Thrift and Sea Campion. The area around Ribble Head and the northern slopes of Ingleborough claims to be the only British habitat of the

Yorkshire Sandwort. Relatively common in local damp pastures there, and above Semerwater, Globe Flower and Bird's Eye Primrose add their distinctive shapes and colours in late spring and early summer. Melancholy Thistle, Meadowsweet, Water Avens, Wood Cranesbill and Giant Bellflower are other common plants of damp limestone pastures, while the dainty little white flowers of Spring Sandwort successfully colonize the arid spoil-heaps of old areas of lead mining.

Upland limestone landscapes may hold greater appeal for botanists, but ornithologists probably prefer the moorlands and open fells. Species and numbers of birds of such habitats may be fewer – about twenty-five birds per forty hectares (one hundred acres) – but they are certainly more distinctive. Most evocative of all moorland sounds are the harsh rasp of Red Grouse and the bubbling call of Curlew, a joyous harbinger of early spring. Golden Plover, Redshank and Snipe soon join them, and you can now expect to see Sandpipers around high tarns and in the upper courses of becks. They nest up to 610 m (2,000 ft), but it is the Black-headed Gull which now dominates many upland tarns. Summer Lodge Tarn, Whitaside Tarn and Locker Tarn, above Wensleydale, Birkdale Tarn, above Keld, and Greensett Moss on the shoulder of Whernside all have a large resident population of these noisy, but graceful birds.

Ravens are less common than they used to be but Buzzards have increased markedly, their faint mewing, and lazily-circling flight readily identifiable over a wide range of upland habitats. Other birds of prey, such as Merlins, Peregrines and Short-eared Owls, are holding their own, and at lower levels Kestrels are relatively common. Ring Ouzels seem to be very patchy in their distribution, and unusually, it is one of the smallest birds, the Meadow-Pipit – that appears to have the widest habitat, extending from the high fells to rough grazing at 244–274 m (800–900 ft), with a consistent distribution of not more than ten birds per forty hectares (one hundred acres). Skylarks can be expected at all but the highest altitudes, and in high summer Swifts swerve and swoop over the fells seeking insects, far from their nesting-sites near farms and villages. Once their breeding-season is over Starlings, too, move to higher pastures, where normally Lapwings are the most prominent spring and summer residents sharing the habitat with Redshanks, Curlew, and Wheatears – so commonly observed perched on stone walls by roadsides and fields any time from March to August, when they leave the uplands.

Woodlands, both in the gills, along the scars, and also at higher levels, give good cover for many species, while rivers of the Dales are commonly frequented by Sandpipers, Pied and Grey Wagtails, and occasional Kingfishers. Dippers, Mallard, Teal and Oyster-catchers are attracted to upper and lonelier reaches of becks which feed the rivers from the upland solitudes. The rivers themselves are well-stocked with fish. Trout are common in clearer, upper reaches, with Grayling in the River Ure below Wensley Bridge. Occasionally Salmon find their way up the main rivers, although they are more likely to be seen in the Lune near Sedbergh. Crayfish live in Malham Tarn and Semerwater but are said to be most common in the River Ure, where fishing for them is locally known as 'crabbing', with liver as bait.

In the world of mammals Grey Squirrels are the most likely to be seen, especially in the gill woods. Badgers and Foxes are not uncommon, although, being largely nocturnal, are rarely observed by visitors. Deer, mainly Roe and Fallow, occasionally stray into the Dales from their Cumbrian habitat, or from private parklands to the east, and owners of woodlands report regular sightings. In spite of myxomatosis and motorists, colonies of Rabbits continue to thrive, especially below limestone scars, on moorland fringes, and along the edge of gill woods, while Brown Hares are widely distributed, particularly on upland pastures and rough grazings.

Conservation of Wildlife

Embracing as they do a great variety of semi-natural habitats as well as a number of important geological sites, the Yorkshire Dales contain many areas which are protected either as nature reserves or as sites of special scientific interest, of which mention has been made of Colt Park and Ling Gill, both near Ribble Head. The Yorkshire Wildlife Trust, founded in 1946, manages five nature reserves, including Grass Wood, near Grassington, Globe Flower Wood (half an acre) above Malham, an area of limestone pavement at South House, above Chapel-le-Dale (ten acres), and a commercial mixed woodland at Tow Hill, near Hawes (a hundred acres). Globe Flower Wood is a damp, lime-rich site whose flora illustrates a fine seasonal succession, including Wood Anemone, Globe Flower, Early Purple Orchid, Melancholy Thistle and Meadow Sweet, almost all of which can readily be seen over its low boundary wall, without the need to enter this delightful little reserve. Most recently acquired is Yellands Meadow, near Muker, covering just three acres by the River Swale, the first Dales hay meadow protected by reserve status, and which continues to be worked traditionally. The National Park Committee has itself recently (1982) bought the thirty-two-acre Freeholders' Wood along the north bank of the River Ure at Aysgarth Falls, one of the oldest remaining coppiced Hazel woodlands in the north of England. It is hoped to reintroduce managed coppicing, with the agreement of the existing freeholders who have certain rights of common in the woodland, and at the same time to improve rights-of-way through the wood to Middle and Lower Falls.

The Nature Conservancy Council has designated twenty-four sites of special scientific interest covering 16,200 hectares (40,000 acres) within the park area, and mainly concentrated in four localities – Ingleborough, Penyghent, Mallerstang Edge, and around Malham Tarn. This latter is probably the best-known of all Pennine Conservation Areas. It is owned by the National Trust, but leased to the Field Studies Council, who use Malham Tarn House as a field studies centre. The various courses are attended by over 1,700 students each year. Field studies are supplemented by laboratory work, and subjects covered include plant life of limestone uplands, bird studies on Malham Moor, fresh-water life in Malham Tarn and the neighbouring becks, and studies in local geology.

Recreation in the Park

Recent surveys show that sight-seeing and touring are the main leisure activities enjoyed by most visitors to the Yorkshire Dales. Although fewer than 40,000 people live within the park, motorways and trunk roads bring the area within a two-hour journey for over fifteen million people in the north of England, making it very popular for day-visitors as well as for those who prefer to make a longer stay. A wide range of services and self-catering establishments is evenly distributed throughout the Dales, together with ten youth hostels, as well as other centres and hostels aimed at providing accommodation for particular groups.

Bunkhouse barns, of which there are now five, at Cam Houses, Catholes, near Sedbergh, Hubberholme, Horton-in-Ribblesdale, and Barden, provide simple, clean hostel-type accommodation for self-catering walkers, and cyclists at a reasonable cost. Each has been converted from a field barn, and can take from twelve to twenty people.

The Yorkshire Dales offer splendid opportunities for many active pursuits, of which walking is by far the most popular. There is a rich network of field paths in the valleys, around villages, or on the wilder tracks among the upland moors, fells and commons, among them the turbary roads to the peatlands, and enclosure roads to upland grazings. Paths used by lead miners of the eighteenth and nineteenth centuries, by quarrymen of last century, by cattle drovers and by packhorse trains, provide historic and rewarding routes into quiet valleys or across the windy hills, while Britain's first official long-distance footpath, the Pennine Way, threads its way for thirty-one kilometres (fifty miles) northwards through the park area, from Airton in Malhamdale to Tan Hill on the Durham border. Its route incorporates many contrasts, including limestone country, gritstone moorlands, a stretch of Roman road, and, especially in upper Swaledale, river scenery of stunning beauty and grandeur. It is Swaledale which is traversed along its northern slopes by

part of an unofficial long-distance route, the Coast-to-Coast Walk, while the Dales Way heading westwards from Ilkley to the Lake District, follows Wharfedale almost to its source, crosses the Pennine Way above Cam Houses, and continues along Dentdale to Sedbergh.

Of the score of summits above 600 m (2,000 ft), the three peaks of Whernside, Ingleborough and Penyghent are undoubtedly the best known, with Ingleborough the favourite, its summit easily reached from a variety of starting-points – Clapham, Ingleton, Chapel-le-Dale, Selside and Horton-in-Ribblesdale. The Pennine Way takes Penyghent in its stride, as it does Great Shunner Fell 713 m (2,340 ft) between Hawes in Wensleydale and Thwaite in Swaledale. The rounded summits and steep-sided secret valleys of the Howgill Fells north of Sedbergh may be less spectacular than Pennine peaks but have their own appeal to those who prefer solitude with wide-ranging views in all directions. A certain amount of rock-climbing occurs on the limestone cliffs near Malham, and at Kilnsey, but this is strictly for the experts, who must seek landowners' permission. Skiing is very limited, for only occasionally is there sufficient snow-cover to create suitable conditions. The Howgills and the fells around the head of Swaledale then offer the best possibilities.

The Great Scar Limestone of the Craven area contains some of the most impressive underground structures and scenery in Britain, making it an important centre for caving and pot-holing. White Scar Cave near Ingleton, Ingleborough Cave, near Clapham, and Stump Cross Cavern between Grassington and Pateley Bridge, are 'show' caves open to the public. Scores of others are the preserve of the properly-equipped, expertly-led, explorers of the various caving clubs. The National Park Committee in 1977 established the Whernside Manor Cave and Fell Centre in Dentdale, which, open all the year round, offers a range of courses to individuals and groups, with a strong bias towards caving and pot-holing. The centre now arranges one-day caving visits to meet demands from people who would like to know just a little more about cave-systems and caving.

Among the more leisurely pursuits pony-trekking is not common in the park area, although there is a centre for it at Sedbusk, near Hawes. Abundant opportunities do exist, however, for fishing, particularly in rivers and their tributary becks. A rod licence, issued by the Yorkshire Water Authority, is necessary for any of the eastward-flowing rivers, while for the Ribble, Lune and their feeder-streams west of the Pennines, the North-West Water Authority issues rod licences. In addition, local permits are necessary from those bodies who own or lease the fishing rights.

On the whole, dales rivers offer few opportunities for canoeing, although the Swale at Richmond is a regular location for slaloms and white-water competitions. Youth groups, and private individuals, use Semerwater for canoe-

The railway viaduct across Blea Moor near the mighty Whernside

ing, sharing its limited facilities for sailing and a decreasing amount of power-boating. The shallow waters of this lake provide some opportunity for swimming, and, if there is a sufficiently prolonged spell of hard frost, skating. Just beyond the park's southern boundary the Leeds–Liverpool Canal is increasingly popular with those who enjoy the peaceful relaxation of canal cruising, for which Skipton is the main Pennine centre.

Limestone scars in Wensleydale and Wharfedale are proving increasingly popular places for hang-gliding enthusiasts, while the more noisy pursuits of motor-cycle scrambles and trials, sponsored by the Auto-Cycle Union and supervised by local clubs, take place regularly in Wensleydale and Swaledale.

The Yorkshire Dales National Park, with its rich heritage of natural history, offers almost unlimited opportunities for its study, as one of the most rewarding and peaceful leisure pursuits. National Park Information Centres at Aysgarth, Clapham and Malham have interpretive displays, and there are a number of self-guiding nature trails. The Park Authority arranges each year a large number of guided walks, usually starting from an information centre, carpark or village pub, and many walks have as their specialist theme some aspect of natural history, local history, or industrial archaeology. These last two interests also feature strongly in good displays in folk museums at Reeth, Hawes, Aysgarth, Grassington and Settle.

Useful Addresses

National Park Offices:
   Colvend, Hebden Road, Grassington, Skipton,
   N. Yorkshire BD23 5LB
   Yorebridge House, Bainbridge, Leyburn,
   N. Yorkshire DL8 3BP

National Park Centres (Open 10.0–5.0 Easter–October):
   Aysgarth Falls (Wensleydale)
   Clapham (between Settle and Ingleton)
   Grassington (Wharfedale)
   Hawes (Wensleydale)
   Malham
   Sedbergh

National Trust (Yorkshire Regional Office):
32 Goodramgate, York YO1 2LG

Yorkshire Wildlife Trust Ltd: 20 Castlegate,
York YO1 1RP

Llangynidr Bridge, built in about 1600, over the River Usk, Brecon Beacons

William Condry

Brecon Beacons
Parc Cenedlaethol Bannau Brycheiniog

SOME OF the most impressive mountains in southern Britain, and the nearest to London, lie within the 1,350 square km (519 square miles) of the Brecon Beacons National Park which was designated in 1957. For over forty miles from east to west they raise their beckoning tops against the sky above a world of green farmlands and leafy streamsides. From north to south the park is not nearly so extensive – there are less than twenty miles between Brecon just within the northern boundary and Merthyr Tydfil which is just outside on the south. But along that north–south axis you go over the highest summits and get the farthest views. From up there you can survey nearly all of this beautiful, heart-lifting park. And you see much good country beyond, especially in the north, where you look into hazy distances across the wild hills and valleys of mid Wales.

The park's uplands are usually thought of as four different ranges though the two westerly ones rather merge into each other. In the east are the Black Mountains which were presumably so-named by people living to the north who looked all day at the shadowy side of these uplands. The Black Mountains march with England but their flank on the Herefordshire side is excluded from the park. Confusingly for visitors the range at the far west of the park is called the Black Mountain (singular) or Mynydd Du. The central uplands are the Brecon Beacons and Fforest Fawr which are separated by the pass containing the A470. The highest summit is Pen y Fan, 885 m (2,906 ft), on the Beacons. The lowest ground is at about 200 ft where the Usk flows out of the park near Abergavenny.

About 35,000 people have their homes in the park, mostly in small market towns and villages or on farms. But in summer their number is greatly increased by tourists, many of them day-visitors from the populous region immediately to the south. The place names on the map give the impression of a thoroughly Welsh-speaking area; in fact, except in the far west, English greatly predominates.

Geology and Landscape

Unlike Snowdonia where sedimentary rocks are jumbled up with huge quantities of igneous material, the Brecon Beacons National Park is a region of sedimentary rocks only, chiefly shales, sandstones and conglomerates of the Devonian period. So although very old (Palaeozoic), most of the park's rocks are not as ancient as those of much of the rest of Wales which belong to the Silurian, Ordovician, Cambrian and Pre-Cambrian systems. But at low levels at the western end near Llandeilo and Llandovery there are Ordovician grits and mudstones as well as Silurian sandstones and shales which contain some well-known fossil beds. All along the southern side the Devonian rocks disappear under the strata of the next geological system, the Carboniferous. There we are on limestone and Millstone Grit, rocks that announce the Coal Measures just outside the park in industrial south Wales.

Much of the park's scenery is eloquent of the age of glaciers. There are cirques, corrie lakes, ice-plucked crags, scarps, moraines, screes, scratched rocks, ice-smoothed pavements, old lake beds, kettle holes and wide spreads of gravels and clays. Some upland areas are peaty and mantled with heathers, as you will see on the Black Mountains, but elsewhere there is much semi-natural, high-level grassland on which large flocks of sheep have pastured for centuries. Valley soils are generally fertile; and farming, mainly stock-breeding and milk production, is prosperous.

If you begin your exploration in the Black Mountains you can start from Llanthony or Hay-on-Wye or Talgarth and make your way up to the heights of Hay Bluff 680 m (2,219 ft) and its slightly superior neighbour, the Tumpa 690 m (2,263 ft). From there you can follow the plateau for miles, eventually coming up to the highest of these Black Mountains – Pen y Gadair Fawr 800 m (2,624 ft) and Waun Fach 810 m (2,660 ft). All the way you will be on a landscape of the Old Red Sandstone and you will have crossed the largest reach of continuous high ground in the southern half of Wales. There is still one peak to conquer – Pen Cerrig-calch 700 m (2,302 ft) – unique amid a sandstone world in being crowned with limestone (*calch* is Welsh for limestone).

The higher levels of the Old Red Sandstone which make up the bulk of the Park's uplands are known as Brownstones, a hard rock that has weathered into rounded hills many of which rise to about 600 m (2,000 ft). The greater heights of

*A pony with her foals in the pass at
Storey Arms*

some of the other summits are due to their being capped by
very resistant conglomerates called the Plateau Beds which
stand up distinctively as flat platforms. On the Black Mountains, for instance, both Waun Fach and Pen y Gadair Fawr
are crowned by these conglomerates.

But though the Plateau Beds and the Brownstones stand
high, their flanks have been enormously eroded and now
show as a beautifully carved escarpment that is one of the
dominant features of the northern half of the park. It begins
in the east above Hay and goes along the Wye valley to
beyond Talgarth, all the way making a splendid plunge from
600 to 90 m (2,000 to 300 ft). It then continues majestically
westwards across the north face of the Beacons and shows as
bold crags here and there on Fforest Fawr and Black Mountain.

Evidence of enormous erosion of the Old Red Sandstone can also be seen in the eastern quarter of the park where
Skirrid Fawr, Sugar Loaf and Mynydd Troed have been left
isolated from the rest of the Black Mountains. South-west
across the Usk from Mynydd Troed is a magnificent prospect of the four-mile ridge of the Beacons crowned by Corn
Du 820 m (2,863 ft) and Pen y Fan. The strata of this high
crest dip gently on the southern side and are covered by

moorland with easy slopes. But the north side is a precipitous
scarp face geometrically carved into a quartet of corries lying
side by side. They look down the long parallel valleys of
Cwm Llwch, Nant Sere, Cwm Cynwyn and Cwm Oergwm,
each divided from its neighbour by long high ridges.

When you climb the Beacons from the north you see
how perfectly horizontal their strata are from that angle and
how colourful are their rocks – not really red in fact but a soft
purple-pink that in spring goes well with the bright-green
vegetation, mainly Bilberry, which makes broad vertical
stripes all down the face of the escarpment. Below these
purple cliffs, on slopes almost as steep, sprawl the huge
spreads of scree which add so much to the wildness of the
scene.

A very popular but boot-damaged path to the Beacons
starts from the Brecon–Merthyr road (A470) at Pont-ar-daf
near Storey Arms. That way you start at 430 m (1,400 ft) and
have to climb only about 460 m (1,500 ft) to reach the top of
Pen y Fan. It is a quick route but one on which you will have
close views of moorlands and mountains only. So to get a real
cross-section of the Beacons country you would do better
to start from some valley in the lowlands. Coming from
Brecon, for instance, you could make your way up Cwm
Cynwyn following a trackway which since prehistory has
crossed over the Beacons and gone down the valley of the Taf
Fechan to Pontsticill. As you come up you will see how a

narrow tongue of broad-leaved woodland reaches towards the hills along the streamside. Then it ends abruptly, leaving the upper two miles of the valley almost without a tree. Once over the ridge you are in a world of wide moorlands and many reservoirs, for the Beacons sandstone is great gathering ground for water, being neither fissured nor porous.

West of the pass at Storey Arms rise the heights of Fforest Fawr, one rounded hill after another beginning at Fan Fawr 734 m (2,409 ft). (*Fan*, a name very frequent on the park map and meaning a high place, is pronounced and often written as 'Van'.) After Fan Fawr we have Fan Llia, Fan Nedd, Fan Fraith and finally, Fan Gihirych. If Fforest Fawr (Great Forest) was ever a forest in the sense of being tree-clad it was so only far back in prehistory. When it first came to be called the Great Forest the name was used in the Middle Ages sense of a hunting ground. Probably by then the native upland forests had long been cleared. Since those days multitudes of domestic animals have replaced the former deer and the valley woodlands have largely gone the way of the rest.

West of Fan Gihirych and across the A4067 you can follow the fine scarp line of Fan Hir as it builds up gradually into the great purple cliffs above the corrie lake, Llyn y Fan Fawr, and culminates on the Brecknock Fan (or Van) at 800 m (2,632 ft), the highest point of the Black Mountain. This summit forms a twin peak with the Carmarthen Fan 750 m (2,460 ft) which has its own corrie lake, Llyn y Fan Fach. These two fans (the plural in Welsh is *fannau* or *bannau*) are celebrated viewpoints that look south to Exmoor, west to Preseli and north to Cader Idris.

The streams that flow in all directions from the uplands rise very quickly in heavy rain and when they come rushing down full of brown spate water you can see at first hand what an active part they play in the shaping of the land. The rainfall on much of the park's high ground is about eighty inches a year and even more on the summits. In the lowlands forty inches is more usual, the driest area being in the east around Abergavenny. Most winters see snow at times on the hills and in hard winters the uplands can be white for weeks. Then there are even ski slopes for a while at Storey Arms and elsewhere.

The park's principal river is the Usk which rises on the far western moorlands and flows east right across the northern edge to Brecon before veering south-east to Abergavenny. Its many sidestreams come from all four uplands, most of them off the Old Red Sandstone. Along parts of the southern edge the streams are different, for they soon leave the sandstone for the limestone where, especially on the slopes of Fforest Fawr, they have cut deep gorges. Pyrddin, Nedd, Mellte and Hepste, slicing their way through these yielding limestones, have created a delightful region of ravines and waterfalls the like of which is not found elsewhere in Wales. This is a land undermined by many miles of complicated caves and underground streams and lakes which have been mapped in recent years by intrepid explorers.

Limestone is likewise a scenic feature of the south-eastern corner of the park on and around the high plateaux of Mynydd Llangynidr and Mynydd Llangatwg. Up there stretch many miles of moorland that is sour and peaty largely because the limestone is capped all over by Millstone Grit which produces an acid soil. Walk across and you soon discover these moors are pitted all over with what look very much like bomb craters some of which are over fifty yards across. These sink holes, in greater numbers here than anywhere else in Britain, occur where the Millstone Grit has collapsed into limestone caves below, the limestone having been dissolved away by acid rainwater seeping through the gritstone.

Prehistoric Man

It is a curious fact that although limestone caves elsewhere in England and Wales have yielded traces of Palaeolithic man yet none have so far been found in the Brecon Beacons. If from the Palaeolithic period we pass over a huge gulf of human time and come to the Mesolithic we are still in very shadowy territory. But as their primitive stone tools have been found locally in the park it may well be that the Mesolithic hunters found their way into most of the Brecon forests. In any case they made no impact on the scene and it was not until the Neolithic peoples arrived in about 3000 BC that man began to change his environment. The remains of a few of the great stone dolmens in which Neolithic people buried their honoured dead are still to be seen in the park, none better preserved than Ty Illtyd at Llanhamlech four miles south-east of Brecon. Britain's first farmers, these New Stone Age people began the attack on the primaeval forests that clothed the uplands to about 600 m (2,000 ft). But far worse was to come for the forests when around 2000 BC the Neolithic phase merged into the Bronze Age as people came from Europe equipped with metal tools that enabled tree felling and ploughing to proceed ever more quickly.

Man in the Bronze Age is thought to have favoured a life on the uplands at a time that was climatically happier than ours. Certainly his traces – round burial mounds (cairns), circles, alignments and single stones – are most frequent on the high ground. Bronze Age cairns can be seen in many places. There are circles on Trecastle Mountain and three miles south in Nant Tarw. A well-known tall stone is Maen Llia which stands solitary on Fforest Fawr and, whatever its primary purpose, probably served later as a marker for trackways across the uplands. Another upright stone, Maen Mawr, is part of a circle in the south-western part of Fforest Fawr. It too stands near an old road.

The Iron Age, which came in with the influx of Celtic tribes about 500 BC, no doubt carried on with the work of forest clearance. But by now the halcyon climate enjoyed by the Bronze Age was of the distant past and the hills retreated ever more often into coldness and clouds – much the sort of climate we know today. So man had to create living space lower down by clearing the jungle-like valley woodlands. His settlements were centred on the semi-upland and low-land hill forts or 'camps' as they are named on many maps. There are splendid examples in the park, notably Pen-y-crug that looks over Brecon town from five well-preserved ramparts – three massive inner banks and two weaker outer ones. And the most extensive fort in Wales, Carn Goch in the north-west of the park near Bethlehem, encloses thirty acres within its great banks of stones.

It is possible that the Roman centuries brought little change in the life-style of Celtic country folk. But the Romans certainly made their mark as military organizers by garrisoning troops at their local headquarters now called the Gaer, two miles west of Brecon, a fort whose ramparts are well preserved even now. From the Gaer they made roads in all directions. One of them headed west up to Y Pigwn then down to Llandovery. Another went south-east with the Usk to Abergavenny, Usk and Caerleon. A third takes us boldly over Fforest Fawr and down to Coelbren and Neath. Another may have gone north to Llandrindod.

The Dark Ages

The museum at Brecon has many reminders of the Roman time – coins, brooches, beads, pottery, tiles and carved stones such as Maen y Morwynion. Here too you can see some of the memorial stones and sculptured crosses of the Dark Ages when the Celtic saints first established the sites of many of today's parish churches and which are still dedicated to Cynog, Catwg, Brynach and other Celtic holy men. Another who has come down to us from that shadowy time is Brychan from whose name we get Brycheiniog, the Welsh name of the district of which he was a fifth century prince. Brycheiniog was later anglicized to Brecknock which was eventually simplified to Brecon. By tradition Brychan had strong links with Ireland, a connection that is adduced to explain the Irish-style Ogam inscribed stones that have been found in Brecknock, some of them on or near the sites of Celtic churches.

The Middle Ages

The princedom of Brycheiniog retained its separate identity until the Normans imposed a new political and social order. We now reach the age of castles – wooden ones of the motte and bailey type as well as those made of stone. Though built

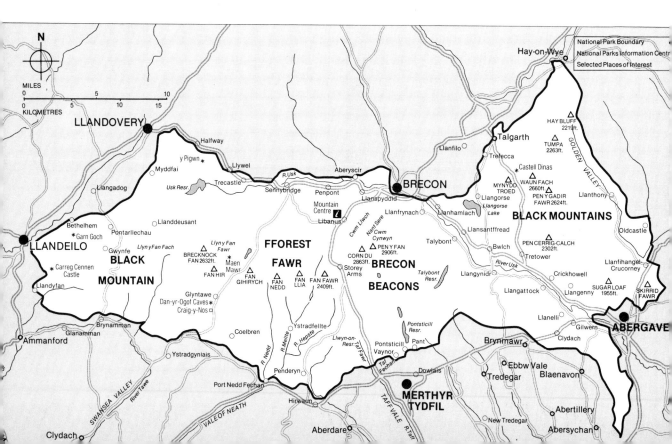

*View of Pen y Fan from Craig Cerrig-gleisiad
National Nature Reserve*

for various local reasons their total effect was the establishment of Anglo-Norman power and a countryside organized on feudal lines. The park has no great stone castles like those Edward I built elsewhere. But three miles south-east of Llandeilo there is Carreg Cennen castle which makes up for its lack of architectural splendour by being one of the most magnificently sited castles in Britain. It is perched on the brink of high limestone cliffs, its walls seeming to grow naturally from the rocks below. Built in the twelfth century with fourteenth century additions its best features are its corner towers and a fine gateway.

At the opposite end of the park was another high-placed castle, Castell Dinas, which is worth visiting simply for its views. That it has long ago crumbled into piles of stones is not surprising: at 450 m (1,476 ft) this presumably small and crude eleventh century structure was probably more battered by the weather than by man. Like so many early castles it stood within the banks and ditches of an Iron Age fort. A castle at Blaen-llynfi between Bwlch and Llangorse, guarded the eastern approaches to the Lordship of Brecknock. Today its walls have largely gone though its embankments remain. Crickhowell too had an important mediaeval castle of which wall fragments and a small tower survive. (The noble gate-

way, Porth Mawr, on the west side of the town, is Tudor; and the multi-arched bridge over the Usk, like the one at nearby Llangynidr, may include work of various centuries.)

Fragments of castles survive also at Hay-on-Wye and at Brecon; and five miles south-west of Brecon on Mynydd Illtyd is the stump of a tower of the thirteenth century castle of Blaen Camlais. All these and other strongholds speak of troubled times but gradually the bloodier side of life gave way to a more peaceful age when it began to be possible to build in less military style. So the later Middle Ages produced Tretower Court which was lived in and gradually altered until the eighteenth century, so providing us with insight into many generations of changing taste in domestic architecture.

Far better preserved than the castles are the mediaeval churches, some of which feature not only splendid stonework but also marvellous woodwork in roofs and screens. And there are many appealing old churches which are altogether beautiful for their simplicity, their quiet settings or perhaps their time-stricken Yews. At Brecon is the cathedral (fine chancel arch and thirteenth century choir) and an early English chapel at Christ's College across the river. But most celebrated of all the park's mediaeval buildings are the twelfth century ruins of Llanthony Priory, beautifully placed amid the Black Mountains in the Vale of Ewyas.

Wild Plants

Varied in its rocks, heights and aspects, and blessed with a temperate climate with a good measure of both sunshine and rain, the park is inevitably of great ecological interest. Certainly the Old Red Sandstone is very rewarding. For while many sandstones produce a limeless soil and a heathy vegetation, the Brownstones are locally rich in lime. So wherever they are broken into crags and screes they may be clothed with calcicole plants, especially where the scarps face the cool north or east, have been softened by the elements and have perennial water seeping out of them.

These are the conditions that favour the development of arctic-alpine communities all over highland Wales but the special interest of the Beacons Park is that here grow arctic-alpines at or near their southernmost British limit. The number of species is small, for many of the Snowdon plants are missing. But there are still enough to make a really fine show. There are sheets of prosperous-looking Roseroot, Mossy Saxifrage and Purple Saxifrage alongside healthy populations of Green Spleenwort (a fern), Lesser Meadow-rue (the mountain form) and Northern Bedstraw. Many of them can be found locally in all the park's uplands from Tarren yr Esgob (Vale of Ewyas) in the Black Mountains to the northern faces of the Beacons; then on Fforest Fawr at Craig Cerrig-gleisiad which, with neighbouring Cwm Du, is a national nature reserve. In the far west, in the cliffs above Llyn y Fan Fach, are still more of these alpine communities.

As elsewhere in Britain these Brecon alpines are not alone on their mountain ledges. Since 600 m (2,000 ft) or so is not a truly alpine elevation, especially so far south, the alpines find themselves challenged by thrusting lowland plants, all eager to get their roots into damp, calcium-rich soils. Prominent among these non-alpines are Cowslip, Primrose, Early-purple Orchid, Burnet-saxifrage, Rock Stonecrop, Wood Anemone and Great Burnet. And there are sheets of calcicole mosses like *Ctenidium molluscum* and *Neckera crispa*.

As often happens in calcareous localities the lime-richness of these Beacons rocks is patchy; and wherever it fails, in come the acid-loving plants to add to the wealth of the flora – Common Heather, Bell Heather, Bilberry, Wood-sorrel, Sheep's-fescue and Sheep's-bit, as well as many mosses, liverworts and lichens. Two calcifuge alpines that are scarce in the park, Parsley Fern and Dwarf Willow, are perhaps much diminished species that are close to the edge of extinction so far south. A plant of opposite fortunes is a very small alien that arrived in Wales this century, the New Zealand Willowherb. Year by year it creeps ever

further into the alpine zone and seems set to become one of the commonest plants though it was not found in the area until 1951.

Away from these crags the flat or rounded uplands are largely covered by acid ground either because there is a layer of peat or limeless glacial clay; or because any lime near the soil's surface has been washed out by the copious rainfall; or because the bedrock is Millstone Grit which is devoid of lime. The resultant vegetation over wide areas is a monotonous grassland of Sheep's-fescue, Common Bent-grass and Mat-grass with spreads of Soft Rush and Purple Moor-grass in ill-drained places. Here and there Heath Bedstraw, Tormentil and Heath Milkwort bring a slight touch of colour to the turf.

Wet peaty moors have heathers, Bilberry, Crowberry, Cowberry, Deergrass, Heath Rush and Green-ribbed Sedge among their typical plants. And where your feet sink into real bogs you can expect Common Cottongrass, Hare's-tail, Bog Asphodel, Bogbean, Round-leaved Sundew and various bog mosses. Keep an eye open for Bog Rosemary and record its locality carefully if you find it, for it seems to be extremely rare here. Among other treasures possible at these bog pools are Lesser Bladderwort, Pillwort and several unusual sedges.

Looked at on a map the narrow band of Carboniferous Limestone that shows itself along the south side of the park may seem rather insignificant compared with the great spread of Old Red Sandstone but its ecological influence is considerable. In the west it comes into the area near where Carreg Cennen castle perches so jauntily on its 90 m (300 ft) cliff. Here begin the Yews, Whitebeams and calcicole wild-flowers that you will find so often along the line of the limestone, especially in the valley of the Tawe around Craig y Nos. Here there are steep screes on which scrub ashwoods have developed and whose ground flora is rich with Lily-of-the-valley, Small Scabious, Autumn Gentian and Common Rockrose along with Broad-leaved Helleborine in rare quantity.

A mile east of Craig y Nos is Ogof Ffynnon Ddu, a National Nature Reserve of about 400 hectares (1,000 acres). Much of it is heather moor (with a few Red Grouse and Ring Ouzels) covering Millstone Grit. But there is also an area of limestone grassland whose choicer plants include Mountain Everlasting, Limestone Bedstraw and Soft-leaved Sedge. The nearby limestone pavement has its own specialities, among them Lesser Meadow-rue and the elegant grass, Mountain Melick. Underground are about twenty miles of cave passages, some of which have been studied by biologists. A public footpath crosses the reserve; but away from it, as in the three other national nature reserves, it is essential to get a visiting permit from the Nature Conservancy Council.

From Ogof Ffynnon Ddu the limestone marches on east over and down to the Ystradfellte country where the Nedd stream and its companions the Mellte, the Hepste and the Pyrddin have gnawed deep into the rocks to create a charming world of ash-shaded gorges and waterfalls. Amid cool green shadows the ferns are a special feature – Green Spleenwort, Hart's-tongue, Brittle Bladder and Hard and Soft Shield-ferns. And there are Globe Flowers, Meadow Crane's-bill, Meadow Saxifrage, Water Avens and many other delights.

The next deep valley sliced out of the limestone is that of the Taf Fawr (along which the A470 runs). On both sides of the road just south of Llwyn-on Reservoir you see high pallid rocks and screes that are known especially for their rare Whitebeams which resemble each other so closely that their identification is a task for experts. Penmoelallt Forest Nature Reserve, high above the west bank of the Taf Fawr,

three miles north-west of Merthyr Tydfil, is a seventeen acre ashwood with a scatter of oaks, Small-leaved Limes and Field Maples along with Ley's Whitebeam which is found nowhere in the world outside this valley. In this scattered, light-filled woodland, wildflowers are abundant in spring, Cowslips especially.

The last great outcrop of the limestone before it goes south-east out of the park can be seen most beautifully from Crickhowell. You look south-west across the wide Usk valley and there along the skyline are the high crags and screes of Mynydd Llangatwg. The flora of this scarp has long been celebrated and now it is protected in the Craig y Ciliau National Nature Reserve. Here are more rare Whitebeams and both Large-leaved and Small-leaved Limes; and under

Harvesting in the Brecon Beacons near Talybont

the trees are Angular Solomon's-seal, Alpine Enchanter's-nightshade among other jewels. In this reserve too is the sole entrance to a cavern, Agen Allwedd, that goes under the mountain for many miles.

Hastening down to the Usk on the south side of Mynydd Llangatwg the Clydach stream has excavated a deep, wide limestone gorge down which you look from the Heads of the Valleys road (A465). Natural beechwoods close to their western limit in Europe were probably far-reaching hereabouts until, in the early days of the industrial revolution, they were destroyed to make charcoal for iron-smelting. But down in the Clydach ravine, which is now a national nature reserve, their inaccessibility saved them and there they still thrive and are regenerating well. Apart from mosses and ferns these shadowy woods have a sparse but interesting flora including, though it is very rare, the Yellow Bird's-nest. But come up into the sunlit clearings and abandoned quarries near the lip of the gorge and you will find many good plants such as Large Thyme, Autumn Gentian, Dwarf Thistle and Limestone Fern. The limestone flanks of the nearby Blorenge are likewise clothed with beechwoods and ashwoods.

Throughout the park the valley bottoms are fertile and until the grassland improvement revolution of recent years they were rich in meadow flowers. But very few of the old fields now survive with their colourful and fragrant communities of Meadow Thistle, Saw-wort, Great Burnet, Pepper-saxifrage, Cowslip, Dyer's Greenweed, Petty Whin, Common Meadow-rue, Whorled Caraway, Creeping Willow, Fen Bedstraw, Globe Flower, Wood Bitter-vetch and many orchids and sedges. So where they survive today, except where they are protected in nature reserves, these plants mostly have to make do with waste corners and hedge banks. The flowers of woodlands do better, provided the woods are fenced, and the soil is moist and base-rich. Their trees are mostly Oak, Ash and Alder with Wild Cherry and Bird Cherry adding the beauty of their flowers in spring. Typical wildflowers are Ramsons, Sanicle, Dog's Mercury, Woodruff and Yellow Archangel, with Toothwort, Bird's-nest Orchid, Alternate-leaved Golden-saxifrage and Herb Paris among the rarities.

Animal Life

Forest destruction was a major factor in the extinction of the formerly common Wolves and Red Deer though both,

Llangorse Lake (Llyn Syfadden) *at Llangasty, a popular fishing place*

May in bloom near Llwyncelyn, which in English means holly grove

especially the deer, may have lingered as late as the seventeenth century. Now Fox, Badger and Otter are the largest wild animals. The Badgers survive with the help of legal protection. But Foxes remain outside the law; and though they may be thriving wondrously in the suburbs of far-off English cities, they may not be able to hold out indefinitely against the implacable persecution they have to face throughout the countryside of Wales.

The problems of the Otter are far more pressing. From about 1950 onwards this once fairly common resident of our rivers was faced with an unprecedented struggle for survival. Threatened by over-disturbance of the rivers, destruction of riverside habitats, water pollution, water extraction and rivalry with American Mink, the Otter has now disappeared from whole districts. That it still lives along the Usk in fair numbers owes much to the Brecknock Naturalists' Trust whose members in the late 1960s became pioneers in Otter conservation by persuading landowners along the river to give sanctuary to Otters by forbidding hunting. Since then the Trust has carried out surveys of the Otter population and landowners have further helped by the creation of Otter havens.

The Otter's three smaller relatives – Stoat, Weasel and Polecat – all thrive in the park, the survival of the Polecat

being the most remarkable because at the start of this century it was expected to become extinct very soon, so intensive was the persecution by gamekeepers. But then came World War I which diverted many keepers to other work just in time to save several hard-pressed species of mammals and birds-of-prey. Game-keeping was never resumed on the pre-war scale and the Polecat has prospered ever since.

Rabbits, often the Polecat's prey, are locally abundant in the valleys except during outbreaks of myxomatosis which occur from time to time with ever diminishing effect. Brown Hares are much more widespread for they live all over the higher ground as well as in the lowlands. They seem particularly common in the west on the slopes of the Black Mountain. The smaller mammals – Grey Squirrel (no Reds these days), Mole, Hedgehog, Field Vole, Bank Vole, Water Vole, Wood Mouse and Common and Pygmy Shrews are all abundant. Much more local are Yellow-necked Mouse and Water Shrew; and most recently detected is the Harvest Mouse whose nest was found during a survey of herb-rich meadows. The Dormouse is possibly not uncommon in sheltered Oak and Hazel woods but its distribution is as yet unknown. A speciality of the park are its bats for there are not only those typical of most Welsh woods and farmlands but also strong colonies of Lesser Horseshoe Bats in the limestone caves. These bats must be very choosy: some have gone three miles underground to find themselves suitable quarters.

Because of the variety of habitats, bird species are numerous, especially in the lowlands. On the high grasslands the only common breeding birds are Skylarks and Meadow Pipits. Some screes and stone walls have Wheatears and Wrens. And in heathery cliffs the piping of Ring Ouzels is a characteristic sound though the birds themselves are not always easy to spot on their high rocky perches. The greater crags are nesting sites for Ravens and Kestrels and, extremely

locally, the Peregrine. On the heather moors is a scattering of Red Grouse and here and there a breeding Merlin. Moorland conifer blocks are a haven for Goldcrests, Coal Tits, Wood-pigeons and sometimes Siskins and Crossbills. But except in their first few years when they attract Redpolls, Chaffinches, Whinchats, Robins, Hedge Sparrows and Willow Warblers, these plantations are poor in birds. In winter most species desert grasslands and conifers alike, leaving the high ground to Ravens and Crows.

In the breeding season it is the broad-leaved woods of the valleys that are liveliest with birds. Some are all-the-year-round residents such as tits, Tree Creepers, Chaffinches, Nuthatches, Robins and the three types of Wood-pecker. These woods are also the strongholds of the Buzzard which thrives so well in a world of pastoral farmlands and

The landscape near Defynnog looking towards Fforest Fawr

tree-shaded dingles. In any month, but especially in spring, you may hear the Buzzards' lovely wailing and see them, usually two at a time, circling and diving gracefully over their nesting places. Sparrowhawks too are quite numerous in the valleys: they forage along woodsides and hedgerows and, like Buzzards, often go up to hunt over high moorlands too.

Among abundant summer woodland and farmland visitors from Africa are Tree Pipit, Spotted Flycatcher, Blackcap, Garden Warbler, Chiffchaff, Whitethroat and Willow Warbler as well as three others which are generally commoner in Wales than in England: Wood Warbler, Redstart and Pied Flycatcher. This very attractive and approachable flycatcher is especially abundant in woods where nest boxes are provided. But it is well to remember that its time in the woods is brief. It sings only from mid-April to mid-June and by early July it can already be hard to find.

Breeding water birds include Dipper and Grey Wagtail, both of which nest, though very sparingly, as high as 460 m (1,500 ft). Kingfishers breed not only along the streams but also by the Usk valley canal; and Common Sandpipers nest by still or running waters from lowlands to uplands. But it is the non-breeding birds that get most attention from birdwatchers – the sometimes rare species that drop in on passage or during winter wanderings. One of the likeliest spots for such casuals is Talybont Reservoir which has many winter ducks and, if the water level is low, attracts mud-loving waders spring and autumn. Most of the other reservoirs, at higher altitudes, attract far fewer birds but some are visited by Whooper Swans and Goosanders.

The only sizable natural lake in the park is five miles east of Brecon at Llangorse. Over a mile long, this water has always been cherished by naturalists for its wealth of plants, its insects, its many breeding birds and its passage terns, waders and warblers. But the glory has departed. Despite years of struggle by conservationists it is acutely disturbed by water sports and grossly polluted by effluents, both sewage and agricultural fertilizers. What ought to be a magnificent nature reserve and one of the chief glories of the park, has been brought to its present plight by problems of conflicting interests and local politics. From afar it still looks beautiful but it is a dying lake which can now only be saved by a truly resolute programme of rehabilitation.

Two kinds of newt live in the park, the Smooth, which is a lowlander, and the much commoner Palmate Newt (formerly called the Alpine) which ranges from the valleys to the mountains. Common Toad and Common Frog are both numerous in the lowlands but even at 790 m (2,600 ft) the frog can breed successfully. The park has three reptiles that are widespread – Grass Snake, Slow-worm and Common Lizard; and one, the Adder, that is local and uncommon.

The fish population shows a typical western bias towards game species. The rivers are full of Brown Trout and along the Usk are many good Salmon pools. The reservoirs are mainly stocked with Brown Trout and Rainbows but some have the more popular American Brook Trout. Llangorse Lake has long been famous for extra-large Eels and for its Pike, Perch, Carp and Roach; and the Usk Valley canal is fished for Roach, Dace and Perch. Some of the streams have Minnow, Bullhead and Stone Loach.

Noteworthy among the butterflies are Comma (increased in recent years); Dark-green Fritillary (thinly distributed); Silver-washed Fritillary; Marsh Fritillary (very local on bogs); Small Pearl-bordered Fritillary; Purple, Green and the very local White-letter Hairstreak and three Skippers, Small (the commonest), Dingy (the rarest) and Large Skipper. Only one species, the Small Heath, is a common resident of the high moors. But up there you may often see

The Monmouthshire and Brecon Canal near Talybont

*Sennybridge market, famous for its sheep and
cattle sales*

migrants, especially Large Whites, and in some years Red
Admirals and Painted Ladies. And the August sunshine
sometimes brings many Small Tortoiseshells up from the
valleys to sip at the heather flowers.

The most striking moorland moth is the Emperor which
you may see on the wing in early spring or, more likely, find
in the larval stage on the heather in summer. Large hairy
caterpillars often found on the high ground are those of Fox,
Northern Eggar and Drinker Moths. Most conspicuous
moths of the lowlands are those which sometimes defoliate
the oaks in spring – Winter Moth, Mottled Umber and Green
Oak-roller. Their super-abundant larvae are crucial in the
successful breeding of many woodland birds. The lepidopt-
era in and around the park are fully recorded in *Butterflies
and Moths of Breconshire* published by the Brecknock
Naturalists' Trust (1978).

Recreation

From Hay Bluff in the east to Carmarthen Fan in the west the
opportunities for ridge walks and other high-level rambles
are infinite. Most people venture forth for just a day or a few
hours but others go in for more ambitious expeditions across
the whole park by staying the night at youth hostels, hotels
or the many bed and breakfast houses; or simply by camping
or bivouacking. In the lowlands there are plenty of footpath
signs to indicate short routes in and around villages and
towns. And along the Usk valley there is often the tow-path
of the canal to help you on your way. The Forestry Commission's plantations are threaded by many miles of roads available to walkers and orienteers. And imaginatively presented
information about the forests, land-use, history and ecology
is provided at the Commission's visitor centre at Garwnant
in Cwm Taf, five miles north-west of Merthyr Tydfil.

The smooth and easily reached uplands attract numerous pony trekkers for whom many far-seeing routes are
available, especially in the eastern half of the park. For the
even more adventurous there is the exploration of the dark
recesses of limestone caves that are among the longest in
Britain. But be warned: do not go caving without proper
training and never enter caves alone and without telling
anyone where you are going. At Dan yr Ogof on the
Brecon–Swansea road (A4067) you can visit brilliantly lit
caverns on conducted tours and with no danger at all. Or if
the troglodyte life has no appeal you can always try the
opposite style of sport: hang-gliding over Hay Bluff or other
windy heights.

Recreation by water is popular especially on the
formerly industrial canal (completed 1812) which has the

distinction of being the only British canal entirely within a national park. For thirty-three miles from Brecon to Pontypool this well engineered waterway winds river-like across the park, often with wide views to the hills. Canoeists use the canal or seek the more exciting waters of the Usk. Anglers fish in lakes, reservoirs and streams throughout the park.

For a family day out that involves no long walks or climbs there is the Country Park at Craig y Nos. For narrow-gauge railway enthusiasts there is a short length of line from Pant just north of Merthyr Tydfil. For naturalists there are courses available on many fascinating subjects at the field study centre at Dan-y-wenallt, five miles down the Usk from Brecon. They might also like to consider joining the Brecknock Naturalists' Trust which has some fine reserves open to members only.

Without ever leaving a main road motorists can see much of this park. There are many minor roads but these are narrow and best left for the use of local people, walkers, riders and cyclists. For information there is the National Park Office in Brecon, or you can drive to the main visitor centre near Libanus four miles south-west of Brecon along A470. There you can take in all the knowledge provided by the excellent display stands and literature; or plan your safaris for the next few days; or simply sit drinking tea while enjoying the views of those lovely Beacons.

Useful Addresses

Brecknock Naturalists' Trust: Chapel House, Llechfaen, Brecon, Powys
Brecknock Museum: Old County Hall, Captains' Walk, Brecon, Powys
National Park Office: Glamorgan Street, Brecon, Powys
National Trust: 22 Alan Road, Llandeilo, Dyfed
Danywenallt Study Centre: Talybont-on-Usk, Brecon, Powys

Water Crowfoot, near St David's Cathedral, Pembrokeshire

William Condry

Pembrokeshire Coast
Parc Cenedlaethol Penfro

PEMBROKESHIRE
NATIONAL
PARK

THE MAGNIFICENT rocky coast of Pembrokeshire reaches out towards the Atlantic between Ireland and south-west England. In Welsh it has always been 'Penfro', the 'Land's End' of Wales, and 'Penfro' was long ago anglicized to become 'Pembroke'. The national park consists largely of a narrow strip of land, much of it on cliffs above the sea, that winds intricately around the coast of the old county of Pembroke which in 1974 was merged into the larger county of Dyfed.

In many ways the Pembrokeshire Coast is unique among our national parks. It is the smallest (583 square km, 225 square miles), the most maritime and the most lowland, much of it not higher than sixty-two metres (200 ft). It has the mildest climate, almost frost-free in the far south-west. It is also the driest with only 812 mm (thirty-two inches) of rain on the west coast. Its farming includes a greater proportion of arable than any other park and is important for early potatoes. It is the park most violently intruded on by heavy industry: since it was designated in 1952 it has seen Milford Haven mushroom from a declining fishing port into Europe's second largest oil port. It is the most densely populated of the parks for it has twice as many people per square mile as the average of the other nine parks. Perhaps most important of all, it is the park most threatened by development (both from tourism and industry) as is shown by the fact that its authorities report that they deal with three times more planning applications, in relation to size, than the average for all the other national parks.

As well as the coastal lowlands there is also an upland section: in the north-east the boundary ventures inland to take in the Preseli Hills (*Bryniau Preseli*) whose highest top, Foel Cwmcerwyn, reaches 542 m (1,760 ft). Because so isolated from the rest of the Welsh uplands these hills are conspicuous in the landscape from far away and are themselves a famous viewpoint. On a reasonably clear day you can see Bardsey Island and the hills of Lleyn in the north, Cader Idris and Plynlimon in the north-east, the Brecon Beacons due east and the Gower coast, ending with shapely Worms Head, in the south-east. In weather of exceptional clarity Snowdon's sharp peak stands up well in the north, especially when white with snow; the high moors of

Somerset and Devon are visible in the south; and in the north-west you could be lucky enough to make out the Wicklow Mountains, especially on a summer's evening when they are cut out black against a sunset sky.

Your near view from Preseli any fine day will take in much of the park and you easily grasp its essential features. You look down over a complex pattern of lowland fields, some pasture, some arable. And all along the north you see that the coast rises high and rocky and that the cliffs continue with only occasional breaks all the way round into the west. Far in the south-west the great inlet (*ria*) of Milford Haven brings a glint of tidal water right into the heart of the land.

Geology

Although occupying so minute a part of the earth's surface the Pembrokeshire park exhibits a remarkable range of rock systems, all the very ancient eras being represented from the Pre-Cambrian to the Coal Measures at the top of the Carboniferous. Such rocks as may have been laid down after that time have vanished, except for a few pockets of Triassic rocks in the limestone cliffs west of Tenby. Broadly speaking the rocks are divided by an east–west line running through Haverfordwest: north of it there is a predominance of Ordovician with some Pre-Cambrian, Cambrian and Silurian rocks; and in the south the rocks are chiefly Devonian (Old Red Sandstone) and Carboniferous. In many places the tensions in the earth's crust have left the strata tremendously distorted and faulted. And erosion has been on an enormous scale.

Up on Preseli the view immediately around you is of heathy or grassy moorland on Ordovician slates and shales. There are also many rocks of volcanic origin – acid lavas, ashes, tuffs, and dolerite – which have resisted erosion while softer rocks have been worn away all round. Their isolated outcrops stand up very strangely in the upland landscape, piles of huge, squared slabs that have been likened to the heaps of mountain-top detritus on Glyder Fach in Snowdonia. From Preseli the hard igneous rocks go on into the north-west to form the massive headland of Strumble, a region of such varied rocks and soils that its ecology may well

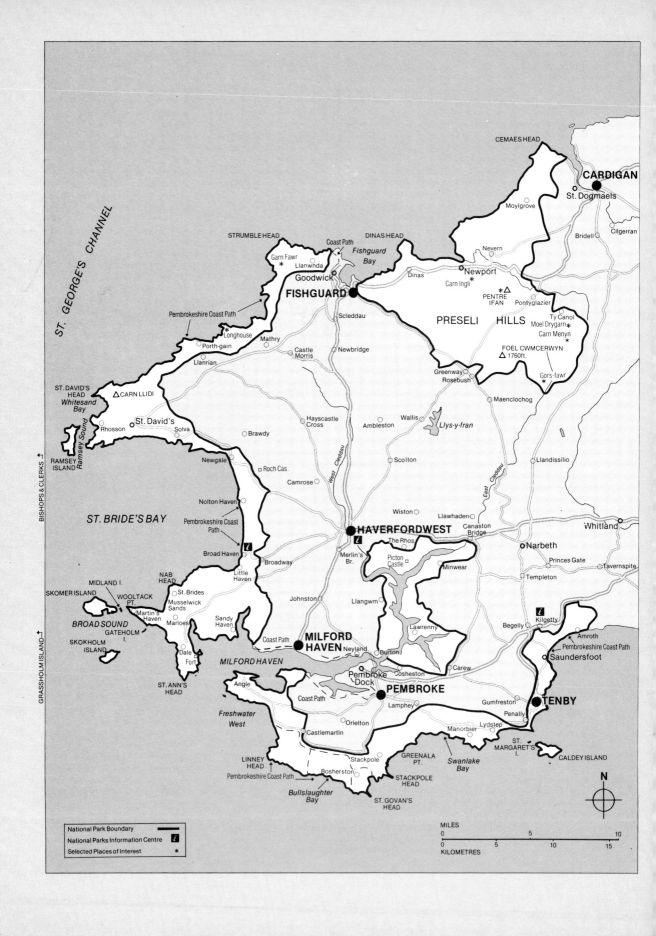

Pentre Ifan, Nevern, one of the finest Neolithic burial chambers in Britain

be richer than that of any other promontory on the coast of Wales.

Strumble's neighbouring headlands north-east up the coast, those of Dinas and Cemaes, are likewise bold and magnificent. But as they continue the Silurian rocks of mid-Cardigan Bay they are lacking in igneous material and therefore have a less varied ecology. Igneous rocks, however, continue west of Strumble all the way to St David's, a headland of resistant gabbro. It is this same tough rock that stands up so boldly just inland to form the conspicuous hill called Carn Llidi. A mixture of acid and basic rocks means that the ecology of St David's Head is comparable with that of Strumble. On this part of the coast too is the geologically well-known Abereiddi Bay where there was a slate quarry till World War I. Here the slates are emphatically fossiliferous: if you pick them up on the old tips or on the beach you will find that many of them have well-preserved tuning-fork graptolites.

The mixture of Ordovician rocks continues out to Ramsey Island and its neighbours the Bishops and Clerks. Ramsey with its two bold summits has quite a mountainous look because, like Preseli, it is made up largely of igneous rocks both acid and basic. Its sedimentary rocks have yielded fossils of the lowest strata of the Ordovician system.

St Govan's Chapel, in a cleft below Trevalen Downs, and St Govan's Head

Many of the rock formations of this coastline, whether island or mainland, can be seen best from a boat. Go south, then east, from St Justinian's and in a few miles you will see cliff after cliff of colourful sandstones, shales and conglomerates of Cambrian age. At Caerbwrdy Bay, for instance, the sandstones are of the delicate purple that you will find in the walls of St David's Cathedral, for it was here that the stones were quarried in the Middle Ages. (The rocks on which the cathedral stands are Pre-Cambrian igneous.) Three miles east of St David's the village of Solva looks down a deep sheltered valley in the Cambrian rocks. Then the cliffs end where the sea has bitten into a softer shore made of the Coal Measures of St Bride's Bay. But do not expect to find any coal mines there, though you would have done a century ago. Today it is hard to imagine that little Nolton Haven once exported coal. Even the quay where the ships tied up has been washed away.

In the southern corner of St Bride's Bay, Little Haven was also a coal mining village which today is unsmirched by industry. It is there we leave the Coal Measures for the broad band of Old Red Sandstone that, with one significant interruption, goes on to form most of the rocks on both sides of Milford Haven including the great St Ann's Head that defies the Atlantic at one of the windiest spots of all the Welsh coast. Nowhere are the Old Red Sandstone cliffs more colourful than from Nab Head to Musselwick Sands. For miles their steeply inclined strata lie neatly side by side making delightful patterns with their various shades of brown, pink and purple. West of Musselwick Sands, the Marloes peninsula is yet another witness to the extra hardness of volcanic rocks. Formerly thought to be of Ordovician age but now regarded as Silurian, they extend out from Wooltack Point to Midland Isle and Skomer and then show up miles out to sea as Grassholm Island and the islets of the Hats, Barrels and Smalls, the most westerly fragments of Wales. At Gateholm, a half-tide island near Marloes, we are back briefly on the Old Red Sandstone but the nearby cliffs,

behind Marloes Sands, are well-known for their superb succession of Silurian rocks. Skokholm, two miles off-shore, is
Old Red Sandstone, as you see clearly from the colour of its
cliffs.

In the far south of the park we come to rocks of yet
another geological era, the Carboniferous, and the coast goes
on as a magnificent sequence of high, vertical cliffs and
headlands. The eight-mile stretch from Linney Head to St
Govan's then on to Stackpole Head is as superb a line of
limestone cliffs as you will see anywhere round the British
coast. Facing south-west into the Atlantic they are often
beaten by enormous seas which come booming into caves
and throw spume high into the air up blow-holes near the
cliff edge. A famous feature here is the Green Bridge of
Wales, a column of limestone standing in the sea and connected with the cliffs by a natural arch. It is a stack rock in the
making: one day its arch will collapse and then it will look
like the two Elegug Stacks nearby. Sadly the path along the
cliffs west from Bosherston is closed much of the time
because the area is a military firing range. But it is usually
open on holidays and summer weekends.

Along the coast path east from Bosherston fine cliffs,
bays and headlands go with you all the way with little blem-
ish to Manorbier, Lydstep and Tenby. Sometimes you are on
the Old Red Sandstone, sometimes on the Carboniferous
Limestone; and you will see from the division of colour in its
rocks that Caldey Island is half sandstone, half limestone.
You get a lovely view of Caldey from the limestone headland
at Lydstep whose strata have in places been turned to a
vertical position. Then as the coast turns northward beyond
Tenby we are soon back on less ancient rocks, first the
Millstone Grit and then the Coal Measures. At Saundersfoot, as in St Bride's Bay, there used to be mining and coal
exporting. The Coal Measures cliffs here are remarkably
crumpled and folded, the Ladies' Cave anticline being one of
the most photographed and sketched geological features in
Britain, appearing in many text-books. A few miles further
east the park comes to an end at Amroth. Here too the Coal
Measures, much distorted, are well exposed in the cliffs.

Early Man

The park is rich in prehistoric remains beginning right back
in the Palaeolithic period. Limestone caves near Tenby and
Pembroke and also on Caldey Island have yielded imple-

Stack Rocks, off Talbenny, in St Bride's Bay

ments dating from about 10000 BC. At that time the Ice Age had not quite ended and man evidently lived by hunting reindeer whose bones are abundant in these caves. The Mesolithic period (about 8000–4000 BC) is represented by the artefacts found at chipping-floors such as those at Nab Head, Caldey, Castlemartin and Swanlake Bay. Among the hunting grounds of these early peoples, as is indicated by weapons found there, were the forests which grew on land that is now just off the present coastline. It was submerged as ice sheets melted and sea levels rose. Traces of these forests (branches and trunks preserved in peat) can still sometimes be seen at low tide on beaches at Newgale, Freshwater West and Amroth.

The Neolithic Age speaks to us vividly when we see great dolmens such as Pentre Ifan on the lower northern slopes of Preseli. Other fine burial chambers are at Trellyfant, Longhouse and Bedd yr Afanc. Most characteristic relics of the Bronze Age which began about 2000 BC, are the circular grass-grown burial mounds or heaps of stones, most of whose contents were removed by the treasure hunters or antiquarians of long ago. At the eastern end of Preseli three prominent cairns stand side by side on Moel Drygarn (or Trigarn), and below the southern slopes of Preseli is another fine Bronze Age monument, the stone circle at Gors-fawr.

Few archaeological theories can have become more firmly planted in people's minds than the claim that the circle of 'blue stones' at Stonehenge was transported there by Bronze Age man from the top of Preseli where the same type of dolerite is found on and around an outcrop called Carn Menyn. The only other possible agent for moving such boulders across country are sheets of ice. But in the 1920s, when the link between Stonehenge and Preseli was first suggested, it was not realized, as it is today, that the glaciers that came across south Wales from the Irish Sea reached as far east as the Bristol–Bath region. So a fashionable conjecture now is that Bronze Age man had to move the 'blue stones' overland for less than thirty miles rather than make the complicated journey of 180 miles by land and water that had been calculated for the transit from Preseli.

If while on Preseli you visit the Bronze Age cairns on Moel Drygarn you will also see a well-known Iron Age hill fort, for these cairns lie within its stony embankments along with many Iron Age hut circles. Except for Moel Drygarn the park is lacking in hill-top forts enclosed within concentric banks, but it has a multiplicity of other Iron Age defence works (often called 'raths'). Promontory forts on the sea cliffs are mostly of the Iron Age. Typically they are headlands defended by banks constructed across their approaches, as you can see on the cliffs at Bullslaughter Bay, between Linney Head and Tenby and at Greenala Point. Two sizeable forts not on the cliffs are Garn Fawr, a mile and a half south of Strumble Head; and Carn Ingli, a mile south

of Newport: both are perched on prominent igneous outcrops and defended by man-made walls. But the best glimpses of Iron Age life are on St David's Head and Skomer: both these sites have hut circles and ancient field systems.

The Dark Ages

The Roman period seems to have had little impact so far south-west and the life-style of the people, the Demetae, probably carried on with little change. For instance some of the Iron Age huts on Gateholm Island are thought to have continued in use into post-Roman times. At St David's, Clegyr Boia, anciently a Neolithic site, then an Iron Age settlement, is connected by tradition with the age of the saints (fifth to the seventh centuries AD), from which survive many inscribed or carved stones. The inscriptions mostly commemorate the names of the dead in Latin; but the cryptic script called Ogam also appears on some stones, testifying to strong Irish influence. Such stones can be seen in museums and in the churches at Brawdy, Bridell, Clydau, Nevern and St Dogmaels. There are also many later Christian stones and

Red Campions bloom in the sand dunes of Freshwater West

crosses in the park. Three of them – at Carew, Nevern and Penally are outstanding for their size and elaborate carvings.

The later Dark Ages are as shadowy as those before. After the age of the saints came the Viking period (ninth to eleventh centuries AD) but it left almost no material trace of itself and would hardly be remembered were it not for Viking place names such as Ramsey, Skomer and Skokholm which suggest that these islands were long used as bases for piratical raids and probably also as trading posts.

The Middle Ages

Norman influences are numerous in the shape of motte and bailey castles and stone castles whose imposing ruins still survive. Of these Pembroke Castle is much the greatest for it was the centre of Norman power in this south-western corner of Wales. It was built in the thirteenth century on a bold limestone ridge overlooking a tidal creek. Among its attractions are its beautiful setting, the immensely thick high walls, the great round keep with wide views from the top, its elaborate gatehouse and a huge, bat-haunted cave underneath through which there is access from the castle to the river.

Commanding one of Milford Haven's higher creeks is the castle at Carew which is so delightful when reflected in the calm waters of a brimming tide. After its military career this castle (*c.* 1300) became a grand private residence and now looks rather odd with Tudor windows cut in its mediaeval

walls. Also beautifully sited is the castle at Manorbier that looks down a partly wooded valley to a rock-girt beach; and up on the north coast the Normans built a castle at Newport which survives partly ruinous, partly as a private house, just above the town.

Roch Castle, prominent on a lava outcrop two miles inland from St Bride's Bay on the road to Haverfordwest, was a mediaeval tower now restored as a private house. It was significant as the most westerly of a line of forts the Normans built to divide the region between the north which, except for the Newport area, was left to the Welsh, and the south which received an influx of Anglo-Normans and Flemish refugees. This twelfth century dividing line was long known as the Landsker and it marks a boundary even today. North of it you will hear plenty of spoken Welsh. South of it is still 'Little England beyond Wales', a name that was in use as early as the Middle Ages. The Landsker castles strung out south-east from Roch were at Haverfordwest, Picton, Wiston, Llawhaden, Carew, Narberth and Amroth.

In the wake of the Anglo-Norman take-over, mediaeval towns grew up at Pembroke, Haverfordwest, Tenby and Newport; and though Pembroke was the military headquarters it was at Haverfordwest that political power eventually became centred. As it grew in importance the town burst out of its original walls which are now lost almost without trace. But you can still see well preserved mediaeval town walls at Tenby where you will also find the original street pattern within the walls, although the houses are mostly Georgian or early Victorian.

As well as in castles and town walls the Middle Ages live on vividly in the churches. There is the small but appealing cathedral in its tranquil setting at St David's. There are also the cathedral-like St Mary's church at Haverfordwest; Manorbier church with its crude interior arches and the very out-of-straight alignment of nave with chancel; the village church and the priory church on Caldey Island; St Brynach's church, Nevern, with its Vitalianus stone and its ancient Yews; and St Mary's church, Tenby, which has a fine late-mediaeval oak ceiling. Other ecclesiastical buildings include the attractive ruins of bishops' palaces at St David's and at Lamphey, two miles east of Pembroke.

Plant Life

The coastline of this park is so celebrated for its wildflowers that visitors scarcely realize that even the acid moors of Preseli have their treasures. For up there in a sheep and pony world of Mat-grass, heathers, Bilberry and Western Gorse there are small boggy patches delightful with Bog Asphodel, Marsh St John's-wort, Round-leaved Sundew, Bog Myrtle, Common Butterwort and Cranberry. Here and there are a few much rarer plants: Oblong-leaved Sundew, Bog Orchid,

Canoeing, windsurfing and sailing at Dale, near St Ann's Head

Ivy-leaved Bellflower, Marsh Clubmoss and, strangely absent from the rest of Wales, Pale Butterwort. Preseli being a hill rather than a mountain, arctic-alpines are lacking except for Parsely Fern but it is exceedingly rare. Strangely absent are two moorlanders so widespread on other Welsh uplands: Crowberry and Cowberry. Stag's-horn and Fir Clubmosses are present but sparse.

Preseli is very colourful in August when the purple of the heathers and the deep yellow of the Western Gorse are most vivid. But spring is the great time for blossom in the lowland farming country where there are long hedges white with Hawthorn and Blackthorn and the banks are bright-yellow with Common Gorse. Sadly the herb-rich pastures and meadows of earlier this century have largely been ploughed and re-seeded by modern grass mixtures and the choicer wildflowers of the fields are only a memory.

So today the chief floral beauty of the farmlands is along the roadsides, especially in the sunken lanes cut in the lime-rich soils of the south. There in late April and May, after most of the Lesser Celandines and Primroses have faded, you will find a wonderful luxuriance of Red Campion mingling with blue carpets of Germander Speedwell; or there are high forests of Cow Parsley often with its fellow umbellifer, the yellow-green-flowered Alexanders. Scurvygrass makes bands of pure whiteness and where there is dampness there are sheets of Ramsons spilling out of woods and spinneys. These are all very common plants but in this southern half of the park they grow with special exuberance of colour and size, often amid a profusion of extra-large Hart's-tongue Fern and Soft Shield-fern. The south is also the home of the Tenby Daffodil, a plant of mystery because botanists cannot decide if it is a wild species endemic to this small area or whether it is of garden origin. It is fairly common about villages and on roadsides in a belt of country stretching for about sixteen miles east of Tenby.

Throughout the park, as spring turns to summer, the hedges are bright and fragrant with Honeysuckle and Dog Rose. More and more umbellifers come into flower and there is much Common Cat's-ear, Smooth Hawk's-beard, Field Scabious, Meadowsweet, Purple Loosestrife and Hemp-agrimony so attractive to butterflies. Here and there certain uncommon or distinguished species are officially protected in roadside reserves recommended by the West Wales Naturalists' Trust.

Sheltered hedge-banks are precious in a park so exposed to the Atlantic that it has very little tree cover. There are widely scattered conifer plantations, even high on Preseli, but none is very extensive. Broad-leaved woodland is like-wise fragmentary. Near Fishguard there is a lengthy tongue of it in the sheltered Gwaun Valley where the West Wales Naturalists' Trust has a reserve: here the typical wildflowers are Lesser Celandine, Wood Anemone, Bluebell and Cow-

wheat. Twelve miles south there are beautiful reaches of woodland along and near the Eastern Cleddau. And a dozen miles further south, on the Stackpole National Nature Reserve, are the tangled woods and thickets around the Bosherston lily-ponds where Black Bryony, Wood Spurge, Early-purple Orchid and festoons of Traveller's-joy pro-claim a limestone soil.

Goultrop Wood, at the south end of St Bride's Bay, is a sea-slope woodland turned away from the south-west winds; and there is also sheltered woodland at Saundersfoot. A distinctive feature of cool, moist woodlands on the higher ground are the many mosses and other flowerless plants. So at Ty Canol, three and a half miles north of Preseli Top, there is a reputedly ancient wood that is especially known for the lichens and ferns of its deep, rocky gullies.

Lowland bogs and marshes survive best around St David's, especially at Dowrog Common (a reserve of the West Wales Naturalists' Trust). Typical plants of these wet-lands are Bogbean, Common Water-plantain and Marsh St John's-wort and there are also Southern Marsh-orchid, Lesser Butterfly-orchid, Lesser Bladderwort, Wavy St John's-wort, Floating Water-plantain and the unfernlike little fern called Pillwort.

Along the south coast there are sand dunes in several places, notably at Freshwater West, Stackpole and Tenby; and along the north coast at Whitesands Bay (near St David's), Newport and the Teifi estuary. All are botanically interesting though there have been some losses where Sea-buckthorn has been planted, as at Tenby, to fix the sands and has spread into impenetrable thickets. Typical dune plants are Marram-grass, Sea-holly, Burnet Rose, Sea Bindweed, Sea Pansy, Carline Thistle, Blue Fleabane, Ploughman's-spikenard, Early Marsh-orchid and Pyramidal Orchid. Three other orchids are uncommon: Bee Orchid, Marsh Helleborine and Autumn Lady's-tresses.

There are several areas of salt-marsh along the shores of Milford Haven, the little estuary of the Gann stream at Dale being a good example. Other saltings have developed along the Cleddau rivers. Characteristic plants include Scurvy-grass, Thrift, Sea Aster, Sea-purslane and, a rare occurrence in Wales, enough Lax-flowered Sea-lavender to turn parts of

the sward into sheets of purple-blue. Muddy areas have long been vanishing beneath forests of Cord-grass which in places has overwhelmed less aggressive species like Glasswort.

Outstandingly beautiful among the plant-rich habitats are the miles of rocky slopes above the sea. Here in the cool ocean breezes are natural gardens bright in spring with the differing yellows of Gorse, Kidney Vetch, Bird's-foot Trefoil and Cowslips alongside white patches of Sea Campion, Scurvygrass and Ox-eye Daisy. And amid all these are pink sheets of Thrift and the blue of Sheep's-bit and Spring Squills. In summer Rock Samphire, Golden Samphire and Saw-wort bring gaiety to the scene. Here and there along the cliffs and headlands are rarer plants: Prostrate Broom, Royal Fern, Yellow Cicendia, Hairy Bird's-foot Trefoil, Spiked Speedwell, Yellow Bartsia, Hairy Greenweed, Wild Chives, Perennial Centaury and two Rock Sea-lavenders peculiar to the British Isles. Roseroot grows in small quantity on the cliffs of St David's Head, its only locality on the coast of Wales.

That Ramsey Island's soils are particularly varied is suggested by the presence there of unusual plants like Royal Fern, Juniper, Yellow Cicendia, Chamomile, Subterranean Clover, Balm-leaved Figwort, Floating Waterplantain, Small Pondweed, Fiddle Dock, Adder's-tongue Fern and Lanceolate Spleenwort. Skomer Island, eight miles south of Ramsey, lacks most of these except the two ferns but has Shoreweed in its ponds and Wild Madder on the cliffs. It also has such sheets of colour in spring that they can easily be seen from the mainland: pink zones of Thrift, marvellous spreads of Bluebells and great white patches of Scurvygrass and Sea Campion. Where nitrogen-rich droppings of gulls accumulate the cliffs may be draped with extra-vigorous Red Campion. With it you will often find a plant especially typical of south-west Britain, the Tree-mallow which stands so admir-

ably erect in the most exposed situations. In fact nowhere does it seem happier than on the very bleakest flat tops of seabird stacks.

Caldey, always the exception among the islands, not only has Carboniferous Limestone and therefore calcicole plants but also enjoys some shelter from long-established groves and monastery gardens. Amongst its lime-lovers are Bloody Crane's-bill, Blue Fleabane, Field Gentian, Burnet Rose and White Horehound. Its Dame's-violet and Sweet Cicely are pretty certainly introductions: so too perhaps are Flowering-rush and Greater Spearwort.

Animal Life

The most distinguished and most easily observed mammals are undoubtedly the Grey Seals. They can be seen at times (and also heard mournfully singing) all round this rocky coast but most commonly in the north and west. At low tide they come ashore, sometimes in large herds, on quiet stony beaches; or they lie out on off-shore rocks. When the tide is high you can often see them as heads sticking out of the water as they eye you with unruffled curiosity. This coast is their stronghold in Wales, their largest breeding colony being on Ramsey Island (about 200 pups a year) and Skomer (about sixty pups). Most young are born in autumn. Their breeding biology has been much studied, especially on Ramsey where marking experiments have shown that some young seals go off on far migrations at a surprisingly early age. These seals have increased in recent years under protection. The other British species, the Common Seal, which prefers shallow, sandy waters, has very seldom been seen along this coast.

While scanning the ocean for seals you may well observe other sea mammals as they surface for a second or two. Most likely are schools of Common Porpoises and Common and

Bottle-nosed Dolphins as they roll up out of the waves. Other cetaceans occasionally reported include Risso's Dolphin, Pilot Whale and the formidable Killer Whale which preys on other whales, dolphins, seals and large fish.

After the Grey Seal the next largest mammals are Fox and Badger, both of which are well established on the mainland. If they were ever on the islands they were probably exterminated long ago along with all other carnivores. On the mainland foxes range from the coast to the Preseli moors. The more stay-at-home badgers belong to lowland woods and coastal valleys but where soils are deep and workable they have their setts on open slopes above the sea. You will hardly ever see a badger except in the lights of a car or by watching a sett at dusk; but a fox you may sometimes meet with in daylight, especially on the sea cliffs. Stoat, Weasel and Polecat are widely distributed; and increasingly reported is the Mink, an alien from America brought here for fur-farming. The much decreased Otter is still occasionally reported from the shore and along streams. The Muntjac is the only deer found in the park, and rarely at that.

Hares have become scarce and have been introduced in a few localities where they were absent. Rabbits are locally abundant, nowhere more so than on some of the islands where they were established in the Middle Ages to provide food at a time when other meat was scarce. Ramsey Island has incredible numbers except when myxomatosis temporarily reduces them. But the most famous rabbits are those on Skokholm because they have never caught myxomatosis despite attempts to introduce it. Their immunity on this one island is explained by the absence there of the Rabbit Flea which is the carrier of myxomatosis in Britain. Why Skokholm's rabbits have no fleas is not clear.

Smaller mammals on the mainland are Grey Squirrels (the Reds are now almost gone), Common, Pygmy and Water Shrews; Mole and Hedgehog; Dormouse (very local and known only in the north); Wood Mouse, Bank Vole, Field Vole and Water Vole; Harvest Mouse (distribution incompletely known); and several common species of bats as well as the Greater and Lesser Horse-shoes. The islands have fewer mammals but those which are present raise some interesting questions. Compare the rodents of Skomer, for instance, with those of neighbouring Skokholm. Why should Skomer have Wood Mice and Bank Voles but no Field Voles despite its moor-like vegetation? By what accident of history does Skokholm have the House Mouse while Skomer does not? And what is it about Skokholm's House Mouse that has enabled it to spread all over the island and, very unusually, become quite independent of man? How is it that Skomer alone among Welsh islands has produced an endemic race of Bank Vole that is bigger, redder and tamer than those elsewhere?

Birdwatchers come to this park mainly for the sea-birds

and migrants on the islands; but to take in the whole range of bird habitats we need to begin on the Preseli uplands in spring among the singing Skylarks and Meadow Pipits. Up there too in rocky places there are breeding Wheatears but they are few. Only gradually as you come down off the hills do the birds increase: occasional Dippers and Grey Wagtails on the streams and waterfalls; and Yellowhammers, Cuckoos, Curlews and Lapwings are noisy on the farmlands. The streams flow down into dingles of Oak and Birch and here are the nesting places of Buzzard, Willow Warbler, Chaffinch, Tree Pipit, Wren and various tits, thrushes and other common woodland birds.

The wilder heaths and marshes near the sea cliffs of the north and west are the chief foraging grounds of Raven, Kestrel and Buzzard and here too are Linnets, Stonechats, Sedge Warblers and Grasshopper Warblers. And wherever you go there is a good chance of seeing Choughs for they are widespread all round the coast, their nests well hidden in sea caves. Look out for Peregrines too along these cliffs for they breed at ancestral sites on several of the headlands. Where the tides of Milford Haven flow into the heart of the park along the wooded Cleddau rivers there are mudflats where many Shelducks feed in summer and where Teal, Wigeon, Mallard and various waders gather in winter. Over the years the Gann estuary at Dale has attracted some notable rarities including American waders.

Of the sea-bird colonies scattered around the mainland cliffs, one is a tourist attraction – the crowd of Guillemots, Razorbills, Kittiwakes and Fulmars on the Elegug Stacks, two huge pillars of limestone standing in the sea within easy viewing distance of the Flimston cliffs. ('Elegug' is a dialect word for Guillemot). Gulls, Oystercatchers and Shags all have breeding stations along the park's cliffs. Cormorants, too, are in small groups here and there but they have one big settlement on St Margaret's Island off Caldey where there are over 300 breeding pairs, the largest colony in Wales. St Margaret's, a reserve of the West Wales Naturalists' Trust, also has a few Kittiwakes, Razorbills and Guillemots.

To see the greatest throngs of sea-birds you must go to the islands, especially Skomer which is a National Nature Reserve open to the public most days and reached by boat from Martin's Haven. A nature trail takes you all round the island and you can see crowds of Puffins, Kittiwakes, Guillemots, Razorbills, Fulmars, Shags and gulls without disturbing one of them. But you need to stay a night on the island (this can be arranged) if you want to get acquainted with Skomer's 25,000 Shearwaters for they do not become active till dark (they will not even tolerate moonlight). All through spring and summer, any really black night, you will hear a wonderful caterwauling, sobbing and shrieking as this great colony of Shearwaters flies wildly about over the island, some coming in off the sea, others emerging from burrows under your feet. Shine a torch and you will glimpse their long-winged shapes in the air or see them standing or walking awkwardly about on the turf.

Skokholm too has a vast colony of Shearwaters and many Puffins but is most distinguished for its 6,000 pairs of Storm Petrels which, like Shearwaters, hide in holes by day and emerge after dark. Here in 1933 the first British bird observatory was established and its work has made the island a famous place for seeing the migrants, some of them very rare, which pass up and down the coast of Wales at passage seasons. Many come from continental Europe and a few even from as far away as Asia and America.

Eleven miles north of Skokholm, Ramsey apparently attracts fewer migrants and has smaller colonies of sea-birds; but it has breeding Shorteared Owls and is easily the best island for Choughs (up to a dozen pairs breeding), the attraction no doubt being the many deep caves where they can hide their nests. Ramsey's satellite islets, the Bishops and Clerks, lie in dangerous waters and are difficult of access: they have small numbers of breeding seabirds. Also hard to get to is Grassholm, an RSPB reserve six miles west of Skomer. Gannets started to breed there in the middle of last century and from small beginnings have grown to a colony so huge (16,000 pairs) and so closely packed that from a distance this humpy island seems to be covered with snow.

In autumn the northern headlands of Strumble and St David's are vantage points for observing sea-bird passage when on some days, especially in strong west winds, endless streams of Auks, Kittiwakes, Shearwaters, Fulmars and Skuas have been moving south-west or south. In early morning, flocks of small land birds such as Starlings, Skylarks, finches and thrushes of various kinds have arrived from the north across Cardigan Bay. Birdwatchers also go to the pools at Bosherston and the reservoir at Llys-y-fran for ducks, grebes and terns on passage.

Hard winters can bring spectacular movements of birds driven into south-west Wales by north-east blizzards: Curlews, Lapwings, Golden Plovers, Snipe, Woodcock and a great many smaller species. Sometimes they find refuge in sheltered coastal valleys but in really arctic weather thousands perish even on this usually mild coast or fly on out to sea to almost certain death. Severe winters are not the only possible disasters. Now that Milford Haven is an oil terminal there is always the danger of huge tankers getting wrecked on this coast, spilling their oil and bringing death on a huge scale to sea-birds, seals, fish and every other form of marine life.

Adder, Grass Snake, Common Lizard and Slow-worm are all found on the mainland. Of these four reptiles, the Lizard probably reaches the highest ground (half-way up Preseli); the Slow-worm is the most abundant; the Adder is only locally common, mainly on heaths and seaward slopes; and the Grass Snake seems to be the rarest, preferring shel-

tered damp places, often near water. Frog, Toad and Palmate Newt are all widespread. On the islands the distribution of these reptiles and amphibians is as erratic as that of the small mammals. There are, for example, Frogs and Lizards on Skomer but not on Skokholm and when both were introduced there they soon died out. In contrast Slow-worms are found on all four of the major islands – Ramsey, Skomer, Skokholm and Caldey.

A glance at a map shows the extreme irregularity of the shoreline with its severely exposed peninsulas and skerries, as well as its comfortably sheltered bays and inlets. There is also great variety in the rock types which range from hard and smooth to soft and full of holes; and there are many different sands and muds on beaches and in estuaries. The result is an immense range of habitats both for life just off-shore and also in the intertidal zone.

All round the coast the sea is rich in fish with the approaches to Milford Haven being regarded by many anglers as the best sea fishing ground in Wales. Round the park's coast nearly forty species are caught including Mackerel, Herring, Bass, Pollack, Conger, Wrasse, various flatfish, Cod, Whiting, Mullet, Dogfish, Tope and Blue and Porbeagle Sharks. Sometimes huge Basking Sharks (plankton-

Freshwater West, a fine stretch of sand, but the sea can be unsafe for bathing

feeders harmless to man) can be seen from the cliffs in summer as they lie motionless on the sea. In the park's fresh waters the species of fish are few. There are Brown Trout, Sea Trout and Salmon in the rivers, mainly the Cleddau and the Nevern; Brown and Rainbow Trout in the reservoirs; and coarse fish (Perch, Roach, Tench, Eel and Pike) in the pools at Bosherston.

Of the many attractive insects those most likely to be noticed are butterflies, moths and dragonflies. On a warm summer's day the slopes above the sea can be marvellous places for butterflies that love sunny, flowery slopes – Graylings, Meadow Browns, Gatekeepers, Commas, Red Admirals, Painted Ladies, Dark-green Fritillaries, Large and Small Skippers. And along this coast there is always a chance of seeing migrant insects. Huge movements of Large White butterflies have been observed and among occasional rarities there are records of Bath White and Camberwell Beauty. Larvae of the Bedstraw Hawk-moth, a rare migrant, have been found at Dale. Passage dragonflies, notably the Fourspotted *Libellula*, have been seen even as far out as Grassholm. There are many resident dragonflies: the best sites for them are probably the bogland pools and wetlands of the north and Bosherston Pools in the south.

Recreation

The making of a splendid path all round the coast (it varies from easy to strenuous) was one of the first projects undertaken by the park authorities. It begins at St Dogmaels in the north and ends at Amroth in the south and on its way it leads you, on its course of 168 miles, to nearly every headland, cliff and bay along this wild shore, giving you far views of sea and hills and all the islands. It calls at or passes close to coastal farms, villages and towns which all offer accommodation at hotels, youth hostels or bed and breakfast houses. Various books and booklets are available describing in detail what to see along the path's entire length.

Besides the one round the coast there are many other public footpaths, the most demanding being those over the Preseli Hills. Up there the longest trail is the east–west ridge walk along the Flemings' Way which, despite its name, is probably prehistoric. These uplands are popular with ponytrekkers as well as with walkers. The boating and sailing paradise is the thirty miles of sheltered waterways inside Milford Haven where the chief centres include Dale, Lawrenny, Burton and Pembroke Dock. Elsewhere there is sailing at Tenby and Saundersfoot in the south, Solva in the west and Lower Fishguard in the north. Bathing and swimming are popular on many beaches especially those at Tenby, Saundersfoot, St Bride's Bay, Whitesands Bay and Newport. But some tempting sands like Freshwater West, fully open to the Atlantic, are dangerous at all times.

Angling is very popular both in salt water and fresh and the *Angling Guide to Wales* by Clive Gammon gives full details of where and how to do it. Underwater swimming and diving mainly in pursuit of shellfish is based on western beaches such as Martin's Haven. It is a worry to conservationists who fear depletion of seabed life, hence the creation of the Skomer Marine Reserve. A more recent sport is the land-yachting which takes place on the long strand of St Bride's Bay in autumn and winter. For seekers of antiquities and ancient monuments there are plenty of guide books available, and for those interested in industrial history there are many old mines, quarries and railways to explore.

Museums at Haverfordwest and Tenby have a full range of exhibits relating to local prehistory, history, land use, folk culture and natural history. There are country parks at Llys-y-fran Reservoir and Scolton, both places just outside the park. Residential courses in a wide range of subjects are available at field-study centres at Orielton near Pembroke and at Dale Fort. Birdwatchers are especially catered for on Skomer (day-trips) and Skokholm (stays of a week or more). In a sheltered valley at Upton Castle a collection of over 250 kinds of trees and shrubs is open to the public. Some hotels arrange weekends for special interests such as music, gastronomics, birdwatching and botany. Many shops sell the creations of local craftsmen; and workshops open to visitors demonstrate how furniture, treen, woollen goods, knitwear, woven fabrics, leatherwork, candles, jewellery and pottery are produced.

Information about the reserves and trails of the West Wales Naturalists' Trust and about visiting Skomer and Skokholm is available at the Trust's office in Haverfordwest. There are park information centres at Fishguard, St David's, Broad Haven (St Bride's Bay), Haverfordwest, Pembroke, Tenby and Kilgetty. From them you can get all the help and guidance you could want, as well as details of expertly led walks to the most interesting places in this delightful park.

Useful Addresses

West Wales Naturalists' Trust: 7 Market Street, Haverfordwest, Dyfed

National Trust: 22 Alan Road, Llandeilo, Dyfed

National Park Office: County Offices, Haverfordwest, Dyfed

Dale Fort Field Centre: Dale, Haverfordwest, Dyfed

Orielton Field Centre: Pembroke, Dyfed

View from the summit of Yr Wyddfa, Snowdonia, looking east over Glaslyn and Llyn Llydaw

William S Lacey

Snowdonia
Parc Cenedlaethol Eryri

THE SNOWDONIA NATIONAL PARK, established in 1951, is the most diverse of the three parks in Wales and includes both coastal lowlands and inland mountainous regions in the north of the country. With an area of 2,170 square km (838 square miles), it is second only to the Lake District Park in size and is the heart of the ancient kingdom of Gwynedd (from which the modern county takes its name), that mountain fastness of the Welsh in mediaeval times and still the stronghold of their culture at the present day.

The park extends some eighty kilometres (fifty miles) from Mynydd y Dref near Conwy in the north to the outskirts of Machynlleth (where Owain Glyndwr's fifteenth-century Parliament House still stands) and the Afon Dyfi in the south; and from Aberhirnant Forest near Bala in the east forty-eight kilometres (thirty miles) to Harlech and the coast of Cardigan Bay in the west.

The word '*Eryri*' in the Welsh name of the park is sometimes translated as 'Land of the Eagles' but according to some authorities its more accurate, if less romantic, meaning is 'ridged land'. Here lies the clue to the nature of the greater part of the park. Ancient earth movements on a massive scale and subsequent erosion have produced a series of mountains and lake-filled valleys which give the country its great beauty. Nine major groups of mountains can be distinguished – the Carneddau, Glyder Range, Snowdon Massif, Nantlle Hills/Moel Hebog, Moel Siabod/Moelwynion, and Arenig Range in the north; Rhinogydd, Aran Range and Cader Idris in the south. Yr Wyddfa, the highest of the five peaks forming the Snowdon Massif, and the highest mountain in England and Wales, reaches 1,096 m (3,560 ft) and is one of fourteen peaks in the park which exceed 900 m. These uplands are dissected by the main access roads, many of which use high bleak passes connecting valleys carved out and deepened by glaciers, to whose action the many lakes and waterfalls are further testimony.

Geology and Landscape

It is not possible to understand the present landscape in the park without knowing something of its geological history.

The rocks which form the physical basis of the land originated in the early periods of the earth's history. The oldest in North Wales are the hard Pre-Cambrian rocks occurring in Anglesey and small coastal areas in Caernarfonshire, outside the northern boundary of the park. Within the park three groups of solid rocks, younger than the Pre-Cambrian, are recognized, known in order of deposition from the oldest to the youngest as Cambrian (about 550 million years old), Ordovician, and Silurian (about 400 million years old). They are named from Cambria, an early name for Wales, and from the Ordovices and Silures, two ancient tribes that formerly inhabited North and South Wales. Strata of all three groups were laid down in the sea as sediments which were originally horizontally bedded and formed gritstones, sandstones and shales. However, great earth movements resulted in lateral pressures from the south-east which forced them against the much older resistant basement Pre-Cambrian rocks in the north-west. This irresistible force crumpled the Snowdonian rocks into two great folds or, to be more precise, one downfold or syncline in the north-west and its complementary upfold or anticline in the south-east, with a 'wave-length' of about fifty-six kilometres (thirty-five miles) from the Bethesda–Llanberis–Nantlle Cambrian slate-belt in the north to the neighbourhood of Corris in the south. The northern synclinal structure can be readily seen in the Carneddau, Glyders Range and Snowdon Massif. Thus, surprising though it may seem at first sight, the summit of Yr Wyddfa is the bottom of a trough and composed of rocks that were laid down in the sea of Ordovician time. Indeed, fossil shells of marine organisms known as brachiopods (superficially similar to present-day cockles) can be found with comparative ease around the summit cairn.

In the Snowdon syncline the Cambrian rocks in the north dip under the younger overlying Ordovician strata and, reappearing as south-east facing outcrops in the vicinity of the Vale of Ffestiniog, form the northern side of the complementary southern anticline. Known to geologists as the Harlech Dome, this structure determines the form of the landscape south to Dolgellau and beyond to Cader Idris, where the Ordovician reappears in north-west facing outcrops.

133

Reflections in Llyn Gwynant at the foot of the Snowdon Massif

accumulating thickness of snow formed upland ice-fields and cwm (corrie) glaciers. These high-level glaciers carved out the flanks of the mountain masses and flowed downwards to fill the lowland valleys with great thicknesses of ice. In this way valley-glaciers were formed in, for example, Nant Gwynant moving south-west towards Beddgelert and Nant Ffrancon moving north-west towards Bethesda. After the ice finally disappeared from Snowdonia, 10,000 to 13,000 years ago, it left evidence of its former presence in the form of high level cwms separated by narrow ridges, over deepened U-shaped valleys, streams descending in striking waterfalls from hanging side-valleys, lakes impounded by moraines of boulder-clay, deposits of sand and gravel, perched boulders, and polished rock surfaces scored with scratches which indicate the direction in which the ice moved. An excellent example of a smoothed and striated rock surface can be seen on the west side of the road a few hundred yards south of Dolbadarn Castle, near Llanberis.

For the geologist Snowdonia is classic ground, for it was here that it was first realized that Britain had once been glaciated. Nowadays this is taken for granted, yet a century and a half ago no less persons than the naturalist Charles Darwin and Adam Sedgwick, a leading geologist of the day, failed to see the evidence. Writing of their visit to Cwm Idwal in 1831 Darwin says '. . . neither of us saw a trace of the wonderful glacial phenomena all around us. . . . Yet all these phenomena are so conspicuous that a house burnt down by fire did not tell its story more plainly than this valley. If it had still been filled by a glacier the phenomena would have been less clear than they now are.'

Other factors affecting the landscape came into play after the Ice Age and are still active today. The very high rainfall, averaging 5,080 mm (200 inches) per year on the summit of Snowdon, results in continuing erosion, washing soils valleywards to fill the lakes gradually with silt. This is very apparent in Llyn Idwal when seen from above, near Twll du (the Devil's Kitchen). Areas of impeded drainage are blanketed with great thicknesses of peat, as in Migneint. On the western borders of the park, in Cardigan Bay, sand carried landwards by south-westerly gales continues to form extensive dunes, particularly well developed at Morfa Dyffryn between Barmouth and Llanbedr and at Morfa Harlech, markedly changing the coastline. Harlech Castle, with its water-gate, was once provisioned by sea but is now a good half mile inland. Man himself is responsible for initiating and continuing the loss of the natural woodland cover of broad-leaved deciduous trees, and replacing it with extensive conifer plantations.

Man in Snowdonia

It is not known with certainty when man first settled in Snowdonia, but it is most likely that it was soon after the

Not all the rocks laid down in Ordovician time were sedimentary in origin; contemporaneous volcanic activity produced vast quantities of ash which settled out in the sea (the fossiliferous rocks on the summit of Yr Wyddfa are of this type) and injected great masses of lava into the mountains around the Harlech Dome from the Carneddau as far south as Cader Idris.

The youngest solid rocks are of Silurian age and occur in small patches between Betws-y-Coed and Pentrefoelas, south-east of Bala and near Llanymawddwy. In these areas the rather softer shales yield a more gentle topography than that found in the country occupied by the harder Cambrian and Ordovician rocks. Strata younger than the Silurian, thousands of feet thick, were deposited over Snowdonia but were subsequently worn away. Indeed, erosional processes cut down the Snowdon syncline until only a little of the youngest Ordovician remains at the centre and reduced the Harlech anticline to expose the oldest Cambrian at its core.

The earth movements which produced the folds had two other important effects. Sediments originally laid down as clays over wide areas were compressed, hardened and given a new structure or 'cleavage', often at a high angle to the original bedding plane, to become the slates formerly so extensively quarried for roofing material.

Sometimes, more locally, the same earth movements that produced the folds and the slate-belts caused fractures or faults that moved adjacent parts of the earth's crust relative to one another vertically, affecting rocks thousands of feet deep, or laterally, with a displacement of many miles. Examples of the latter type of faulting are seen in the long narrow valley occupied by Llyn Tegid running south-west from Bala and in the Tal-y-Llyn valley south of Cader Idris.

Some of the most striking features of the modern landscape in the park owe their origin to the Ice Age, which began to affect Britain about two million years ago. Deterioration of the climate caused snowfalls at the higher altitudes in excess of the loss by summer melting and the pressure of the

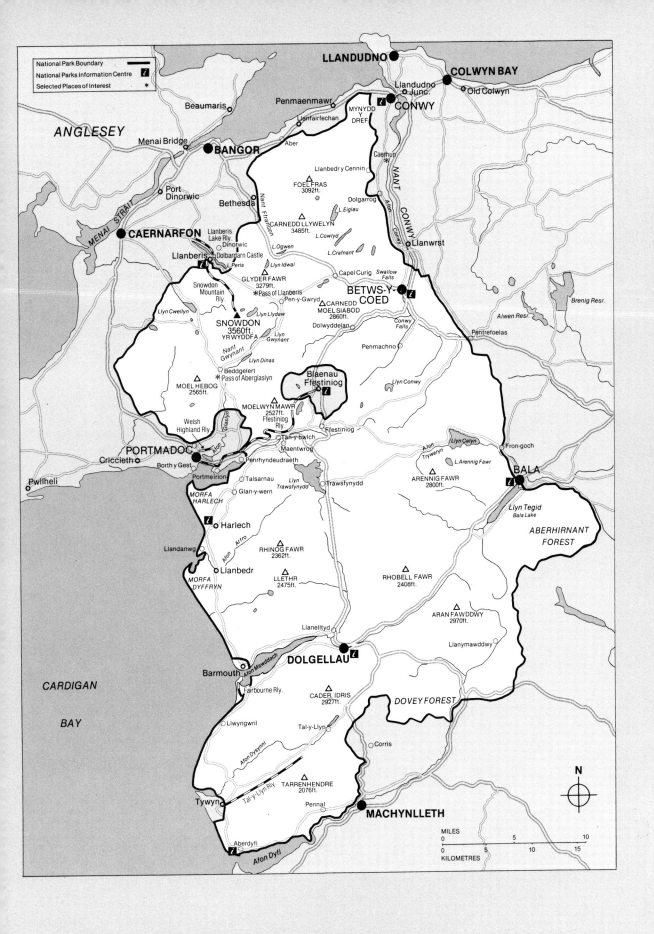

glaciers finally retreated from the region. What is clear, however, is that early man was excluded by marshes from most of the valleys and from the foothills, perhaps up to 600 m (2,000 ft), by impenetrable forests. The higher mountainsides above the tree-line were unsuitable for habitation and were used only for hunting. For these reasons most of the oldest archaeological sites occur in those parts of the park which are at or near the coast, that is from Afon Dyfi to Traeth Mawr in the west and from Conwy to Bangor in the north. The earliest examples are the great burial-chambers erected by settlers who came from the Continent between about 4000 and 2000 BC by a west coast sea route or by inland trade routes across southern Britain. These megalithic tombs were built of massive slabs of local rock, sometimes weighing many tons, and are now mostly exposed. In this condition the tomb is called a 'cromlech' or 'dolmen'. Originally it was completely covered by stones and earth in a form known as the long barrow. There are good examples a short distance from the coast between Barmouth and Harlech. The Neolithic people who built these burial places used stone implements. Stone axe 'factory sites' of Late Neolithic age utilized the local igneous (volcanic) rock at Graig Lwyd, near

The start of many a climb of Snowdon in Llanberis Pass

Penmaenmawr, just outside the northern boundary of the park.

After about 2000 BC the discovery of tin and copper in Britain and the ability to make bronze tools from these metals led to great changes in the way of life. The Bronze Age peoples, who succeeded the Neolithic, ceased to use the long burial chambers, but cremated their dead and interred the ashes in pottery vessels in round barrows. This custom was used for at least a thousand years and many such barrows (shown as 'cairns' on OS maps) can be seen on the hillsides between Tywyn and Talsarnau and between Llanllechid and Penmaenmawr.

About 500 BC Britain was invaded by a Celtic-speaking people, the Brythons, from Western Europe. According to some authorities, it is from the language of the Brythons, the 'Ancient Britons' of school history-books, that modern Welsh is derived. Evidence for its continental origin can still be found today in the many linguistic features common to Welsh, Cornish and Breton.

Soon after 500 BC the adoption of iron for the manufacture of weapons seems to have led to a period of unrest. At any rate, the most striking remains of the work of the Celtic Iron Age people are hill-forts constructed with strong walls of earth and stone. Examples can be seen on Conwy Mount-

ain and a few miles south at Pen y Gaer, near Llanbedr y Cennin. These hill-forts remained in use until the Roman invasion and were doubtless centres of resistance for a long time, but eventually all but a few fell into disuse.

The Romans did not really settle Wales as a province of their empire but rather they occupied the country as a frontier district and held it so for over three centuries from 78 AD. They achieved this by constructing numerous forts with linking roads. *Kanovium* (Caerhun), four miles south of Conwy, lay on the road from *Segontium* (Caernarfon) to *Deva* (Chester) and from it branched off the main road to South Wales, crossing the centre of the park to link with forts at Bryn y Gefeiliau (near Capel Curig), Tomen y Mur (near Trawsfynydd, perhaps the best preserved Roman fort in North Wales), Brithdir (near Dolgellau) and on to Pennal (near Afon Dyfi) on the southern boundary of the park.

During the Roman occupation the native inhabitants of the park lived in circular houses built with a low stone wall and thatched roof. These hut-circles, known as *Cytiau'r Gwyddelod*, are the earliest habitation sites to be seen in the park. They occur on the northern and western foothills and in Cwm Ystradllyn and Cwm Pennant in the north-west corner of the park.

When the Roman armies left Britain at the end of the fourth century AD the language of the native people was still Brythonic with an admixture of Latin. This early form of Welsh was spoken throughout almost all of the country as far north as the Clyde valley, but in 500 AD Cunedda led his compatriots from northern Britain to settle in the region now known as North Wales and in due course Wales was surrounded by Saxon settlements reaching into Cheshire, Shropshire and the Border country of the South. But the Welsh language has survived the centuries to this day. It is important for the visitor to recognize that Welsh is a living language – and that Snowdonia is its stronghold. In Wales as a whole some twenty per cent of the population are Welsh-speaking but in the park Welsh is habitually spoken by more than seventy per cent of the people.

The first Christian missionaries arrived in Wales not long after the Romans departed, travelling both by sea along the west coast and inland by the roads left by the Romans. The fabric of their churches has not survived but the founders are commemorated by inscribed stones of the fifth, sixth and seventh centuries AD. One of the best collections can be seen in the church at Penmachno, four miles south of Betws-y-Coed.

Churches with work dating from the twelfth to the sixteenth centuries are well represented, good examples being at Beddgelert, Dolwyddelan and Tywyn. Llanrwst Church (just outside the park) has stone effigies of knights carved by Welsh sculptors.

The park is noted for its castles. The earliest type, built

Tryfan (3010 ft), from the north-west

both by the Normans and by the Welsh princes copying the Norman style, consisted of an earth mound surmounted by a wooden stockade and is known as a motte-and-bailey castle. An early Norman example, within the walls of the Roman fort of Tomen y Mur, is believed to have been built by William Rufus in 1096. Another mound marking the site of an early castle of Llewelyn the Great can be seen at Aber, just inside the northern boundary of the park. The Welsh princes started to build their castles in stone in the tenth century and placed them within the comparative safety of the mountains. Three good examples can be seen at Dolbadarn (near Llanberis), Dolwyddelan, and Castell y Bere (near Tywyn). The castles built by Edward I to contain the Welsh after the Conquest of 1282–3 were placed round the coasts so that they could be supplied by sea. As a result, only Harlech Castle actually lies within the park but the castles of Conwy

Harlech Castle looming through the mist above Harlech Beach

vated bleak mountain tops, craggy outcrops and high moorlands, the people of Snowdonia have relied for centuries on the rearing of stock – goats, cattle and sheep. There is comparatively little arable land, but some crops are grown in the drier parts of the valleys and hay can be taken from the valley bottoms and upland pastures. Although they are no longer kept on farms, herds of feral goats still roam free on the higher parts of the Glyder Range and the Rhinogydd, coming down to the lowlands in hard winters. Cattle-rearing is not as extensive as it once was, but Welsh Black Cattle are still a characteristic feature of the lowland landscape. The emphasis nowadays is on sheep. However, the practice of transhumance, whereby the whole farm household moved with the flocks of sheep from the main farmstead (*hendref*) to a summer dwelling (*hafod*), situated, like the Norwegian *seter*, on the mountain pasture, has ceased long ago.

While farming, and especially sheep-farming, remains the main source of livelihood in Snowdonia there are other occupations which contribute to the *per capita* income. Slate-quarrying, which used to employ several thousand men, is now in decline, but still provides work for some hundreds. Forestry work, both for private land-owners and for the Forestry Commission, has in some respects taken over, recruiting some of its labour force from quarrying and mining. Traditionally many quarry workers used to run a smallholding part-time to supplement their income. This practice has been maintained by forestry workers. The Forestry Commission retains better agricultural land unplanted with trees and offers to its employees forest holdings consisting of a small acreage of good land round a farmhouse and grazing rights in the higher land above the forest. Catering for visitors is also a valuable source of income. Recent years have seen a considerable development in this field, both in the form of simple farmhouse bed-and-breakfast accommodation and in the provision of an ever increasing number of static and touring caravan sites.

Flora and Fauna

It is one of the many attractions of Snowdonia that the visitor can see for himself a great variety of plants and animals with comparative ease. To present a complete picture of this rich wildlife in the space of a few pages is an impossible task. All that is attempted here is a brief sketch of some of the more interesting features.

It is necessary to go back some thousands of years to the early Post-glacial period which followed the final retreat of the glaciers from Britain. The study of fossil leaves, seeds and pollen preserved in peat and in lake sediments has shown that the ground left bare by glacial processes became colonized first by a 'tundra' type of vegetation, such as is found in arctic regions today. This consisted largely of mosses, lichens,

and Caernarfon lie only a short distance outside the northern boundary.

The early residences of the Welsh princes and later mediaeval houses were built of timber and no vestiges of them remain. Indeed, it was only from the fifteenth and sixteenth centuries onwards that Welsh landowners living in the mountainous parts of Snowdonia could afford to build in stone. Two examples, both still occupied, are Cochwillan Hall just outside the park near Bangor and Gwydir Castle near Llanrwst.

In addition to the many noteworthy scattered individual buildings there are whole settlements beautifully executed in local stone. The village of Maentwrog, in the Vale of Ffestiniog, is one such place and well merits its designation as a conservation area. In striking contrast is the Italianate village of Port Meirion, near Portmadoc, conceived and built by that colourful figure, the late Sir Clough William-Ellis, as an unusual kind of holiday resort.

The economy of the park as a whole is essentially rural. With some seventy per cent of the land consisting of unculti grasses, sedges and a few low-growing shrubs, including the Dwarf Birch (no longer found in Wales). As the climate improved, trees spread throughout Wales, at first predominantly Common Birch, then Oak, until, in a period of the most favourable climate since the Ice Age, in Early Flandrian time (about 8000–4000 BC), most of the country became forest-covered up to a height of about 600 m (2,000 ft). The highest cwms of Snowdonia, with their crescentic cliffs, remained largely tree-less, however, and continued to provide the conditions necessary for some arctic plants to survive. This they do to the present day, although they have long since disappeared from southern and eastern Britain. The subsequent history is one of climatic deterioration, accompanied by the ever-increasing impact of man on his environment, leading to almost complete eradication of the original broad-leaved forest, whose natural regeneration is prevented by his grazing animals.

To the casual observer the general impression is one of extensive areas of monotonous rough grassland and moorland, locally blanketed with conifer plantations, and interspersed with barren rocky outcrops. Nothing could be further from the truth. In fact, the very varied plant and animal life in the park is a reflection of the many environments or 'habitats' found within it. Since animal habitats are determined mainly by the nature of the vegetation and this in turn is influenced by such factors as climate and soil, it is possible to describe the chief plant habitats and the animal life together in a simple physiographic scheme. In this account four broad habitat categories are recognized – uplands, wetlands, lowlands and coastal areas – and the wildlife of their various subdivisions is outlined.

In the uplands, montane grasslands are certainly the major component, occupying hundreds of square miles. All

The Snowdon Lily (Lloydia serotina) *– which in Britain is found only in Snowdonia*

MICHAEL PROCTOR

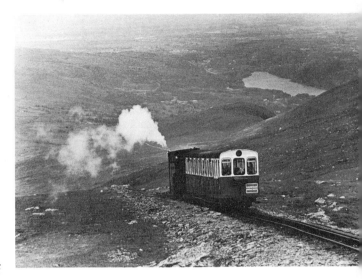

The Snowdon Mountain Railway on its way up from Llanberis

are grazed by sheep which, by their selective feeding, exercise a controlling influence on the composition of the vegetation. On poor soils, derived from acid rocks, the land is dominated by the unpalatable Mat-grass; where the soil is more mineral-rich Fescue-grass and Bent-grass provide better bite for the sheep. Superficially uninteresting, both kinds of grass land are enlivened in spring and summer by a generous scattering of small flowers: blue Milkwort, four-petalled yellow Tormentil, and white Heath Bedstraw. On many hillsides the summer-flowering Western Gorse makes a colourful show. Three kinds of Club-moss, relative of the ferns, also occur here. Heather is attractive to sheep and is one of the plants rapidly suppressed by grazing. To some extent this also applies to the Bilberry. Consequently, there is comparatively little of these two plants except on islands in lakes, on acid rocky crags too steep for grazing and in areas where grazing is intentionally excluded. Indeed, the only parts of the park where heather is abundant are places like the block-scree slopes of Cwm Bychan in the Rhinogydd east of Harlech and the moors kept for grouse on the Berwyn in the east. In such places, besides the Red Grouse, the Black Cock and Merlin make their home. Upland butterflies are not common; apart from migrant Red Admirals and Painted Ladies, the Small Heath is the most frequently seen, but the Large Heath and several kinds of Fritillaries can be found. Moths are more abundant, including several of the larger ones, like the Emperor, with its conspicuous bright green caterpillars marked with rings of yellow spots.

Rough pastures extend to the tops of most of the peaks but on Cader Idris and above about 900 m (3,000 ft) on the

Carneddau, Glyder Range and Snowdon Massif the grass cover becomes sparse and the summits have more moss and bare stony ground. But montane grassland and moorland are the places in which to see the Peregrine Falcon and Kestrel hunting, or the Buzzard soaring high overhead, or to hear the guttural 'kronk' of the Raven on its leisurely flight.

From a botanical standpoint the richest upland habitats are undoubtedly to be found on rocky crags and on cliffs at the heads of cwms. Here, if the rock is acidic, like the Idwal Slabs in Cwm Idwal, heathers dominate the vegetation; but if the strata are base-rich and contribute lime to the soil, luxuriant growth of many more kinds of plants occurs. Examples of these species-rich habitats can be found on the Ordovician Volcanic rocks outcropping in the cliffs above Llyn y Gadair on Cader Idris, in Cwm Glas under Crib y Ddysgyl on the Snowdon Massif, on Ysgolion duon (the Black Ladders) on Carnedd Dafydd, and on each side of the Devil's Kitchen in Cwm Idwal. Indeed, so luxuriant and colourful are some of the ledges that the name 'Hanging Gardens' has been given to them.

In such places, safe from marauding sheep and goats, representatives of Snowdonia's 'arctic-alpine' flora are to be found. Some are relatively common, like the Purple Saxifrage, flowering in February and March (quite the earliest of the mountain flowers), followed much later by the white-flowered Mossy Saxifrage; the pink-flowered cushion-forming Moss Campion; the succulent Roseroot, whose rootstock emits a fragrant scent when broken; and the yellow Globe Flower, large relative of the lowland Buttercup. Some are rare, such as the Holly Fern and the two Woodsia Ferns; the Mountain Avens, with its eight-petalled white flowers and leaves like those of the Oak; and the delicate white Snowdon Lily or Mountain Spider-wort. This last plant is not found anywhere else in Britain. Here, too, grows the yellow Welsh Poppy, not really one of the 'arctic-alpine' plants, but characteristically associated with them on the rock ledges. On the screes below the crags the Parsley Fern grows in abundance; it is easily known in summer by its dense tufts of bright green leaves which later turn brown.

The higher crags provide nesting sites for the Buzzard, Peregrine Falcon and Raven, as also for the red-legged, red-billed Chough, a member of the Crow family, usually thought of as a bird of sea cliffs. One undoubted sea-bird, the Cormorant, regularly fishes inland lakes and for several hundred years a colony of them has nested on the crags of Craig yr Aderyn (Bird Rock), more than five miles inland in the Dysynni Valley.

On the lesser cliffs and screes the Wheatear and the Ring Ouzel can be heard, the latter a shy bird and not readily seen.

On the screes and in the woods lower down the hillsides one of the rarest British mammalian carnivores, the Pine Marten, still survives, along with his much commoner cousin, the Polecat.

Among all this wealth of rare plants and animals living at high altitudes it is surprising to find with them such common lowland plants as the Red Campion, Wood Sorrel, Wood Anemone, and Dog's Mercury; and surprising also to hear the strong, confident song of the Wren perhaps 600 m (2,000 ft) up in the rocky cwms.

Wetlands include bogs and marshes, streams, rivers and lakes, both upland and lowland. In Snowdonia bogs are found most commonly at high levels in poorly drained areas where the ground water is acid. The peat-forming Bog-moss or *Sphagnum* moss is one of the most characteristic plants but associated with it and also at the sides of streams draining

The River Dovey (Dyfi) which is the Park's southernmost boundary

from the bogs are many colourful plants, such as the pink-flowered Heath Spotted Orchid, the yellow Bog St John's Wort, the pale blue Ivy-leaved Bellflower and the yellow Bog Asphodel. The Asphodel has been given the undeserved name of 'bone-breaker' because it was once thought to be the cause of brittle bones when eaten by cattle, but really it should be regarded as a useful indicator of mineral-deficient soil. In these situations also grow two insect-eating plants, the Round-leaved Sundew, with its leaves fringed with red sticky hairs, and the Common Butterwort, with its pale yellow-green leaves and long-stalked bluish-purple flowers. In the marshy areas of lower ground, as in the Glaslyn and Ogwen Valleys, the Willow-like Bog Myrtle grows, easily recognized by the strong, pleasant smell given off by its leaves and catkins when bruised.

Beside the mountain streams, in addition to flowers mentioned already, the Golden Saxifrage, Starry Saxifrage and Water Avens can be found. These streams, especially the

fast-flowing ones, are the haunt of the Dipper, a fascinating bird which gets its name from its habit of standing on stones at the water's edge and bobbing up and down. It feeds under water, using its wings to assist its passage forward.

The upland lakes contain several interesting aquatic plants. In those with stony shores grows the bottom-dwelling Water Lobelia, with pale blue flowers borne above the water on long slender stalks. The peculiar Quill-wort, relative of the Club-moss, can be found totally submerged at depths of six feet or more. The Common Sandpiper and Grey Wagtail frequent these shores, but on lakes with peaty margins, fringed with the Water Horsetail and Bottle Sedge, the Mallard and Teal are more common. Occasionally there are nesting colonies of the Black-headed Gull.

In general the rather acid waters of the upland rivers and lakes provide a poor food supply for fish but the Brown Trout and several other kinds do occur. The lowland rivers and lakes support good-sized fish; the migratory Salmon and Sea Trout sometimes ascend to the shallow moorland streams. Several of the lakes in the park are particularly interesting in having certain kinds of fish restricted to them. The Char is found in the Llanberis lakes and Llyn Cwellyn near Beddgelert, and the Gwyniad is known only in Llyn Tegid, near Bala, and does not occur anywhere else in Britain. Where there is a plentiful supply of fish and a minimum of disturbance the Otter can be expected. Although it appears to be verging on extinction in some parts of the country, it is still to be found in the rivers and estuaries of the park.

The lowland fields and lane-sides in the park have plants and animals common to most other parts of Britain and with which the ordinary country-goer is familiar, but sometimes their distribution is a little unexpected. The Bluebell, for example, usually a woodland flower in most of England, often grows in the open in lowland Snowdonia. The lower slopes of Nant Ffrancon and many other valleys are carpeted blue with it in late spring, before the Bracken Fern provides its masking cover. This particular kind of distribution probably indicates areas which have been cleared of woodland. Certainly the woodlands were more extensive a few hundred years ago and reached much higher up the hillsides than the present tree-line at about 220 m (700 ft).

The isolated patches of broad-leaved woodland that survive still provide the best habitat in the lowlands for plant and animal populations. The dominant tree is the Oak (usually the Sessile Oak), though other native trees such as the Ash, Birch, Elm, Mountain Ash, Holly and the introduced Sycamore are not uncommon. Where the woodlands border streams the Alder is common. Towards the upper limit of the woods the Oak gives place to Birch and the tree cover becomes gradually thinner until the woods pass into open moor. Snowdonian woods in general are characterized by an open canopy and the ground beneath is usually carpeted with grass and moorland plants. Natural regeneration of trees is prevented as a result of grazing by stock, since it is a common practice of hill farmers to use the woods for shelter in winter. Despite the comparative paucity of flowers, one oakwood plant, the yellow-flowered Cow-Wheat, provides a brave show in high summer. What the woodlands may lack in showy flowers they make up for with a wealth of mosses, liverworts and ferns. In moist places among boulders, shaded from the direct rays of the sun, two kinds of the delicate Filmy Fern can be found, but, since they are no bigger than the mosses with which they grow, some searching is usually necessary. Coed Crafnant in the Artro Valley is a splendid example of this kind of oakwood. Such woods are also rich in animal life. Of the carnivores, Fox and Badger,

Fishing on Llyn Ogwen

Stoat and Weasel, Polecat and the rare Pine Marten make their home here. The Red Squirrel, too, can still be seen occasionally. Alas, its numbers have been much reduced in recent years and replaced by the introduced American Grey Squirrel, attractive enough to look at perhaps, but an aggressive animal which does lethal damage to broad-leaved trees. Bird life is almost overwhelming in its abundance and variety. The Pied Fly-catcher is surely the most characteristic bird of these western oakwoods, but Nuthatches and Tree-creepers, Redstarts and Woodpeckers, Buzzards and Sparrow Hawks also nest here.

The plantations of conifers, such as Spruce and Fir, which are increasingly replacing the native oakwoods and often extend from the valleys to the high moorlands make a different contribution to the overall picture in Snowdonia. For the economic good of Britain, some afforestation with conifers is certainly necessary and such forests are not without their own complement of wildlife. In the early stages of a plantation there is usually an increase in the numbers of such birds as the Short-eared Owl, Kestrel, Meadow Pipit and Yellowhammer, but this may be at the expense of the loss of birds of the open moorland, such as the Merlin, and in any case the gains are transitory. The mature forest of close-planted trees, with closed canopy and almost non-existent ground flora, is a disappointing place in which to look for wildlife. It would be a great loss if the oakwoods still remaining in the valleys were clear-felled to make way for more conifers.

The coastal areas on the western side of the park consist principally of the two great sand-dune systems of Morfa Harlech, and Morfa Dyffryn, interspersed with mudflats in the estuaries of five rivers from the Afon Dwyryd in the north to the Afon Dyfi in the south. Short lengths of cliff, composed of glacial boulder clay or of rock, but of no great height, occur here and there. The muddy stretches and the cliffs each harbour their own particular kinds of plants and animals, but it is the sand-dune systems which provide the richest coastal flora. In its way this is hardly less attractive to the botanist than the 'arctic-alpine' flora of the lime-rich upland crags. In autumn and winter the dunes appear drab with their covering of the sand-binding Marram Grass, but in spring and summer the scene changes. Then there is a riot of colour, provided by the blue, yellow or bi-coloured Dune Pansy; the tiny blue Forget-me-not; pink Storksbill, and purple Wild Thyme. The wet hollows or 'slacks' between the sand-hills also appear uninteresting early in the year, due to their cover of the Creeping Willow, but from about the end of May into early August a whole succession of orchids is in bloom. The flesh-coloured or crimson Early Marsh Orchid is the first to appear. It is followed by the deep purple Northern Marsh Orchid, the magenta Southern Marsh Orchid, white-flowered Marsh Helleborine and a form of the greenish-yellow Dune Helleborine. Less conspicuous, but equally interesting, are the Adder's Tongue Fern and Moonwort Fern which also grow in the slacks.

Wildlife Conservation

All British wildlife is threatened to some degree by man's varied, but necessary, activities. The spread of towns into the countryside, the building of power stations, new roads and reservoirs, drainage of wetlands, afforestation and newer agricultural practices, all reduce the extent of the remaining wildlife habitats. Wild, remote and unspoiled as Snowdonia may appear to be, its plants and animals are not exempt from the effects of these developments. All have taken place at one time or another within the boundaries of the park and are likely to continue. To them must be added another factor – the increasing pressure from the numbers of visitors, resulting from the rapid growth in all kinds of outdoor pursuits and leisure activities.

Several statutory and voluntary bodies exist whose functions are to safeguard the landscape of the park and its wildlife. The Nature Conservancy Council is the official government body concerned with wildlife. It manages sixteen National Nature Reserves in Snowdonia – four mountain reserves, of which Cwm Idwal was the first established and is probably the best known; one partly woodland, partly rocky hill-side reserve with 'arctic-alpines' growing at an unusually low altitude; two coastal reserves in parts of Morfa Dyffryn and Morfa Harlech; and nine broad-leaved woodland reserves, of which one, Coedydd Maentwrog, was acquired by the joint efforts of the National Trust and the North Wales Naturalists' Trust. Both the Conservancy and the Naturalists' Trust make their nature reserves accessible to visitors whenever possible, but in some cases it is necessary for scientific reasons to control access by a permit system. In other cases restrictions may be imposed to respect the rights of private owners and tenants, but public rights of way are not affected. The North Wales Naturalists' Trust, established in 1963, promotes nature conservation in Gwynedd and Clwyd. Four of its nature reserves lie within the park. The Trust also manages two centres which provide wildlife information for visitors, one jointly with the Nature Conservancy in the Coedydd Aber National Nature Reserve, the other at Penmaenpool near Dolgellau, a cooperative venture with the Snowdonia National Park Authority and the Royal Society for the Protection of Birds. As the latter and the North Wales Naturalists' Trust are entirely voluntary bodies they will always welcome help from new members.

Recreation in the Park

There are many leisure activities possible in Snowdonia. One of the most popular is walking, for which there is ample opportunity, both during a day visit by car and for the longer-stay visitor using strategically sited hotels or good accommodation provided by the Youth Hostels Association. For those who do not wish to climb high mountains there are lowland walks in the Forestry Commission's forests or along estuaries such as the Mawddach. For the more energetic there is the challenge of the mountain peaks. Almost all have well-defined routes. Yr Wyddfa has six good paths to the summit. The visitor who has no inclination to reach the top under his own steam can do so by the rack-and-pinion railway, one of six working narrow-gauge railways within the park or nearby. In one way or another more than 200,000 visitors reach the summit of Yr Wyddfa every year.

Northern Snowdonia has been a centre of the specialized pursuit of rock-climbing for generations and

Rock climbing on Crackstone Rib in Llanberis Pass

much of the preparatory work for the first successful ascent of Everest in 1953 was carried out here. There are over 1,500 listed routes in the park where the climber can test his skill on slabs, buttresses and gullies.

There are limited opportunities for skiing. Natural snow can be used between January and March (but usually only intermittently) on some slopes, particularly on the Carneddau and in Migneint. A nylon slope is available at the National Mountaineering Council Centre at Plas y Brenin, near Capel Curig.

The Forestry Commission's forests provide splendid locations for the popular Scandinavian sport of orienteering and most of the residential Outdoor Pursuits Centres in the park list it among their activities.

A relatively recent development is the sport of hang-gliding from some of the more accessible mountain slopes.

Among the more leisurely pursuits, pony-trekking, though catered for in some areas, is not common. This cannot be said of fishing, for which there are abundant opportunities in streams, rivers, lakes and the sea. A licence, issued by the Gwynedd Division of the Welsh Water Authority, is required to fish inland waters in the park and usually also a permit from those bodies who own or lease the fishing rights. No licence or permit is needed for sea fishing.

Lakes, rivers and estuaries all provide suitable locations for canoeing. The Afon Tryweryn, north of Bala, is popular for 'white-water' canoeing and international slaloms are held there. Parts of the coast are also suitable for sea-canoeing, with surfing at Harlech.

Llyn Tegid is the most favoured location for sailing on inland waters and there are also stretches of coast in or near the park suitable for sea-sailing. Club sailing predominates, but non-club sailing is possible from some lake-sides and from beaches.

Although power-boating and water skiing have taken place on Llyn Geirionydd, these pursuits are discouraged within the park because of the disturbance caused in tranquil situations and possible physical danger to other water users. They are pursued in parts of the Mawddach estuary, however, and on the sea off Barmouth and Morfa Harlech.

The many fine beaches round the coast of Caernarfonshire from Conwy to Borth y Gest and of Merioneth from Harlech to Aberdyfi provide safe locations for swimming, sun-bathing, and children's games, in addition to the interests of the water users already mentioned.

Several car rallies are organized annually in certain parts of the park, mainly using roads on Forestry Commission

land. They are held under the auspices of the Royal Automobile Club and comply with legal requirements. Motorcycle scrambles, sponsored by the Auto-Cycle Union and supervised by local clubs, take place on private land near Bala.

The list of amenities would not be complete without reference to the study of natural history as a leisure pursuit. As mentioned already, several bodies provide interpretative centres and nature reserves, many of the latter having self-guiding nature trails. The Park Authority provides lecture courses at its Residential Centre at Plas Tan y Bwlch in the Vale of Ffestiniog and also organizes guided walks. Several rather different centres lie just outside the park. The Llechwedd slate caverns and the Gloddfa Ganol slate mine at Blaenau Ffestiniog are concerned mainly with industrial archaeology, while Oriel Eryri, an outstation of the National Museum of Wales at Llanberis, interprets the general environment of Snowdonia.

It can be fairly claimed that the Snowdonia National Park has something for everyone and offers facilities second to none in Britain for the appreciation and enjoyment of the countryside.

Useful Addresses

Snowdonia National Park HQ: Penrhyndeudraeth

Snowdonia National Park Study Centre: Plas Tan y Bwlch, Maentwrog

Information Centres at:
  Aberdyfi
  Bala
  Betws-y-Coed
  Blaenau Ffestiniog
  Conwy
  Dolgellau
  Harlech
  Llanberis

Nature Conservancy Council HQ for Wales: Penrhos Road, Bangor

National Trust, North Wales Regional Office: Dinas, Betws-y-Coed

North Wales Naturalists' Trust: 154 High Street, Bangor

THE NATIONAL SCENIC AREAS

OF SCOTLAND

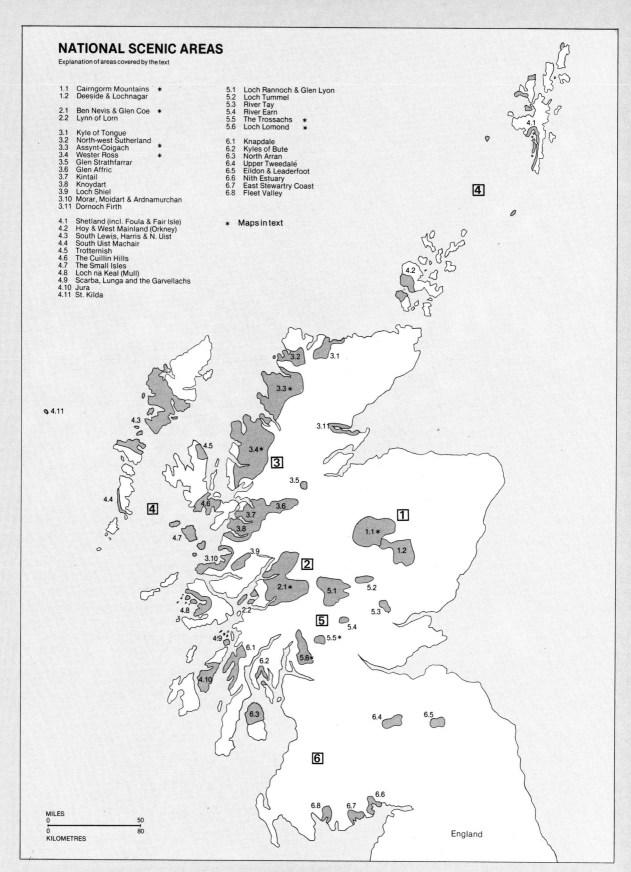

NATIONAL SCENIC AREAS

Explanation of areas covered by the text

1.1 Cairngorm Mountains *
1.2 Deeside & Lochnagar

2.1 Ben Nevis & Glen Coe *
2.2 Lynn of Lorn

3.1 Kyle of Tongue
3.2 North-west Sutherland
3.3 Assynt-Coigach *
3.4 Wester Ross *
3.5 Glen Strathfarrar
3.6 Glen Affric
3.7 Kintail
3.8 Knoydart
3.9 Loch Shiel
3.10 Morar, Moidart & Ardnamurchan
3.11 Dornoch Firth

4.1 Shetland (incl. Foula & Fair Isle)
4.2 Hoy & West Mainland (Orkney)
4.3 South Lewis, Harris & N. Uist
4.4 South Uist Machair
4.5 Trotternish
4.6 The Cuillin Hills
4.7 The Small Isles
4.8 Loch na Keal (Mull)
4.9 Scarba, Lunga and the Garvellachs
4.10 Jura
4.11 St. Kilda

5.1 Loch Rannoch & Glen Lyon
5.2 Loch Tummel
5.3 River Tay
5.4 River Earn
5.5 The Trossachs *
5.6 Loch Lomond *

6.1 Knapdale
6.2 Kyles of Bute
6.3 North Arran
6.4 Upper Tweedale
6.5 Eildon & Leaderfoot
6.6 Nith Estuary
6.7 East Stewartry Coast
6.8 Fleet Valley

* Maps in text

England

MILES
0 _____ 50
0 _____ 80
KILOMETRES

Previous page: *Hebridean croft on the island of Coll*

Alan Hamilton

Introduction

*I*T IS A source of mystery and wonder to a great many of the thirteen million tourists who visit Scotland each year that in a country acknowledged throughout the world as one of the most sublimely beautiful corners of all Europe, there does not exist a single national park.

That such an apparently glaring omission should exist suggests to the outsider that the Scots do not care for the fate of their surroundings, or at best they take them for granted. Nothing could be further from the truth; the Scots know intimately and appreciate keenly the land they inhabit; the literature and songs of few other peoples are so occupied with description and celebration of their physical surroundings.

All Scotland, some would claim, is a national park in itself. After all, nearly two-thirds of the land area is officially classified as rough grazing – mountain and moorland – and to delineate certain areas as worthy of particular attention and protection is merely to ignore countless others. But the real reason for Scotland being without formally designated national parks, when England has had them for over thirty years and the United States for more than a century, is the combined product of circumstance, tradition and, inevitably, politics.

Scotland is a land with more than its share of breathing space. Its 77,852 square km (30,414 square miles) support a population of little more than five million, at an average density of only sixty-six to the square km (170 per square mile). As three-quarters of that population live in a narrow belt barely thirty miles wide in the central lowlands, sometimes in the most overcrowded urban conditions in Europe, it leaves much of the rest of the country with an enviable emptiness. Much of the emptiness stems from a history which is far from enviable; the essence of the Highland Clearances was the wholesale eviction of humans from their ancestral acres by southern landlords to make room for the infinitely more profitable sheep and, more recently, for deer forests. But it has meant that, during the present century with its burgeoning pursuit of leisure, the Scottish countryside has suffered much less from pressure of numbers than have the scenic areas of England and Wales.

With much of the native population evicted to colonize North America and the Antipodes, and with those who remained squeezed into the central belt and kept from wandering far by the sheer oppression of poverty, there has always been in Scotland more than enough countryside for everyone. In this decade of largely enforced leisure, that is no longer as true as it was.

At the same time, Scots have regarded it as a more or less self-evident truth that they should have completely free access to their mountains and other wild areas, whoever the landowner might be. So ingrained is the tradition of the owners of scenic land allowing the public relatively free access that the entirely erroneous belief has gained hold of there being no law of trespass in Scotland. It may be invoked only rarely, but the law of trespass does exist, and it is not greatly different from the law of trespass in England and Wales. It is a civil offence, and for an action to succeed, damage must be proved. In addition, strictly speaking, it is a criminal offence to camp or light fires on private land without permission, a Victorian hangover originally intended for moving on gypsies.

Despite the establishment in recent years of Scotland's first three long distance right-of-way footpaths, the West Highland Way, the Speyside Way and the Southern Upland Way, the latter opening in 1984, most steps taken on a Scottish hillside are still through the grace and favour of the landowner rather than of right. It is a tribute to tolerance that the system works on the whole without friction, except when walkers and sportsmen get in each other's sights during the grouse shooting season beginning on 12 August, and the deer stalking season which lasts from mid-August to October.

In 1884, in the infant days of outdoor leisure as it is now understood, an attempt was made in Parliament to formalize the long-standing informal custom in the Access to Mountains (Scotland) Bill. But there was felt to be no great necessity for it, and the landowners preferred to retain the greater degree of control that a voluntary and informal system offered them. The bill never reached the statute book.

In the immediate post-war years after 1945, when a government-sponsored committee was considering the establishment of national parks in England and Wales, a similar committee chaired by Sir Douglas Ramsay was undertaking the same exercise for Scotland.

The Ramsay Committee recommended the creation of five Scottish national parks enclosing a total of 484,000 hectares (1,870 square miles) of the finest of the country's landscape. The areas chosen were: Loch Lomond and the Trossachs; Glen Affric–Glen Cannich–Strathfarrar; Ben Nevis and Glencoe; the Cairngorms; and Loch Torridon–Loch Marees–Little Loch Broom. In addition the committee nominated three other areas that might be placed on a reserve list for consideration as national parks at some future date: Moidart–Morar–Knoydart; Glen Lyon–Ben Lawers–Schiehallion; and St Mary's Loch in the Borders.

In 1949 the publication of a further report on the national parks question confirmed Ramsay's findings, and made the added recommendation that national nature reserves be set up in appropriate areas of Scotland. But when the National Parks and Access to the Countryside Act became law in 1949 and enabled the first parks to be established in England and Wales, it contained no provision for Scotland. Again, north of the border, it had been felt to be an entirely unnecessary measure.

The public, after all, enjoyed virtually all the access it wanted to the Scottish countryside. The landowners faced no particular problem, as the numbers enjoying their grace-and-favour access were well within manageable bounds. There was a feeling too that to identify selected areas as formally designated national parks would lead to their over-use, and would destroy that essentially Scottish quality of unspoilt wildness. And quite apart from that, there was no great enthusiasm from any quarter for large tracts of countryside being taken into public ownership, an essential prerequisite for the establishment of national parks in the view of the Ramsay Committee.

So Scotland decided that it neither needed nor wanted national parks at that time, but the proposals of the park lobby did not go entirely unheeded. The five potential park areas named by the Ramsay committee were declared by the Secretary of State for Scotland to be 'National Park Direction Areas,' which meant that central government agreed to exercise a modest and rather inadequate degree of overall planning control in those areas as a means of preventing the worst excesses of development and despoliation. Scotland also adopted those parts of the national park legislation which established national nature reserves, and today there are over fifty in Scotland which owe their existence to the 1949 Act.

The establishment in 1968 of the Countryside Commission for Scotland as the government agency responsible for the overall strategy towards open spaces gave fresh impetus to the idea of formally designated parks. In the meantime, other bodies had been making some progress of their own. Since its establishment in 1931 the National Trust for Scot-

land has acquired a number of scenic areas, most of them relatively small, for the nation, and the Forestry Commission, Scotland's largest landowner despite a supposed dislike of state land ownership, has turned five of its largest plantations into forest parks, the first as long ago as 1935, allowing public access to its land and providing some recreational facilities like picnic sites and nature trails.

In 1974 the Countryside Commission for Scotland produced its proposals for an integrated park system, and once again the drum was beaten for the establishment of national parks. They avoided the precise term and chose instead to call them 'special parks', suggesting as prime candidates the Cairngorms, Ben Nevis–Glencoe, and Loch Lomond–Trossachs.

Such parks, the Commission suggested, would be areas 'already under substantial recreational pressure and having particular attributes of scenic character which give them a national rather than a regional or local significance'. Each should be run by its own park authority, with two-thirds of the members appointed by the existing local authorities in the area, and one-third by central government. The park authorities would take over from the local councils a high degree of planning control, and would be largely funded direct from the Exchequer.

Some of the Commission's other proposals of the time did come to pass and are now in existence, notably small local country parks with their emphasis on recreation, and regional parks, with Clyde–Muirshiel south-west of Glasgow likely to be first, and others proposed in the Lomond Hills of Fife and the Pentland Hills behind Edinburgh. But as for national parks, they once again failed to materialize. Resistance this time came chiefly from local authorities, who were reluctant to give up their traditional planning powers to a new and outside body, despite the offer of being able to nominate two-thirds of that body's members.

Scotland is still without its national parks, but there are now one or two instances where pressure on the countryside has become so great in recent years that some kind of overall planning control has become patently urgent to prevent overdevelopment ruining the land altogether, and to arbitrate between the sometimes conflicting interests of skier and climber, stalker and walker, camper and forester. The need is most urgent in the Cairngorms, where man threatens to overwhelm what was once a wilderness, and in the Loch Lomond area, where tourism and farming are making uneasy bedfellows. Loch Lomond is an unusual case in that the four local authorities concerned are actually in favour of the area having national park status. At the time of writing, however, the Secretary of State remains unconvinced.

Having again failed to establish national parks, the Countryside Commission for Scotland nevertheless felt that some action was necessary to safeguard the finest areas of

Scotland's landscape. Accordingly in 1978 it published a report identifying forty locations which it named 'National Scenic Areas', and proposed that central government should exercise a greater degree of influence over development within them.

The choice of areas was necessarily a somewhat subjective one, there being no objective measure of beauty, and there are plenty who will disagree with the selection. The areas chosen did however include substantial parts of the eight possible national parks identified by Ramsay in 1945. The forty areas are now established, and the Secretary of State exercises a degree of planning oversight which, although still modest, is a great deal better than none at all.

There are six categories of proposed development within the national scenic areas over which central government can intervene: schemes for five or more dwellings outside towns and villages; sites for five or more caravans; all non-residential developments occupying more than 0·5 hectares (1·2 acres); all structures over twelve metres (thirty-nine feet) high; vehicle tracks other than forestry roads at more than 300 m (980 ft) altitude; and any new roadworks away from existing highways costing more than £100,000. In addition, the Countryside (Scotland) Act of 1981 gives planning authorities and the Countryside Commission for Scotland power to negotiate land management agreements with landowners, and to make payments in cases where the landowners agree to put amenity before agriculture.

The national scenic areas cover a total of just over one million hectares, or one-eighth of the total land area of Scotland, from Shetland to the Solway, from Royal Deeside to the outermost Hebrides. The emphasis is very much on conservation rather than on organized recreation, and the visitor to them must not automatically expect the provision of campsites or visitor centres, waymarked walks or nature trails. Many of the areas are remote, and difficult of access. Visitor facilities do exist throughout Scotland (although signposted footpaths are in general much rarer than in England and Wales) but they are provided very much on an *ad hoc* basis, and vary greatly from one area to another.

Apart from those few areas where pressure of numbers has generated a conflict of interests, like the Cairngorms and Loch Lomond, Scotland remains largely an open and unspoilt land. Countryside 'management' can be a mixed blessing, and is not always conducive to an atmosphere of solitude, remoteness, and nature unsullied by the footprint of man. There is still a great deal of Scotland which, thankfully, retains that essentially untamed character.

The Cairngorms, Deeside and Lochnagar

National Scenic Areas:
The Cairngorms
Deeside and Lochnagar

THE BROWS of the morning beetled with the dark threat of rain as I struck out with Captain Birdseye on the longest of Scotland's classic hill walks, the 32-mile route march across the Cairngorm range by the Lairig Ghru pass. It held every promise of a filthy day.

The Captain was dressed for the occasion, having acquired from an unspecified source a complete set of trawler skipper's bright yellow oilskins, including broad-brimmed sou'wester. His back bore the day's supplies in a papoose bought from a chain store by his wife for the original purpose of transporting a wriggling infant to the shops. Not a conventional man, the Captain, but practical.

It was, as I recall, the day before Midsummer, and every promise that the dawn held was fulfilled when we had gone barely a mile. Scottish rain is the wettest that falls anywhere on the planet; it does not so much fall from the sky as ooze from the air, in droplets so fine that its powers of penetration are unmatched by the fiercest tropical storm. Our path was turned to a torrent of mud, and to tread the heather was to walk on sponges that yielded water the colour of malt whisky.

For six hours we toiled upwards between the bleak frowning battlements of the mountains, peering under dripping eyebrows for the indistinct way ahead. Desert travellers dream of cool mountain streams; we dreamed of deserts, and of a public bar with a roaring log fire dancing its warm light on a row of the finest malts. The Captain sweated buckets inside his oilskins, and only the constant hosing from the skies prevented his engine from overheating. To pass the time, we discussed our joint insanity.

We breasted the summit at two, and the rain suddenly stopped as though a tap had been turned. We gazed north at the great green carpet of the Rothiemurchus Forest laid below, bathed in bright summer sun.

The first of the day's walkers from the north passed us with economical Scots grunts of greeting; they gazed at our soaking clothes incredulously. We knew what they were in for. The Captain disrobed, stuffed his oilskins into his papoose, and we descended the northern slopes of the Cairngorms, from the high bare hills into the ancient pine forest, on a brilliant summer afternoon, sauntering the last gentle miles to the bar of the Coylumbridge Hotel and two generous glasses of Macallan, a fine whisky that never tasted finer.

'It is a great pity,' observed the Captain, draining the last drops of liquid gold in his glass, 'that you need that sort of rain to make that kind of whisky.'

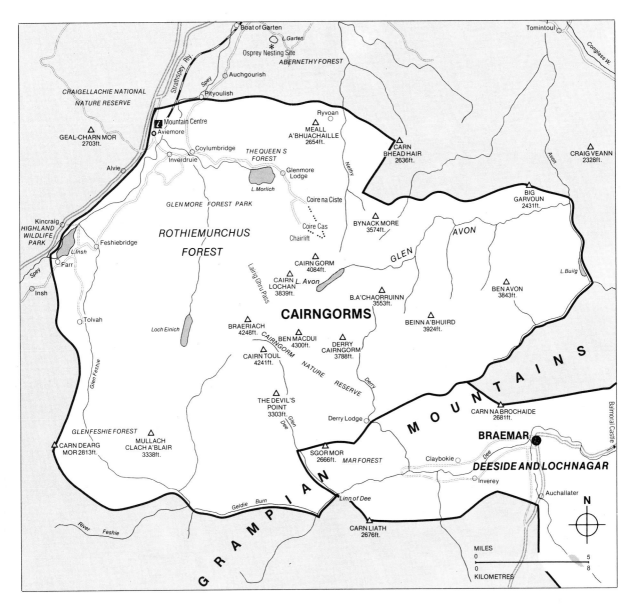

THAT THE weather can be so dramatically different on opposite sides of the range is an indication of the immense size of the Cairngorm Mountains, the greatest upland mass in the British Isles, and the most extensive area over 900 m (3,000 ft) anywhere in these islands. The railway and the main A9 road from Perth to Inverness, picking their way side by side along the convenient river valleys of the central Highlands, are forced to make a long and bulging detour to the west just north of Pitlochry to avoid the forbidding barrier of the Cairngorms.

What first impresses about these mountains is not their height, but the sheer immensity of their bulk. Yet within the range are four summits of over 1,220 m (4,000 ft), including the highest mountain in the British Isles after Ben Nevis, and three more which closely approach it. These ought to be the highest British summits, and only an accident of nature has allowed Nevis to take the honours.

The Cairngorms National Scenic Area encompasses 67,200 hectares (165,984 acres), from the meandering course of the Spey in the west to the slopes of Ben Avon in the east, from Glenfeshie Forest in the south to the Queen's Forest in the north. Its area covers the principal summits of the range, a high, bare and bleak plateau with a sub-arctic climate and vegetation not found in such quantity elsewhere in Europe below the latitudes of Scandinavia.

Once a wilderness crossed only by sheep drovers, the Cairngorms are now a highly developed playground, at least on the fringes. It is now the premier winter sports area of Britain, and a ski lift will whisk visitors winter and summer close to the 1,240 m (4,084 ft) summit of Cairn Gorm, to the distress of those who seek the reward of solitude for the effort of making the ascent on foot. Aviemore, the area's principal centre, has grown in two decades from a village to a full-blown tourist resort of hotels and bright lights.

In 1951 the Cairngorm plateau was created a national nature reserve, one of the largest in Europe, yet at the same time its high moors are among Scotland's finest gun country, and there is no more glaring evidence of that than the dozens of high altitude Land-Rover tracks which scar many a Cairngorm hillside, bulldozed to ease the ascent of elderly sportsmen and the descent of their quarry of grouse and deer. The Cairngorms are still big enough for the walker to find emptiness, yet because of conflicting pressures the area has for long been Scotland's prime candidate for the creation of a national park.

The Cairngorms are rounded red granite mountains, quite distinct from the grey trackless heights of the Monadhliaths ('Grey Mountains') which rise west of the Spey and reach barrenly north-west towards Inverness and the Great Glen.

To understand their creation is is necessary to recall the Caledonian Orogeny, the great period of mountain building 400 million years ago when much of what is now Scotland and Scandinavia was uplifted in a massive geological convulsion into a range of mountains equivalent in scale to the present-day Alps.

Most of the Scottish Highlands are the remnants of that mountain chain, ground and planed to their present relative insignificance by millenia of weathering and glaciation. But the Cairngorms were formed by the intrusion into the roots of those mountains, from the intense heat of the earth's core, of a vast body of magma, or molten rock, metamorphosed by heat and pressure into granite. The overlying mountains have long been worn away, and only the granite intrusion, or pluton, remains, a vast mass covering 409 square km (160 square miles). Granite is composed of quartz, mica and feldspar, which in the case of the Cairngorms is predominantly red orthoclase, giving the mountains their characteristic rosy tint.

As the granite mass cooled, its cracks and air bubbles were frequently filled with quartz which, crystallized and coloured with impurities, is now sought after as the semi-precious smoky Cairngorm gemstones. You will not, unless you are very fortunate, find them lying about on the ground; professional collectors keep their sources of supply well hidden.

For all its reputation as the most durable of building materials, granite in its natural state wears much less well than most igneous rocks, and it is highly susceptible to breakdown by the forces of weathering and glaciation.

The typical profile of a Cairngorm mountain is a rounded hulk like an elephant at rest, and its smooth sandpapered summit is a disappointment to some climbers who prefer to aim at a more obvious soaring needle. But the forces of nature have carved on the flanks of these hills some of the most splendid corries in Scotland, great hollows gouged by ice and water backed by horseshoe walls of granite sometimes hundreds of feet high, with an icy-cold lochan at their foot. One of the finest is that which separates the peaks of Braeriach and Cairn Toul; other spectacular hollows on the north side of the Cairn Gorm–Cairn Lochan summit ridge are so deeply hidden from the summer sun that they shelter patches of lingering snow for most of the year.

These corries offer a testing range of rock climbs, although those who tackle them know well the principal attendant danger of climbing on granite – rotted rock. The Cairngorms are still being worn down apace, as is evident from the shattered boulder-strewn summits. Geologists debate how much of the Cairngorm topography was moulded by the moving ice sheets of the last glacial period,

The Bluebells of Scotland near Loch Insh

and how much had already been carved by wind, water and the shattering action of frost.

Granite is highly susceptible to the action of frost, its coarse crystalline structure opening easily into vertical and lateral splits which create the typical tor landscape of upland granite country, be it Cairn Gorm or Dartmoor. One undoubted effect of the ice sheets, however, was to gouge the great gash which crosses the range from south-east to north-west, the long dolorous pass of the Lairig Ghru.

Bleak though the Cairngorm uplands may be, one of the beauties of the plateau is that it is skirted up to a tree line of 458 m (1,500 ft) by rich forest, some of it modern forestry planting of the inevitable Sitka Spruce, but much of it a remnant of the great native Scots Pine wood of Caledon which once clothed much of the Highlands. Major remnants of this native pine cover exist in the forests of Glen More, Rothiemurchus and Abernethy on the northern slopes, and the forests of Glenfeshie and Mar on the south. Beneath the Scots Pines of the upper forest, which give way to a mixture of Scots Pine, Common Juniper and Common Birch and finally to the rich cultivated woodlands of the Spey valley, lies a rich undergrowth of heathers and Blaeberry carpeting the forest floor.

But it is on the very top of the plateau that the uniqueness of the Cairngorms is to be found. Here, grouped closely together, are Britain's second mountain and its attendants: Ben Macdui, 1,321 m (4,296 ft); Braeriach, 1,299 m (4,248 ft); Cairn Toul, 1,297 m (4,241 ft); and Cairn Gorm, 1,249 m (4,084 ft), with its neighbour Cairn Lochan standing beside and only a whisker below at 1,191 m (3,893 ft). A little to the east, Beinn a'Bhuird, 1,200 m (3,924 ft) and Ben Avon, 1,175 m (3,843 ft) almost match them. At such altitudes the vegetation is sub-arctic, the product of combined height,

Water sports on Loch Morlich, Invernesshire

View from Cairngormside over Loch Morlich and the Spey Valley

distance from the moderating influence of the sea, and the ferocious weather which is never far away and can descend with sometimes fatal suddenness even in high summer. Too many ill-advised adventurers have died on these moors.

The vegetation of the high Cairngorms has much in common with that of Greenland and Spitzbergen. Above 612 m (2,000 ft) what grows underfoot is firstly of alpine character, a thick carpet of heathers interspersed with Bearberry, Crowberry and Dwarf Azalea, a mass of tiny pink flowers in June. As the altitude rises the heathers and copious Starry Saxifrage give way to a true tundra of mosses and liverworts, although the heather growing at 1,100 m (3,600 ft) on Beinn a'Bhuird is probably the highest that it grows anywhere in Britain.

The hills support a rich variety of wildlife, none of it rarer than the herd of Reindeer introduced from Scandinavia in 1954, which thrive on the Reindeer Moss of the high plateau and have now expanded their population to more than a hundred, all of them Scots born. The native Scottish reindeer is thought to have become extinct in the twelfth century; today the offspring of the immigrants can be seen browsing in summer near the summits of Ben Macdui and Cairn Lochan.

The Red Deer are the dominant mammals of the region, a thriving and numerous indigenous breed. In summer they generally remain above 612 m (2,000 ft) where the air is cool, the pasture sweet, and there is a welcome absence of bothersome flies. Often in the evening they will descend to the glens to drink. The Roe Deer is less common, but is

nevertheless well established in the forests of Glenmore and Rothiemurchus.

The high plateau is also the hunting ground of the king of British birds, the Golden Eagle, which will also nest at lower altitudes in the old Caledonian pinewoods. The moors are the home of Red Grouse, Lapwing, Meadow Pipit, Ptarmigan, Golden Plover and the rare Dotterel, as well as the predatory Peregrine Falcons and Sparrowhawks. Just outside the national scenic area, at Loch Garten in the Abernethy Forest, is the celebrated nesting site of the Osprey.

The sub-arctic vegetation of the high plateau is matched by a climate of due severity. This is by far the snowiest part of Britain; snow falls on an average ninety days a year on the highest ground, and lies on the summits for an average of a hundred days a year, from early January until mid-April. In some of the high north-facing corries it may lie for much longer; in one hollow on Cairn Gorm a patch of snow lay for ten years until melted by the mild summer of 1969. The plateau is subjected to constant and often severe wind, which whips the winter snow and can pile it in tremendous drifts. Gusts of up to 125 knots have been recorded on the anemometer on the Coire Cas ski lift.

A number of minor roads and tracks strike off the A9 between Perth and Inverness to nibble at the foothills of the Cairngorm mass. From Kincraig a track leads south-east past the lovely Loch Insh, where the meandering Spey broadens into marshes and there is a bird reserve, into Glen Feshie, wild and stern, where the old Caledonian Scots Pines stand mixed with Juniper. The River Feshie dominates the glen, rushing and tumbling in its tearing hurry to join the Spey at Loch Insh.

From Aviemore the A951 leads east to Coylumbridge and is the main gateway to the Cairngorms, leading all the way to the shoulder of Cairn Gorm from where a chair lift continues to the summit. Three miles south of Aviemore is a visitor centre at Loch an Eilan, a tree-fringed gem to which there is a signposted nature trail giving high promise of a sight of Golden Eagle, Ptarmigan, Capercaillie and Osprey.

A pond in the Insh Nature Reserve

Beyond Coylumbridge the A951 leads past the clear waters of Loch Morlich, another highly favoured bird observatory, and into the Queen's Forest to Glenmore Lodge, where the Scottish Sports Council maintains an adventure training centre. Nearby the Forestry Commission has a good information centre, and from it trails of varying length meander through the ancient pinewoods. Adjoining Glenmore to the west is the great private forest of Rothiemurchus whose owner Mr John Grant has done much to encourage visitors, and who provides maps of his forest walks at the Inverdruie visitor centre near Coylumbridge.

But there is no walk in the Cairngorms to match the thirty-two-mile traverse of the range through the Lairig Ghru. It is not a trek for the faint-hearted, the unfit, or the ill-equipped, although the experienced walker should have no difficulty in accomplishing it in a day.

The walk properly begins at Braemar on the A93 Perth to Deeside road, but a few short miles can be saved by driving up the dead-end road to Linn of Dee, abandoning the car, and striking up the mountain track to Derry Lodge. The ascent from the south is long and occasionally hard, but it presents no particular difficulty. The effort is rewarded as the path ascends to the high plateau with the immense granite bulk of Ben Macdui rearing up on one side, and Cairn Toul on the other. Only on the top of the pass is there a slight difficulty, where the walker has to negotiate a boulder field reminiscent of those wartime coastal tank defences built of square concrete blocks. The descent on the northern side takes the walker down through the forest and deposits him most conveniently by the Coylumbridge Hotel.

A major problem of walking the Lairig Ghru is that, if you drive to the start, you are a very long way from your car at the end. The difficulty is often solved by two parties agreeing to start from each end simultaneously, exchanging car keys at the summit. If they miss each other in the mist, they are in serious trouble.

From its birth at the summit of the Lairig Ghru, the River Dee tumbles eastwards off the plateau, through the cauldrons and pools of the Linn of Dee, and from Braemar to Ballater runs through the lushly wooded valley of Upper Deeside, which with the overlooking mass of the mountain of Lochnagar forms a separate national scenic area.

This is the much-visited Royal Deeside, discovered by Victoria and Albert. The bare wilderness of the high Cairngorms is replaced by an altogether richer and more managed landscape, with great stretches of pine and birch wood, and tall stands of Douglas Fir filling the side glens.

On the south side of the valley between Braemar and Balmoral Castle is Ballochbuie Forest, a fine and substantial

A shooting party on a grouse moor, Royal Deeside

remnant of the old Caledonian pinewood that would have been felled to its last tree had not Queen Victoria bought the entire estate to preserve her view from Balmoral.

The whole area is dominated by what Byron described as 'the steep frowning glories of dark Lochnagar,' a mountain more recently immortalized by Prince Charles in his children's story written to amuse his younger brothers, *The Old Man of Lochnagar*.

The 1,158 m (3,786 ft) mountain is, like the Cairngorms, another massive intrusion of granite into the roots of the old Caledonian ranges, and it exhibits the typical granitic features of tremendous corries, their sheer walls plunging hundreds of feet from the summit. The upper reaches of Lochnagar are clothed in a similar alpine vegetation to that found in the Cairngorms.

Lochnagar is approached from Ballater along a delightful minor road that follows the east side of Glen Muick to the Spittal of Glenmuick. From there a steep path leads directly towards the mountain, and to follow it all the way to the plateau top is to discover breathtaking views of the north-eastern cliff face, and of the great south-western corrie, one of the largest in Scotland. An additional bonus is the distant view of the grey granite walls of Balmoral Castle nestling in its well-manicured woodlands, and the consequent appreciation of why Victoria chose this location as her holiday retreat and thereby founded the Scottish tourist industry more or less single-handed.

Loch Lomond and the Southern Highlands

National Scenic Areas:
Loch Lomond
The Trossachs
River Earn, Comrie to St Fillans
River Tay, Dunkeld
Loch Rannoch and Glen Lyon
Loch Tummel

L OCH LOMOND should really be a fjord, a bony finger of the sea pointing deep into the Highland mountains. But an accident of geology has made it instead the largest inland body of water in Great Britain, and so celebrated in a single song that its name is known to people across the world who could not summon to memory a single other feature of the Scottish landscape.

The loch is twenty-four miles long and varies in width from five miles to less than one mile, covering a total of 6,500 hectares (16,055 acres) and studded with thirty islands. It owes its existence to the last Ice Age which ended in Scotland some 10,800 years ago, a mere tick on the clock of geological time. The ice sheets which covered Scotland had one final burst of expansion, concentrated in the south-western Grampians and now known as the Loch Lomond Re-advance.

Slow-moving glaciers exert tremendous power, the more so because they pick up countless fragments of rock which become frozen into their lower surfaces and act like a giant and fearsome rasp, grinding out a course for the advancing ice.

The ice sheet advancing in the south-west Highlands gouged out deep channels on its way to the sea, the most prominent of which are Loch Lomond and Loch Long. When the climate warmed and the glaciers melted, three things happened. First, the sea level rose as it filled with the meltwater, so the Loch Long channel flooded and is today a classic fjord. Loch Lomond should have flooded too but the second thing to happen was that the land, relieved of the tremendous weight of ice, rose up out of the sea, and indeed is still rising.

The third effect was that where the glaciers had reached their limit of advance before melting they left enormous piles of debris, known as terminal moraines, composed of all the shattered and splintered rock they had collected on their journey. As the land rose, the pile of debris cut off Loch Lomond from the sea, and now forms the narrow coastal plain between Dumbarton and Balloch, threaded by the loch's only outward drainage, the little River Leven which carries its overflow into the Clyde. How close Loch Lomond came to being a fjord may be deduced from the fact that its surface is only eight metres (twenty-seven feet) above sea level.

The loch displays another primary lesson in geology, for it is bisected at Balmaha near its southern end by the Highland Boundary Fault, the obvious and clear-cut division running south-west to north-east right across Scotland from Helensburgh to Stonehaven, which delineates the end of the midland valley and the beginning of the Highlands. North of the boundary fault Loch Lomond is truly a fjord in character, a narrow glacial trough hemmed in by crowding mountains, and an average of 180 m (600 ft) deep. South of the fault, where the softer Old Red Sandstone fashions the landscape, the loch broadens out into a lowland mere, up to five miles wide and only twenty-three metres (seventy-five ft) deep, sprinkled with lush wooded islands.

The boundary fault, where the hard Dalradian rocks of the Grampians meet the soft sandstone sediments of the lowlands, can easily be traced, from Conic Hill on the eastern shore opposite Luss, through the line of grassy islands Inchcailloch, Torrinch, Creinch and Inchmurrin, to the western shore at the village of Arden. North of the fault line the glacial nature of the loch is enhanced and underlined by the many waterfalls that tumble from hanging valleys, watercourses whose progress was interrupted by the passage of the ice.

To gaze on the shining ribbon of the loch from its southern end is to be beckoned by Highland mystery, for the ribbon, which cannot quite be seen for its entire length, disappears among the gathering mountains, imploring the watcher to follow it and discover what lies at the other end. The view is greatly enhanced by the acres of deciduous woodland, particularly towards the southern end and on the islands, giving way to dark hillsides of planted conifer on the

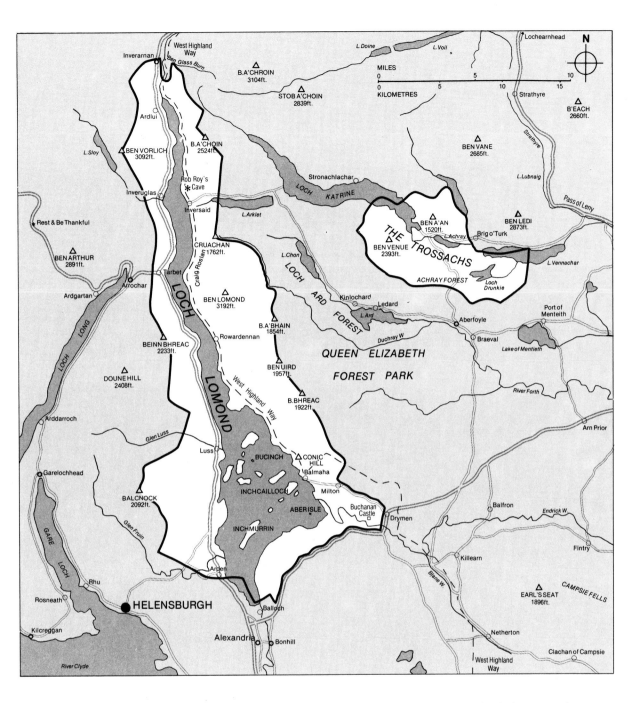

eastern shore, the beginning of the vast Queen Elizabeth Forest Park.

North of the boundary fault the lochside is dominated by the great Grampian hump of Ben Lomond, at 976 m (3,192 ft) the most southerly of Scotland's Munros, a Munro being any Scots peak of 917 m (3,000 ft) or over named after Sir Hugh Munro, a remarkable late Victorian explorer who climbed all but two of them – and there are 279. Two-thirds of the way up on the western side, set back behind the village of Tarbet, rise the finest group of mountains in the south-west Highlands, known as the Arrochar Alps and compris-

ing three knobbly summits of which Ben Arthur, more commonly known as the Cobbler, is the most familiar.

Loch Lomond's glorious situation is also the source of its present-day problems. Its glacial trough provides an excellent route into the Highlands, and the wholly inadequate A82 road hugging the western shore carries one-third of all the traffic entering and leaving the Highlands. In summer months the road can be badly clogged, as those who want to stop and stare conflict with those in a hurry. Improvements are on the drawing board, but it will be a long time before they are complete.

The upper lochside also provides part of the route for one of the outstanding scenic railway journeys in Britain which should not be missed while the line, under constant threat of closure because it is so hopelessly uneconomic, remains open. The West Highland Railway runs from Glasgow to Mallaig, and nowhere in the country can finer views be had from the window of a train. Opened in 1894, it had a briefly profitable life carrying fish from Mallaig, but now all the fish goes by road, and with the closure of the short-lived pulp mill project at Fort William, the line's future is in even graver doubt.

Loch Lomond has always been the great playground of Glasgow, being rapidly and easily accessible from the centre of the city by both road and the now-electrified railway which runs right to the waterside at Balloch Pier. The crowds and the congestion make the area a prime candidate for the overall planning control of a national park. The loch's broad southern end is under pressure from all manner of aquatic sports, and the Loch Lomond Association has drawn up a voluntary code of safety and good manners in the hope that by following it the sportsmen, be they cruisers, divers, water-skiers or windsurfers, will manage to keep out of each other's way.

Water lilies on Loch Chon

View over Loch Lomond to Ben Ime

The western shore is much the busiest, but it is possible to rise above the madding crowd at Luss, where a single track road from the Colquhoun Arms Hotel leads into the Luss Hills behind. It is a short climb from its end on to the Luss Ridge and its highest point of 736 m (2,408 ft) on Doune Hill, affording a fine view down the Clyde estuary.

The eastern shore is much more unspoilt, there being no road traversing its entire length. The B837 road from the village of Drymen leads to Balmaha and the Loch Lomond National Nature Reserve. The reserve covers the shore at the south-east corner of the loch around Endrick Water, together with the five adjacent islands of Inchcailloch, Clairinsh, Torrinch and Creinch, all of which form part of the Highland boundary fault, and the tiny Aber Isle just to the south. Inchcailloch, the only one which provides for visitors, is reached by small boat from Balmaha. The main interest of the reserve is its oak-dominated woodland which once covered so much of Scotland, and its rock formations, seen at their best on Inchcailloch, where the conglomerate sandstone of the lowlands meets a band of lava-like serpentine on the boundary fault. The freshwater marshes on the mainland part of the reserve are a noteworthy remnant of formerly extensive Scottish wetlands that have been lost through land drainage.

A little to the north of the nature reserve the thickly wooded islets of Bucinch and Ceardoch are owned by the National Trust for Scotland. Bucinch has a considerable stand of Yews, said to have been planted originally by Robert the Bruce to provide the raw material for bows.

From Balmaha the road continues a few further miles along the lochside to a dead end at Rowardennan where the car must be abandoned, but from where it is possible to travel for days on foot. This is the western edge of the huge Queen Elizabeth Forest Park, covering 172 square km (sixty-seven square miles), encompassing the three forests of Buchanan, Ard and Achray, and clothing the great sweep of country from Loch Lomond to the Trossachs in an almost unbroken carpet of afforestation. Within the park there are no less than 170 miles of forest road open to the public on foot.

Rowardennan, with its hotel and forestry campsite, is a good base from which to explore the forest. From here the walker is spoiled for choice. He is standing astride the West Highland Way, Scotland's first properly negotiated and waymarked long-distance footpath stretching 150 km (ninety-four miles) from the outskirts of urban Glasgow to Fort William.

Southwards from Rowardennan the path takes an easy and level route back to Drymen; northwards it follows the loch shore all the way to its northern end, climbing on its way through the splendid hillsides of Craigroyston, where there are dire threats to build a hydro-electric scheme. To be met by a car at Inversnaid further up the loch, at the dead end of the public road from Aberfoyle, is the ideal end to one of the finest short walks in the Highlands, although it should be

Loch Ard, by the Pass of Aberfoyle

noted that parts of the West Highland Way are over rough ground, and the loch is not always in view.

Alternatively the medium distance walker can traverse the entire forest park, tackling the thirteen-mile route over fine hill country from Rowardennan to Aberfoyle. The walker hungry for wider vistas will want to tackle the path to the summit of Ben Lomond, a three-hour ascent that is arduous but presents no great difficulty, and offers the reward at the top of a tremendous panorama of the Clyde estuary and the southern end of the Inner Hebrides. It is one of the easiest and most accessible of all Munros, but those who do not know them, and who attack even this relatively gentle giant ill-equipped, are liable to be shocked by the cold at the top even on the sunniest days.

Across the Queen Elizabeth Forest Park and forming its northern and eastern boundaries, is the region known as the Trossachs, which thanks to the attention of some particularly eminent publicists is almost as well known as Loch Lomond. It is the land of Rob Roy Macgregor, romanticized by Scott into a folk hero, a kind of Scottish Robin Hood, but in truth an outlaw, a rogue and a sheep stealer who ran a protection racket. Scott more or less invented the Trossachs as a tourist attraction, chiefly through his narrative poem *The Lady of the Lake*. Dorothy Wordsworth visited Loch Katrine, but thought it inferior to Ullswater. Scott, however, gave it all the good reviews it needed: 'The rocky summits, split and rent, formed turret, dome or battlement.'

Trossachs is a corruption of the Gaelic meaning 'bristly country'. The hills here are not unduly high: Ben Ledi, 879 m (2,873 ft) and Ben Venue, 732 m (2,393 ft) are modest by Scottish standards. But they have a jagged ruggedness which compensates for their lack of stature, and stands in stark contrast to the gentler lowlands immediately to the south. Again we are at the very edge of the Highlands, with the boundary fault running just to the south of Aberfoyle.

The Trossachs have been called the Scottish Lake District, and are essentially a string of three lochs: Katrine, Achray and Vennachar, which fill the floor of a glacial trough, one of those like Loch Lomond which radiate from the south-west highland glacial centre of the last Ice Age. The rocks here are hard schistose grits, and evidence of their resistance to the scouring of the ice can be seen around the Trossachs Hotel, where the valley narrows noticeably. The jaggedness comes partly from the hardness of the rocks, but also from the fact that the dominant geological structure here is an intense folding of the strata, so that bands of rock are lying at sixty or seventy degrees and outcropping on the skyline. There are great bands of slate, once worked commercially at Aberfoyle.

But the ruggedness is softened by the thick cloak of forest, and it is the combination of water, wood and wildness that gives the area its potent attraction, with the added bonus of Hen Harrier, Sparrowhawk, Buzzard and the occasional Peregrine Falcon wheeling in the skies above. There are areas of greater grandeur, but the Trossachs are the quintessence of Scotland, a condensed introduction to the Highlands that lie beyond.

Aberfoyle is the centre of the region. One mile north of the village is the David Marshall Lodge, visitor centre of the Queen Elizabeth Forest Park, which in addition to being the starting point for many forest walks is the base for two unusual Forestry Commission facilities, a seven-mile forest drive for cars, and a forest cycleway. The motor drive is open only from March to October.

Ben Venue is easily climbed by the experienced walker, either from the Inversnaid road at Ledard, four miles west of Aberfoyle, or from the A821 at the western end of Loch Achray. Both routes are of about three miles, and need care in poor visibility. Lower but rockier is BennA'an, 463 m (1,520 ft), a two-mile climb from the Trossachs Hotel through beautiful birchwoods to a fine panoramic view. There is another fine high-level viewpoint on the Menteith Hills, at the summit of a five-mile circular walk from Braeval on the A81 just east of Aberfoyle.

A longer but flatter walk follows the north shore of Loch Katrine from Trossachs Pier to Stronachlachar, a model village built by the Victorian city fathers of Glasgow when they appropriated the loch for their water supply in 1859. The walker or cyclist who makes it that far can return to Trossachs Pier by the *Sir Walter Scott*, the Victorian steamer that plies the eight-mile long, 152 m (500 ft) deep loch in the summer months.

Four other national scenic areas lie in the southern Highlands. The first is away to the north-east of the Trossachs, on the A85 road that strikes west from Perth to Crianlarich and makes its way through Strathearn to the head of Loch Earn. This upper part of the strath, between the little town of Comrie and the village of St Fillans, lies at the conjunction of highland and lowland scenery, and although not dramatic the various elements of hillside and well-tended wood and farmland effect a particularly pleasing combination. Not unlike the Trossachs, the hilltops have a bare, rugged character which contrasts with their wooded lower slopes and the prosperous farms of the valley floor.

The next national scenic area is north-east again, on the main A9 road between Perth and Inverness where it follows the valley of the River Tay through the tiny and ancient cathedral city of Dunkeld. Again it is the harmonious combination which creates beauty: rugged tops, lower slopes richly clothed in coniferous and broadleaved forest, and beneath the hills the Tay curling in great loops of peaty water. At Dunkeld the Tay is joined from the west by the faster, busier River Braan, tumbling over the Falls of Braan and through a narrow gorge overlooked by the Hermitage, a curious little folly of 1758 set in fifteen hectares (thirty-seven acres) of fine woodland.

Pleasure boats at Inversnaid on Loch Lomond

Although Dunkeld was first established as an ecclesiastical centre in the tenth century, most of the present town dates from the eighteenth, and the centre, largely in the care of the National Trust for Scotland, displays a pleasant formality that is somewhere between Scots vernacular style and formal Georgian elegance.

North-west of Dunkeld lies Aberfeldy, and from there a minor road leads to Fortingall and the hidden entrance to what is claimed as Scotland's longest glen, the thirty beautiful miles of Glen Lyon, which manages to sustain along almost its entire length a near-perfect combination of bare but colourful hills, rich woodland, and a sparkling river well endowed with gorges and waterfalls.

It begins as a wide and prosperously farmed strath, and ascends into the hills until it becomes a high bare mountain glen. A minor road travels most of its length from Fortingall to the Loch Lyon reservoir. One of the great pleasures of Glen Lyon is that it is so secretive; its entrance is not apparent until you round a corner at Fortingall and come upon what appeared to be an impenetrable line of hills; and the glen itself is deeply entrenched between mountains of over 917 m (3,000 ft), the principal peak on the south being Ben Lawers, a summit of particular interest.

The National Trust for Scotland, which owns the ben, has established an informative visitor centre high on its western shoulder on the hill road from Loch Tayside to Bridge of Balgie in Glen Lyon. The ben, at 1,218 m (3,984 ft), is the highest in the southern Highlands, and being largely composed of limestones and lime-rich schists has long been a place of pilgrimage for botanists because of its splendid arctic-alpine flora. The mountain is a national nature reserve of international significance. Its unique flora occurs chiefly between 765 and 1,162 m (2,500 and 3,800 ft), and is a rich carpet of pink Moss Campion, purple Saxifrage, yellow Mountain Saxifrage, Alpine Mouse-ear, Chickweed, Cyphel, Alpine Gentian, Globe Flower and Mountain Pansy.

Continuing northwards from Dunkeld, the A9 road comes to Pitlochry and the national scenic area of Loch Tummel. The road passes through the gorge of the river at Killiecrankie, the scene of the first battle, in 1689, of the long and sporadic Jacobite rebellion which finally ended at Culloden in 1745. A National Trust for Scotland visitor centre in the pass explains the history in detail. Until the coming of General Wade and his military roads in the late eighteenth century, this gorge was one of the most formidable obstacles on the road into the Highlands.

To the west of the pass the B8019 road follows the shores of Loch Tummel to the celebrated Queen's View, a fine panorama which looks west along the glen and offers a view that, despite its altitude, is a remarkably soft sylvan scene, with the quite superb backdrop of Schiehallion, not only Scotland's most mellifluously named mountain, but one of the most elegant, with its perfect cone soaring to 1,085 m (3,547 ft).

The road continues westwards to Loch Rannoch, part of the traditional Road to the Isles: 'by Tummel and Loch Rannoch and Lochaber I will go,' the song has it. The loch, easily circumnavigated by car, has above its southern shore the great Black Wood of Rannoch, the largest surviving remnant of the Caledonian Pine forest south of Rothiemurchus.

Loch Rannoch forms the northern part of the Glen Lyon National Scenic Area. The road continues for some miles west of the loch and ventures to the edge of the great bleak Moor of Rannoch, described in the next chapter. The ultimate end of the track is the West Highland Railway station at Rannoch, one of the remotest halts in Britain.

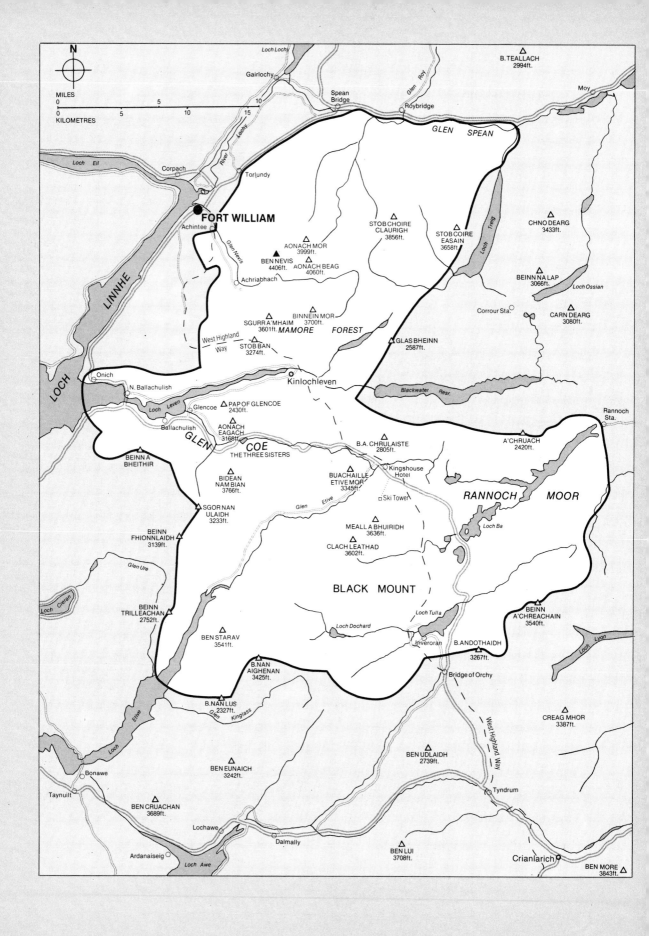

Ben Nevis and Glencoe

National Scenic Areas:
Ben Nevis and Glencoe
Lynn of Lorn

ONCE, AND only once, I dragged a caravan all the way from the south of England to the north-west Highlands. So wearisome and frustrating was the haul that there came a point when I refused point-blank to drive another yard, despite the exhortations of Madame to press on, and I pulled my rig on to the grass verge in the dark brooding vale of Glencoe. I was soon asleep in my fold-down bunk, drifting deeply to a distant land where all the roads were six-lane highways and a motorist was being lynched on a wayside elm for being in possession of a mobile home.

I was brought sharply back to Glencoe by violent shaking of my right shoulder. Madame was sitting bolt upright in bed, ghastly pale and quaking in the narrow shaft of moonlight. 'Burglars!' she breathed through quivering lips.

Burglars in Glencoe I regarded at that moment as about as likely as the imminent appearance of a squadron of flying pigs, but she had a point. There was undoubtedly an irregular and deeply ominous tapping on the outside of the paper-thin caravan walls, as though not one felon, but several, were feeling for the entrance in order to burst in and commit nameless pillage. 'The poker!' breathed Madame. 'We are,' I reminded her, 'in a caravan.'

A large climbing boot came to hand, and I peeped through the curtains. Nothing. Short burglars, clearly. There was nothing for it but to step out and confront them; they might be armed, they would certainly be wearing something more than blue pyjamas, but Madame was about to enter a paroxysmic state of terror. Gingerly I opened the door and peeped out, whereupon four magnificently antlered red deer stags, disturbed at their browsing directly under my bed, took sudden fright and fled through the moonlight.

'The Campbells,' I announced to a mightily relieved Madame, 'are not coming after all.'

THE A82 FROM Glasgow to Fort William is no place for such midnight frights. Having followed the gentle, friendly shores of Loch Lomond and forged up Glen Falloch, now beyond Bridge of Orchy it enters upon such a scene of desolation as is without compare in those parts of Scotland accessible from a main road. Before entering the gloomy vale of Glencoe, the road skirts the awesome empti-ness of Rannoch Moor, an almost featureless slough of 154 square km (sixty square miles) stretching away to the east. You feel that if it rained on the moon, and rained a very great deal, this is what the moon would look like.

The moor is a virtually trackless waste shot through its heart by, of all things, a railway. The builders of the West Highland line in 1894, with a boldness that only Victorians

163

would have attempted, floated their tracks across the bog on a raft of brushwood and cinders, and there it still rides, defying the sodden and waterlogged peat as though it were walking on water.

Readers of Stevenson's *Kidnapped* will already be familiar with the moor, described therein as 'as waste as the sea' and 'a wearier looking desert man never saw'.

Today, when the aesthetics of emptiness are more keenly appreciated than they were in Stevenson's time, Rannoch Moor is a national nature reserve, although there is no facility, indeed no road, for the public to enter it. It is one of the best examples of blanket bog to be seen anywhere in Britain, its treacherous brown ground and numberless lochans alive with Dunlins, Greenshanks, ducks, divers and plovers.

Being ringed around with jagged mountains, the flat waste of Rannoch has the appearance of a depression. It is in fact a plateau, underlain with granite which outcrops all over the peat, and with an elevation of 306 m (1,000 ft). It is ringed by hills of harder rock: quartzites and mica schists to the east, north and south, and the rhyolites and other resistant volcanic rocks of Glencoe to the west. As the Pleistocene ice moved across the face of Scotland to sculpt it into its present form, it found the rotten granite of Rannoch much more yielding, and ground the area to flatness.

Trapped by poor drainage and subjected to heavy rainfall, the region has become thickly covered with acid blanket bog, a sudden carpet of *Sphagnum* Moss and Bog Myrtle, grey-green Cotton Grass and Moor Grass, enlivened with Bog Asphodel and tiny orchids; everywhere there are buried tree roots from the ancient Caledonian forest, a reminder that the area was not always so barren. From the main road near Loch Ba, six miles north of Bridge of Orchy, look east

Highland Cattle in Glencoe

across one of the wildest tracts in Scotland to the cone of Schiehallion rising to 1,085 m (3,547 ft) in the far distance.

Rannoch Moor and the Black Mount, the shoulder of hill that abuts its western edge and is traversed by the modern road, were always major obstacles on the old route to the isles. At Bridge of Orchy, General Wade's eighteenth-century military road strikes west towards Inveroran, and now, no longer used by traffic, offers an excellent short walk to the Inveroran Hotel on Loch Tulla over the Mam Carraigh pass, with excellent views of the moor and of the Black Mount. The main road can be rejoined by a track along the north shore of Loch Tulla. Even before Wade's day this was a drove road, and an old inn, long demolished, was a favoured resting place of the drovers taking Highland sheep to the great market at Falkirk.

Immediately on leaving the wastes of Rannoch Moor, the A82 road enters upon a desolation of an entirely different kind – the sombre grandeur of Glencoe, the Glen of Weeping. It is a forbidding place, even at high noon on a summer day, a place of dark, damp shadows heavy with the smell of menace. It would have been difficult to find a more appropriately theatrical and melodramatic setting for one of the great acts of treachery in the bloody history of Scotland.

In the early, snowy hours of 13 February 1692, 120 members of the Campbell clan, enlisted in the Duke of Argyll's Regiment and loyal to the new Protestant King, William III, slaughtered in cold blood thirty-eight men, women and children of the Macdonald clan upon whom they had been billeted in their tiny townships in the glen. Those who escaped the sword fled into the hills, many to die of exposure in the cruel winter cold.

It had been the sin of the Macdonalds to be tardy in swearing allegiance to the new monarch in the aftermath of the flight of King James II to France in 1688 and the subsequent collapse of the Jacobite cause. In all probability the King himself connived at the extermination of the recalcitrant clan.

The stones of the Macdonald townships are long scattered, and nothing remains in Glencoe of that evil night except the brooding memory of a great treachery.

But to Glencoe itself. It is a splendid example of a glacial valley carved out by the ice cap that covered Rannoch Moor and sought an escape route for its advance. The rocks of Glencoe are volcanic, chiefly of hard and resistant rhyolite, much harder than the Rannoch granite. As the advancing ice squeezed its way through the defile it left characteristic marks of its progress: grooving and polishing of the rocks and, most remarkably, great boulders of granite plucked from the floor of Rannoch and deposited on the mountain tops that form the northern wall of the glen.

As the road leaves Rannoch Moor there rears up on the left the 1,112 m (3,636 ft) peak of Meall a Bhuiridh, known to

climbers simply as 'M & B', with its chairlift opposite the lonely Kingshouse Hotel giving access to winter ski runs that offer a deal more speed and excitement than the gentler shoulders of the Cairngorms.

The glen proper begins a short distance further on, where its portals are guarded on the south side by the tremendous bulk of Buachaille Etive Mor, the Great Shepherd of Etive, with its cliff wall rising to a summit of 1,023 m (3,345 ft), and offering some of the most challenging rock and ice climbing in Britain. Beyond it is the Little Shepherd, Buachaille Etive Beag, 926 m (3,029 ft), and next to that westward the mass known as the Three Sisters of Glencoe – Beinn Fhada, 954 m (3,120 ft), Gearr Aonach, 765 m (2,500 ft), and the black rhyolite walls of Aonach Dubh, 871 m (2,849 ft) with Ossian's Cave visible on its north face. All three are outliers of the peak which rises behind them, Bidean Nam Bian, at 1,152 m (3,766 ft), the highest mountain in what used to be called Argyllshire.

There are no easy paths to the summits of these mountains, although the main shoulder of the Buachaille can be reached by a minor road and track which leaves the A82 about two miles beyond Kingshouse Hotel. The summit is more difficult, although it offers fine views of Ben Nevis to the north and the wild recesses of Glen Etive to the south.

As you enter the glen you can see on the north side the original route of General Wade's military road to Fort William, built in the 1790s, heading directly for Kinlochleven over the dauntingly steep path of the Devil's Staircase. The rest of the north side of the glen is formed by the superb six-mile mountain ridge of the Aonach Eagach, topping out at 969 m (3,168 ft) and offering exhilarating high-level walking for the sure-footed and experienced.

As the road approaches Glencoe village the dark vale opens out, the valley floor becomes lusher owing to an underlying outcrop of limestone, and the oppression of the inner valley is lifted. At Clachaig, at the western end of the glen, a visitor centre is operated by the National Trust for Scotland, today's owners of Glencoe. Just beyond the village of Ballachulish, whose ugly and now disused quarries once produced huge quantities of blue roofing slate, the Glencoe forest office marks the start of a short scenic walk to the Signal Rock; a tradition, unsupported by much fact, has it that from here the signal was given for the start of the Macdonald massacre.

From Ballachulish village the walker can tackle the horseshoe ridge of Beinn a Bheithir, 1,004 m (3,284 ft), somewhat less taxing than the Glencoe mountains and offering splendid views down Loch Linnhe and out to Mull and the Inner Hebrides. Alternatively, there is an eight-mile one-way expedition to be undertaken through the forest following the Laroch river from Ballachulish and crossing into Glen Creran.

North Ballachulish, at the mouth of Loch Leven

of hydro-electric power attracted an aluminium smelter, opened in 1907. Power was provided by damming the River Leven above the village and creating the huge artificial Blackwater Reservoir. Kinlochleven is a wet and gloomy place, made gloomier by the decline of the aluminium industry.

Across Loch Leven, with the distinctive quartzite Pap of Glencoe, 743 m (2,430 ft), rising above the surrounding schists and limestones of Glencoe village, we are now in the district of Lochaber. The main road wastes no time in heading directly along the eastern shore of Loch Linnhe to Fort William and the star attraction of the region, the highest mountain in the British Isles.

Ben Nevis excels not only in height, but in bulk. At 1,347 m (4,406 ft) it is an enormous lump, and its scale is not always appreciated because it is so often seen from close quarters. It is worth heading out of Fort William on the Mallaig road as far as Corpach in order to look back at the big ben; you need to be a little way away to appreciate it.

Nevertheless, seen from Fort William it looks impressive enough with its great western screes rising sharply from sea level on the Loch Linnhe shore. As a view, it will certainly do to be going on with.

It would be wrong to leave Glencoe without mentioning the lonely winding road that leaves the A82 not far from Kingshouse Hotel and heads south into Glen Etive. It is a long and ultimately dead-end track but it is worth exploring, for it is the only road to penetrate the southern battlements of Glencoe into the hinterland beyond. Loch Etive is an exceptionally long fjord with sides steep and narrow even by Scottish standards. The hills which press upon the glen and provide the valley walls which in some places drop 612 m (2,000 ft) into the loch, are of granite, in contrast to the volcanic lavas of Glencoe. The region is one of the largest granite intrusions in the Highlands, although considerably younger than the Cairngorms.

The Etive region is an excellent example of cauldron subsidence, where the ancient rocks have collapsed inwards not unlike the crater of a volcano, and the underlying molten granite has boiled upwards to fill the gap, being subsequently carved into its present shape by the passage of ice down Glen Etive. Nowhere is the grinding passage of the glacier more evident than in the great bare slabby sides of Ben Starav at the head of the loch.

But to return to Glencoe. Having passed out of the narrow defile the main road to Fort William passes over the new Ballachulish Bridge spanning the narrow entrance to Loch Leven where there was formerly a ferry. An alternative route is to drive round Loch Leven, taking the old road at its rightward fork in Glencoe village up to the little town of Kinlochleven, an oppressively dark industrial settlement created in the early years of this century when an abundance

Shaggy, long-horned Highland Cattle

The geology of Ben Nevis is complex, but in essence it is a mass of granite capped with hard lavas of the Old Red Sandstone period, the whole having been ground down by the passage of ice and of time. It exhibits the typical features of granite: tremendous corries and cliffs whose scale is without equal in Britain, displaying sheer precipices of up to 612 m (2,000 ft), particularly on its north-western flanks. In its north-facing corries patches of snow will lie easily from one winter to the next, a demonstration that the last Ice Age, and possibly the next, are not that far distant, and that it would take only a moderate change of climate for glaciers to form again in the high corries.

A glacier is, after all, only one winter's snow piled upon the last, and compressed to ice by the weight of succeeding winter snows.

More often than not the summit of the big ben is shrouded in cloud, and many a day tripper who treks to the summit by the easiest route is deeply disappointed that the drape seems resolutely unwilling to lift. The climate at the top of Nevis is vastly different from that at sea level in Fort William; the summit sits directly in the path of the vilest weather that may be driven in from the Atlantic.

It was because of the climatic difference between bottom and top that in 1884 a meteorological observatory was built on the summit, together with a pony track to give access to it. The opening of the observatory, which operated for some years with a staff of four, generated a great public desire to climb the mountain, and people ascended it in droves despite being charged a toll of one shilling to walk the pony track, or four shillings to ride a pony. The opening of the West Highland railway in 1894 brought even greater crowds to the mountain, and there was serious talk of building a railway to the summit in the manner of Snowdon.

At one time, and for a brief spell, there was a small hotel at the top, an extension to the observatory, built for the benefit of those who wished to be there for the sunrise. There are two kinds of people who go up mountains: those who pray for a hotel at the top, and those for whom a hotel destroys all reason for going up there. It should be well noted that there is now no hotel on the top of Ben Nevis.

Even the observatory has long gone, although its ruins remain. But the pony track is still there, and it affords the easiest ascent of the mountain, a long test of stamina rather than a climb full of interest, a lengthy expedition for which at least seven hours should be allowed, and the proper footwear and protective clothing worn. Do not be lured by tales of fell runners who make it from Fort William to the summit and back in under an hour and a half; fell runners are not like the rest of us. Do not be beguiled either by the story of the first motor car, a Model T Ford, to reach the summit in 1911. The descent may have taken two and a half hours, but the ascent took three days. And do not ever forget that, however soft the day in Fort William, the summit is subjected to constant howling, freezing wind.

The finest approach to Ben Nevis is undoubtedly by Glen Nevis, which strikes east from Fort William and curls round the south and west of the great ben. Others have described the glen as the only example of Himalayan scenery in Britain, reminiscent of the gorges of Nepal. It starts at sea level as a broad valley of cultivated fields and oakwoods and then, round a well-placed bend, enters the Nevis gorge where the river tumbles over a hard outcrop of quartzite, and high waterfalls cascade from the towering crags above. Nowhere else in Britain is it possible to stand and gaze up through 1,223 m (4,000 ft) of relief, and in more or less continuous slope. To do so, however, it is necessary to leave the car and climb, for the main summit is hidden from the Glen Nevis road. After passing through the Himalayan gorge, the glen path ascends to alpine high meadows, and eventually proceeds to the summit.

To the south is the Mamore range, a belt of schistose mountains topped with white quartzite rock which can easily be mistaken for a capping of snow. Two peaks, Stob Ban, 1,001 m (3,274 ft) and Sgurr a'Mhaim, 1,101 m (3,601 ft) can

Photographing Buachaille Etive Mor and Glencoe from Rannoch Moor

Sunset over Castle Stalker and the Lynn of Lorn

be approached by the track that leads from Achriabhach in Glen Nevis. From the head of the glen, where the metalled road ends, a twenty-five mile footpath strikes south-east across rough country to Rannoch Moor.

There are many other ways up Ben Nevis, almost all of them for the experienced. Every year the mountain claims more lives than any other in Britain. It is a tremendous challenge, its corries and huge rock walls providing un-rivalled sport for those who like to go up hills with little or nothing under their feet. Its summit is a bleak, boulder-strewn plateau devoid of vegetation, unlike the lower slopes which exhibit typical alpine and sub-arctic growths of mos-ses, lichens and saxifrages amongst the scree.

But from the top, on the occasional day when the brisk wind briefly whips away the trailing scarf of cloud, it is possible to see the saw-teeth of the Aonach Eagach ridge to the south, Ben Lawers in the central Highlands to the east, the Cuillins of Skye and the Paps of Jura seventy-seven miles

to the west, the peaks of the island of Rhum ninety-two miles towards America, and even the far hills of County Antrim at a distance of 120 miles. It is the ultimate view in Britain, but the mountain which offers it demands in return a substantial measure of respect.

To return for a moment to Glencoe. If, instead of cros-sing Ballachulish Bridge and heading north to Fort William, you continue to follow the A828 road south round the coast towards Oban, you come eventually to the national scenic area of Lynn of Lorn, at the mouth of Loch Linnhe. The area comprises part of the Appin shore with its fine old coastal castles of Stalker and Barcaldine, and the long narrow island of Lismore.

The area is unusual in the Highland scene because it is a substantial outcrop of limestone, producing a landscape that is not only lush, but small-scale and secluded. The island of Lismore, reached by ferry from Oban, still supports a popu-lation of 200 on a land that is rich with wild flowers and the scents of Wild Rose and Honeysuckle.

The North-West Highlands

MAINLAND SCOTLAND is only 440 km (275 miles) at most from north to south, yet its wildly indented coastline extends to more than 3,680 km (2,300 miles). The western seaboard from Kintyre to Cape Wrath is wondrously fretted with sea lochs and promontories, made all the more appealing by the constant yet ever-changing views west to the Hebrides, so tantalizingly near when the sun turns the sea to sapphire, yet so far on a winter ferry ploughing through the furious Minch.

It is the first long-awaited glimpse of those enchanted isles that thrills, and nowhere more so than when you are nearing the end of the traditional Road to the Isles, the route westward from Fort William occupied both by the much-improved A830 to Mallaig and the final miles of the West Highland Railway. That first electric sight, assuming the weather to be kind which often it is not, comes soon after Lochailort, where the hills of Moidart fall away and there, riding the sea, are the Small Isles dominated by the unmistakable peaks of Rhum. It is that view more than anything that makes the coast of Moidart and north Ardnamurchan a national scenic area.

Although deeply indented by the sea it is a gentle, intimate coast, well wooded and with occasional beaches of sparkling silver sand ground from the mica-rich igneous rocks. The road passes the heads of Loch Ailort and the wide Loch nan Uamh, the Loch of the Caves. From Lochailort a recently-built road has opened up the formerly trackless emptiness of Moidart, joining at Salen with the old and still inadequate road out to Britain's most westerly promontory at Ardnamurchan Point.

Something of the former silence of Moidart can still be captured by taking the minor roads which strike west from the new route at Glenuig, Blain and Acharacle, leading to the coast and further views of the isles.

Moidart's principal geological feature merits an adjoining national scenic area of its own. Loch Shiel is another of those long, deep trenches like Loch Lomond that ought to have been a fjord, but is only just prevented by a terminal moraine of glacial debris that blocks its mouth. Shiel, whose water is only six metres (twenty feet) above sea level, is a magnificent glacial trough when seen from the Glenfinnan end, its enclosing hills forming an interlocking pattern of purples and greens as far as the eye can see. The National Trust for Scotland maintains an information centre at Glenfinnan, by the monument marking the spot where Prince Charles Edward's standard was raised for the start of the 1745 rebellion.

The lower end of the loch is much less visited, but is accessible from the A861 road at Tarbet, where a minor road to Ariundle and Polloch leads into the Sunart Forest, to a nature trail through oakwoods leading to old lead mines and a splendid waterfall, and eventually to a fine viewpoint overlooking Loch Shiel and Loch Doilet at the foot of the deep, remote and heavily wooded Glen Hurich.

North of Mallaig the countryside immediately becomes infinitely wilder across the mouth of Loch Nevis in the peninsula of Knoydart, one of the roughest and emptiest areas of mainland Britain. Its value as a national scenic area stems from its penetration by the two sea lochs which form its southern and northern boundaries, Nevis and Hourn. Nevis is a typical western seaboard loch, but open of aspect because of the low hills on its southern side. Hourn, dark, gloomy and oppressively enclosed, is of all the ice-gouged sea lochs of the west the one which most closely approaches the proper definition of a Norwegian fjord, particularly in its sombre inner reach entrenched between steep and massive mountains, and with the fjord characteristic of a bar of terminal moraine not far below the water surface at its mouth.

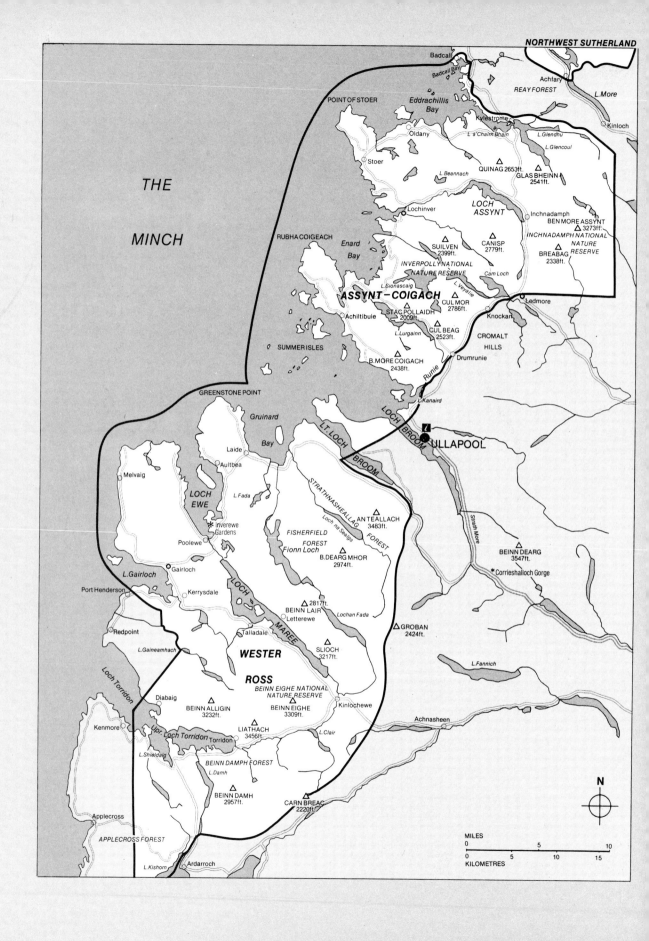

THE

MINCH

POINT OF STOER

Badcall

Badcall Bay

Eddrachillis Bay

Achfary

REAY FOREST

L.More

Kylestrome

Kinloch

Oldany

L.a'Chairn Bhain

L.Glendhu

Stoer

L.Glencoul

L.Beannach

QUINAG 2653ft.

GLAS BHEINN
2541ft.

Lochinver

LOCH ASSYNT

Inchnadamph

BEN MORE ASSYNT
3273ft.

RUBHA COIGEACH

Enard Bay

SUILVEN
2399ft.

CANISP
2779ft.

INCHNADAMPH NATIONAL NATURE RESERVE

BREABAG
2338ft.

INVERPOLLY NATIONAL NATURE RESERVE

L.Sionascaig

L.Veyatie

Cam Loch

ASSYNT–COIGACH

Achiltibuie

STAC POLLAIDH
2009ft.

CUL MOR
2786ft.

Ledmore

L.Lurgainn

CUL BEAG
2523ft.

Knockan

CROMALT HILLS

SUMMER ISLES

B.MORE COIGACH
2438ft.

Drumrunie

Runie

GREENSTONE POINT

L.Kanaird

Gruinard Bay

LT.LOCH BROOM

LOCH BROOM

ULLAPOOL

Laide

Aultbea

Melvaig

LOCH EWE

L.Fada

Strath More

STRATHNASHEALLAG

AN TEALLACH
3483ft.

Loch na Sealga

FOREST

*Inverewe Gardens

FISHERFIELD FOREST
Fionn Loch

B.DEARG MHOR
2974ft.

BEINN DEARG
3547ft.

Poolewe

*Corrieshalloch Gorge

L.Gairloch

Gairloch

LOCH MAREE

Kerrysdale

2817ft.
BEINN LAIR

Lochan Fada

GROBAN
2424ft.

Port Henderson

Letterewe

Redpoint

Talladale

SLIOCH
3217ft.

L.Fannich

L.Gaineamhach

WESTER

L.Clair

ROSS

BEINN EIGHE NATIONAL NATURE RESERVE

Kinlochewe

Achnasheen

Loch Torridon

Diabaig

BEINN ALLIGIN
3232ft.

BEINN EIGHE
3309ft.

Kenmore

Upr. Loch Torridon

LIATHACH
3456ft.

Torridon

L.Shieldaig

BEINN DAMH FOREST

L.Damh

BEINN DAMH
2957ft.

CARN BREAC
2220ft.

Applecross

APPLECROSS FOREST

L.Kishorn

Ardarroch

N

MILES
0   5   10

KILOMETRES
0   5   10   15

Before the Clearances this peninsula supported a population of over 1,000, mainly on the northern shore of Loch Nevis, but it is now a desolate and empty place, a huge private estate virtually uninhabited and crossed by no road. Its topography is rough and bare, carved mainly from metamorphosed sandstones and shales rather than from the usually more resistant Lewisian gneiss. To the east of this trackless waste, to be explored only by ardent lovers of rough country, the mountains rise to 1,043 m (3,410 ft) in Sgurr na Ciche. Its beauty is in its very wildness and inaccessibility, for there is no road access to its depths from the landward, only by sea from Mallaig to the tiny settlement of Inverie on the Nevis shore, the only remaining habitation in Knoydart, or by private boat across Loch Hourn from Arnisdale.

Loch Hourn is accessible to the motorist, but only by long journeys on narrow, steep and hairpinned roads. One of the loneliest roads in Scotland leaves the main A87 Invergarry to Kyle of Lochalsh route by the shores of Loch Garry, and strikes west through the emptiness of Lochaber, across the great divide of the north-west Highlands by Glen Garry and Loch Quoich, to descend by a staircase of hair-raising hairpins through a waterfall filled gorge to arrive at a dead end by the grim and sunless headwaters of Hourn. The alternative approach is to leave the A87 at the head of Loch Duich, follow the footsteps of Boswell and Johnson over the Mam Ratagan pass, and take the narrow road round the coast from Glenelg to Corran on Hourn's northern shore. The two road ends are eight miles apart, and are joined by a rough path along the northern lochside.

The head of the Mam Ratagan pass between Shiel Bridge and Glenelg is one of the best points from which to view a range of Highland mountains which, although not the highest, are certainly among the most elegant, and are rightly named as a national scenic area.

The Five Sisters of Kintail rise sheer from the Glen Shiel roadside, and are among the steepest and highest grass-covered slopes in Scotland. The majestic range reaches its highest peak in Sgurr Fhuaran 1,072 m (3,505 ft). Facing this handsome battlement across Glen Shiel is the 1,014 m (3,317 ft) height of The Saddle, and behind them to the north rises the 1,035 m (3,383 ft) mass of Beinn Fhada. This is the watershed of Scotland, despite its being much nearer the west coast than the east. The River Croe rises near Kintail's highest peak and rushes westwards towards Loch Duich and the Inner Sound of Raasay. A short distance away the River Affric rises on Beinn Fhada at the start of a course which leads it at a less hurried pace to the Beauly Firth near Inverness.

Sgurr Fhuaran is an outstanding viewpoint, reached most easily by way of its western ridge on a track that begins a mile and a half east of Shiel Bridge. Although not difficult,

Loch Loyne, desolate and dramatic

it is an unrelieved uphill slog all the way. Glen Croe, which forms a deep gully between the Five Sisters and Beinn Fhada behind, is also the first section of an eighteen-mile walk across rough country over the watershed and into Glen Affric to meet the dead-end road from Cannich to Affric Lodge.

The streams which tumble down the western side of the Highland watershed here are short, fast and steep and one of them, the Glomach Burn, provides one of Britain's highest waterfalls. The burn flows northwards off the slopes of Beinn Fhada, and soon enters a narrow gorge on a rapid descent through 229 m (750 ft). The most spectacular part is where the burn plunges over a ledge for a sheer drop of 92 m (300 ft), bounces off a rock ledge, and tumbles another fifty feet into a boiling pool. To reach the falls entails a long, rough but ultimately rewarding walk from Morvich at the head of Loch Duich.

Since 1944 the whole area has been owned by the National Trust for Scotland; their visitor centre at Morvich gives helpful guidance on walking, climbing and how to avoid the guns in the late summer deer-stalking season.

Behind the Kintail ridge, stretching far away to the north-east, is one of Scotland's longest and loveliest glens, Glen Affric. Only hardy walkers will enter it from this, its western end; the more normal approach is by the A831 road from Drumnadrochit on Loch Ness to Cannich, and then by minor road which follows river and lochside to Affric Lodge. Affric was suggested as a national park in 1948, for it is a classic Highland glen with all the necessary components, blending into a scene which, while less grand and wild than the far north-west, is still the very essence of Scottish upland scenery, and well deserves its national scenic area status.

On its north side Glen Affric is bounded by the highest mountains in the north-west Highlands, Carn Eige 1,186 m (3,877 ft) and Mam Soul 1,181 m (3,862 ft), yet the lower slopes and the valley floor are richly clothed in one of the finest remaining remnants of the native Caledonian Scots Pine forest, overlooking the bright waters of Loch Affric and Loch Beneveian. The glen is almost entirely owned by the Forestry Commission, and the forestry office has details of walks through the pinewoods and other marked forestry trails in this loveliest of glens, whose waters are harnessed in a hydro-electric dam at Fasnakyle. Besides the old Scots Pine forest the slopes are clothed with Birch, open enough to permit a rich undergrowth of heathers and Blaeberry, and to be home to Red and Roe Deer, Fox, Badger, Wildcat and Pine Marten. Its essential romantic Scottishness was appreciated by Landseer, the master of Victorian romantic painters.

A short distance to the north of Glen Affric is another of the long deep eastern-facing troughs whose waters feed the River Beauly. Glen Strathfarrar, reached from the A831 on its continuation north from Cannich, is less majestic than Affric, and has been somewhat spoiled by a hydro-electric scheme, but its middle portion from Loch Beannacharan to the Culligran Falls rates as a national scenic area, where again the steep hillsides are clothed in rich old Scots Pine, and the shining River Farrar alternately rushes towards the falls or meanders placidly through the glen's two lochs. Part of the pine forest is a national nature reserve.

To return to the main A87 road, which after passing through Glen Shiel proceeds towards Kyle of Lochalsh, the main ferry port for Skye. Shortly before there the route to the far north-west branches off to the right as the A890 and strikes north into the entirely different landscape of Wester Ross, which at 145,300 hectares (359,000 acres) is by far the largest of Scotland's national scenic areas.

Wester Ross national scenic area stretches from the shores of Loch Carron to Little Loch Broom, and encompasses some of the very finest of Scottish scenery in a land already replete with grandeur. Not only does it include six of the great mountain groups of Scotland, it contains one of its best freshwater lochs, one of its premier national nature reserves, and one of its outstanding sea lochs. The region is sometimes called the last great wilderness of Britain, but wilderness is a grossly over-used term; Wester Ross contains a wealth of scenic and geological interest, and its ruggedness is softened by much that is undeniably picturesque.

Journeying north from Kyle of Lochalsh, the traveller almost immediately crosses a geological watershed and enters upon a topography that is essentially different from the rest of the Highlands. This far north-western seaboard is built chiefly from Lewisian gneiss and Torridonian sandstone, the two oldest rocks in the British Isles and among the oldest known rocks in the world.

The vast convulsions occurring over millions of years which shaped the Grampian highlands did not reach this far. The thrusting and folding of rocks which gave the rest of Scotland a perplexingly complex geological structure ran out here. The great period of mountain building, the Caledonian Orogeny, when the face of Scotland was put in the melting pot, came up against the ancient unyielding gneiss of the north-west, and stopped; the gneiss would not be moved. The line of meeting between the southern rocks and the immovable table of gneiss is well charted and is known as the Moine Thrust, a well-defined line which runs from Loch Carron to the Kyle of Durness in Sutherland. Along it can be seen evidence of shattering and immense folding where the forces of mountain-building met their match. To the west of that line the landscape is unimaginably old, an ice-scoured platform of tough, hummocky gneiss which refuses to break down into fertile soil, overlain with great mountains of Torridonian sandstone, rounded and massive.

The high ground of north Sutherland, looking towards Ben Hope

Cloud on the peak of Arkle, after which the famous racehorse was named

North of Loch Carron, the first major part of Wester Ross is the bulge of the Applecross peninsula, carved from Torridonian sandstone into a high rough moorland, reaching a summit of 898 m (2,936 ft) in Beinn Bhan. It is a somewhat featureless landscape, and its chief source of interest is the dizzy mountain road, one of the highest in Britain, which crosses it. The road, Bealach na Ba, the Pass of the Cattle,

begins at the head of Loch Kishorn, within sight of the oil platform building yard where in 1978 was built and launched the world's largest movable object, a massive concrete platform for the Ninian field. Using the sides of a huge corrie sculpted by ice from the walls of the plateau, the road rises in a series of wild hairpin bends with superb views (for the passengers at least) back down to Kishorn, until it reaches its summit of 628 m (2,053 ft) and looks down on a magnificent panorama of Skye and the inner isles. From there the road descends to the tiny village of Applecross, where an outcrop of limestone provides a coastal band of lush vegetation in sharp contrast to the high dun moorland.

Until 1976 this difficult, exposed and dangerous road was Applecross's only landward link with the rest of the world, and it continues a further four miles to the tiny harbour of Toscaig, which used to be the peninsula's main link with the outside world. In recent years a new road has been driven round the north of the peninsula from Shieldaig, offering little in the way of remarkable scenery but promising a glimpse of Sea Otters.

After traversing the waist of Applecross, the main A896 road descends into Shieldaig, bursting upon the bright white village through a stand of pines which provide a curtain of surprise to the view which awaits. You are now on the southern shore of Upper Loch Torridon surrounded by a tremendous arc of some of Scotland's finest mountains while just offshore the National Trust for Scotland's Shieldaig Island carries a fine stand of nineteenth-century pines that offset the bareness of the encircling hills.

Before you are the mountains of Torridon, the oldest mountains on earth, which at 750 million years make the Himalayas mere geological infants.

They are not high mountains by world standards, reaching a maximum of only 1,057 m (3,456 ft). But they are

Oldshoremore Beach, North-West Sutherland

beautiful mountains by any standard, their grandeur and emptiness softened by the waters of Loch Torridon and its tree-clad shores. To the west, directly opposite Shieldaig on the north Torridon shore, is Beinn Alligin, its three peaks reaching a top summit of 988 m (3,232 ft), and the least arduous for the hill walker. At the head of the loch is the tremendous skyline of Liathach, a great five-mile ridge of seven craggy peaks, the highest reaching 1,057 m (3,456 ft). Liathach is a mass of ancient sandstone, but the ridge is topped by a capping of sparkling white Cambrian quartzite like the icing on a cake, which can give the appearance of midsummer snow.

Liathach means 'The Grey One', probably from the mass of screes that spill down its precipitous southern slopes. The quartzite capping is even more pronounced on the huge seven-mile long summit ridge of Beinn Eighe which rises to 1,012 m (3,309 ft) and exhibits on its north face a stupendous corrie with 398 m (1,300 ft) sheer sandstone walls plunging from the summit to a lochan below.

This is mountain walking country without equal in Scotland, although the summit ridges of Liathach and Beinn Eighe are the exclusive province of the experienced. But there is much exploration of a less arduous kind to be done, and the National Trust for Scotland's visitor centre on the main road at Torridon will provide details, as well as a full exposition of the region's wildlife.

The mountains can be seen to great benefit and without too much difficulty by driving the minor dead-end road from Torridon along the north shore of the loch; the road which twists and heaves over the hummocky shore is an exploration in itself. From near Torridon House there is a fine ten-mile mountain walk over the shoulder of Beinn Alligin and down Glen Grudie on the far side to Loch Maree. The path has the double attraction of displaying the spectacular northern side

of Beinn Eighe, while at the same time keeping in view the superb slab of Slioch, a great square mountain that soars from the northern shore of Loch Maree.

The long-distance walker may prefer to continue along the north Torridon shore from Diabaig where the road peters out, stopping overnight at the lonely youth hostel of Craig, and continuing to join up with the minor road at Redpoint. There have been proposals to join these two roads to make one of the most dazzling round trips in the Highlands.

In 1951 the eastern side of Beinn Eighe northwards to Loch Maree was created the first national nature reserve in Britain, chiefly to preserve a substantial remnant on the loch shore of the Caledonian Pine forest which covered much of northern Scotland from the end of the last Ice Age some 8,000 years ago. Many of the Scots Pines still standing are 250 years old, a tiny portion of the forest that has been felled continuously since the coming of man to build boats, smelt iron, or flush out wolves. The reserve has a nature trail exhibiting the typical flora of Scottish deer forest country and the geology of the Moine Thrust, including the tiny half-inch fossil worm casts in the quartzite that are among the earliest known signs of life in the British Isles. Visitors should call at the reserve centre at Aultroy on the A832 just west of Kinlochewe; as the reserve is part of a larger red deer management programme covering much of Torridon, guidance on where to walk is advisable from late August until November.

Besides the Red Deer which roam Torridon in great numbers, the region is also the home of Roe Deer, Pine Marten and Wildcat, while the skies are the province of Golden Eagle, Buzzard, Ptarmigan and Merlin.

At Kinlochewe the Torridon road meets the A832 which has struck across country from Inverness, and continues west along the southern shore of Loch Maree, a handsome ribbon of water that is one of the key elements in this national scenic area. The northern shore of the loch is remarkably straight, having been gouged by the ice along an existing fault line in the gneissic rocks. The juxtaposition of gneiss and sandstone is nowhere better displayed than in the majestic slab of Slioch, raising its broad shoulder 984 m (3,217 ft) above the still blue water. The division between the two rocks can be plainly seen; the lower gneissic part of Slioch is an ancient landscape indeed, being the face of Scotland as it was 600 million years ago, before the gneiss was overlaid with sandstone. Now the sandstone has weathered away again to expose the original landscape.

Besides the pinewoods of the Beinn Eighe reserve, much of the southern shore of Loch Maree is clothed in native Oak; this indeed is the northern limit of Oak in the British Isles. The Oak too was almost a threatened species, being felled in the eighteenth century in huge quantities to provide charcoal for what was then the largest iron smelter in the Highlands, across the loch at Letterewe. The iron ore came from Cumberland, shipped to Poolewe.

The road leaves Loch Maree and strikes west to the coast and to an entirely different landscape, a scene of beaches and caravans and holidaymakers in crowds, a shock after the solitude of Torridon. Gairloch is the main settlement between Kyle of Lochalsh and Ullapool, and has all the facilities of a small tourist centre. The minor B8021 road out of the village leads to a succession of beaches and crofting townships on its way to Melvaig and a peninsula which is otherwise unexciting. But a short way along the main road,

at Poolewe, you come upon a most unlikely sight – palm trees growing by the shore of Loch Ewe amid a startling blaze of rhododendrons.

The creation of the sub-tropical gardens of Inverewe was the inspiration and life's work of a determined Victorian laird, Osgood Mackenzie, who in 1865 set out to tame a bare windswept peninsula covered with barren and unyielding Torridonian soil. He began by planting a shelter belt of Scots and Corsican Pines without which his garden could not flourish, for although the Gulf Stream brings exceptional mildness to this shore it also brings an average of sixty inches of rain a year, mostly delivered in salty squalls by tearing gusts of wind. The soil had to be brought in a basket at a time and fertilized with seaweed and dead fish. The story of its creation is told best by Mackenzie himself in his memoir, *A Hundred Years In The Highlands*.

Today the garden's ten hectares (twenty-four acres) exhibit some 2,500 species. It is best known for its rhododendrons, but many other exotic plants flourish in the improbable atmosphere of Wester Ross: Flame Flowers of Chile, Coral plants and Glory Flowers, *Clematis*, *Hydrangea*, American Avalanche Lilies, *Eucalyptus*, and what is claimed to be the largest *Magnolia* tree in the world with a circumference of over twenty-one metres (seventy feet). The garden, owned by the National Trust for Scotland, is at its best in May and June when the rhododendrons are in full flower.

North of Inverewe, what is now the continuation of the A832 by Gruinard Bay and the southern shore of Little Loch

Eilean Donnan Castle, Dornie

Broom was once known as Destitution Road. It was built by virtual slave labour in 1851 by crofters driven to extremes of hunger by the potato famine, who sold their labour to build this highway in return for miserable amounts of food. As the road skirts the loch and out of the national scenic area the prospect ahead is of the great jagged mass of An Teallach raising the Torridonian sandstone to 1,065 m (3,484 ft) in this northern outpost of the Torridon range, before the even wilder country of Assynt–Coigach begins.

Before leaving Gruinard Bay, however, you should be aware of Gruinard Island just off-shore, which was used for bacteriological warfare experiments in 1940 and remains infected with deadly anthrax to this day.

The north shore of Loch Broom marks the beginning of the national scenic area of Assynt and Coigach, geologically similar to Torridon yet quite different in appearance, exhibiting a wildness that is almost lunar and is certainly unique among British landscapes.

We are still in the ancient land of the Lewisian gneiss. But here its overlayer of only slightly younger Torridonian sandstone has been ground and weathered away much more

than in Torridon, and the result is a vast, low, flat and knobbly sea of gneiss from which rise a few steep and isolated sandstone peaks, producing a landscape which many claim is the most dramatic in Scotland. The mountains are of modest height, generally between 765 and 917 m (2,500 and 3,000 ft), but their isolation and their often near-vertical sides give them the appearance of being much higher as they rise suddenly and unexpectedly from the ice-scoured platform of gneiss, pitted with countless tiny lochans and dressed in the drab garb of moorland peat.

Beyond Ullapool the A835 road first skirts the landward end of the peninsula of Coigach, dominated by the first of those isolated peaks, Ben More Coigach 746 m (2,438 ft), a relatively flat-topped dome rather less wild and weird than those still to come. A minor road winds round the peninsula to the remote crofting settlement of Achiltibuie overlooking the enchantingly-named Summer Isles, an archipelago of eighteen sandstone islands that once supported a population of several hundred but which have been deserted for many years. They can be visited by boat from Achiltibuie, a charming excursion that has the distant mountains of Torridon for a theatrical backdrop.

Ten miles north of Ullapool the main road is overhung by a dark mile-long cliff that is one of the key sites of Scottish

The ruins of Ardvreck Castle, Loch Assynt

geology. This is Knockan Cliff, where all the principal rocks of which Scotland is built are laid open for inspection, and where in 1883 the existence of the Moine Thrust was proved. The thrust was discovered because the schist rocks at the top of the cliff are older and more altered than those which lie immediately beneath, thus defying the normal geological order of having the oldest rocks at the bottom and the youngest at the top. It was therefore deduced that the schists had arrived there from somewhere else, from the east, and had been pushed in some cataclysmic earth movement on top of the existing rocks of Knockan. It was a major scientific discovery and led to the discovery of many other similar mountain-building movements elsewhere on the earth.

The cliff forms part of the Inverpolly national nature reserve, the second largest in Britain. A visitor centre and a one-and-a-half-mile nature trail explain the cliff fully and simply. The trail rises to 321 m (1,050 ft), requiring care and good footwear.

A short distance to the west, lying in the heart of the nature reserve, the splendid peak of Stac Polly rears up from the low hummocky gneiss, its summit ridge rising to 614 m (2,009 ft). Like the Torridon peaks it was once capped with tough white quartzite, but it has long been worn away and the remaining sandstone has been weathered and splintered to a spiky coxcomb. Stac Polly is reached with relative ease by a track from the Achiltibuie road.

To the west of Stac Polly another minor road strikes north towards Lochinver and an attractive and little-visited stretch of coast where the Lewisian platform slides under the sea in a pattern of skerries and tiny bays. As the road approaches Lochinver it offers to the east the remarkable sight of Suilven, which although far from being the highest Scottish mountain, at only 734 m (2,399 ft), it is perhaps the most unusual and dramatic of all. From the low, treeless landscape of naked gneiss it rears with breathtaking suddenness on all sides, a startling sugar loaf surrounded by near-vertical cliffs, a lonely pillar of sandstone that is un-questionably one of the finest and least-expected views in the north-west. To its east is the slightly higher and only slightly less dramatic peak of Canisp at 850 m (2,779 ft), another eruption from the barren plain that is so unyielding that not even heather will grow on it.

Every so often, however, the moorland drabness changes to a patch of much more vividly green vegetation, an almost certain indication that an outcrop of limestone has intruded into the gneiss. Such an outcrop exists at Inchnadamph, on the main A837 road as it approaches the eastern end of Loch Assynt with its picturesque ruin of Ardvreck Castle. Whereas the gneiss supports little more than lichens and coarse grasses, the Assynt limestone abounds in Mountain Avens, Bladder and Holly Fern and Purple Saxifrage.

To the east of Inchnadamph rises the region's highest peak, Ben More Assynt 1,000 m (3,273 ft); it is different in character from the isolated peaks of Stac Polly and Suilven, being altogether more massive, formed from a complex structure of Lewisian gneiss and sedimentary rocks of the Ordovician–Silurian period, younger than the Torridon sandstone. For Ben More Assynt is east of the Moine Thrust, and belongs therefore to the main Highland mass rather than to the ancient floor of the earth exposed in the far north-west.

Just beyond Skiag Bridge on the A894 road to the north-west, the knobbly mountain of Glas Bheinn 777 m (2,541 ft) on the east side of the road conceals Britain's highest waterfall. The little burn of the Eas a Chual Aluinn leaps 202 m (660 ft), about four times the height of Niagara, although the volume of water spilling down the cliff is only a fraction of that other more celebrated cascade. Access is not easy, and requires a three-mile trek across rough country from the main road two miles south of Kylesku.

Beyond Loch Assynt the scene is dominated by the lone peak of Quinag 811 m (2,653 ft), another sandstone hump with a white quartzite capping.

As the main road approaches Kylesku to cross Loch a' Chairn Bhain, the Sutherland mountains become ever more bare and bleak, but the coastline around the shores of Eddrachillis Bay more than compensates. The minor road west from Unapool, steep and winding, travels through some of the best of the gneiss country, ending at the Point of Stoer where the old red sandstone takes over in cliffs of 122 m (400 ft) and in the 61 m (200 ft) sea stack of the Old Man of Stoer, a sheer sandstone needle considered utterly unclimb-able until it was finally conquered in 1966.

One final example of the gneiss country is designated a national scenic area, the bare shores of Loch Laxford to the north of Eddrachillis Bay. Between the A894 and the sea is a good example of knock-and-lochan topography, the essence of gneiss landscape with ice-shaved hummocks, bare rock outcrops and countless lochans, so many that few even have a name. The coast is largely remote and inaccessible, but one minor road leads to the hamlet of Tarbet, where in summer a launch plies regularly to Handa Island.

Handa is an outcrop of red Torridon sandstone, inhab-ited until the potato famine of the 1850s, and still displaying the ruins of a settlement and a graveyard. Today it is a major bird sanctuary in the care of the Royal Society for the Protec-tion of Birds, the home of more than 100,000 Guillemots, Kittiwakes, Herring Gulls, Fulmars and Puffins, packing every ledge of the 300 ft cliffs. Visitors may follow a nature trail.

Handa is also as good a place as any from which to look back into the empty heartland of Sutherland, the most thinly populated area of Britain, and to what are almost the last

A keeper and his terriers, Kinbrace, Sutherland

Though we have almost reached the northern limit of mainland Britain, the Highland mountains still have one final display in hand. The A838 road which winds a tortuous and lonely route round the north-western corner comes eventually to the broad inlet of the Kyle of Tongue. This deep tidal inlet, picturesque in itself with its varied woodlands, crofting settlements, indented bays and sandy beaches, is framed in the last great mountain backdrop of all, the assymetric cone of Ben Hope 930 m (3,040 ft) and the four granite peaks of Ben Loyal 766 m (2,504 ft). The policies* and gardens of Tongue House on the eastern shore of the Kyle help to soften and humanize what would otherwise be a stern prospect.

This is the last Highland outpost. To continue east on the A836 is to enter the drab flatland of Caithness, a county famed not for mountains, but for paving stones.

The eastern seaboard of the northern Highlands is of a character entirely different from the west, less riven by the sea, less barren, and less grand. But it has pleasures of its own, particularly in the only inlet of great size, the Dornoch Firth, the sole national scenic area of the far north-east.

The firth is the drowned valley of the River Oykel, which rises high on Ben More Assynt and flows into the sea here through the least spoilt of all the great eastern Scottish estuaries, and the only one not to have attracted some kind of heavy industry. High hills crowd down to its shore, which is variously and luxuriously wooded, while the tidal water itself is a constantly changing pattern of bays, beaches and sand spits, the result of glacial debris brought down from central Sutherland. Good pasture and arable land abound on the alluvial flood plain and the whole scene, although less majestic than the stern west, remains pleasantly untouched by the twentieth century.

* In Scotland the word 'policies' means pleasure gardens surrounding a mansion.

outliers of the Scottish Highland massif. Ben Stack, Arkle and Foinaven are of gneiss with cappings of ancient quartzite, but no sandstone, that having been worn away even before the quartzite was laid down. Arkle 789 m (2,580 ft) has a great corrie on its northern face, hung with waterfalls. They are remote, forbidding mountains, far from any road, but their fame has spread far beyond the circles of dedicated climbers; the late Duchess of Westminster, who owned this barren tract, bestowed the names of her mountains upon her racehorses.

The Scottish Islands

National Scenic Areas:

Shetland	St Kilda
Hoy and West Mainland, Orkney	South Uist Machair
Trotternish, Skye	Loch na Keal, Mull
The Cuillin Hills, Skye	Scarba, Lunga and the Garvellachs
The Small Isles	Jura
South Lewis, Harris and North Uist	North Arran

IT WAS a chastening lesson to stand on the ramparts of Edinburgh Castle one crisp April day and overhear a Birmingham schoolteacher test her charges' knowledge of British geography. She directed their gaze across the five-mile wide estuary of the Firth of Forth and asked them what they could see. The consensus of twelve-year old opinion was that the low hills of Fife were the Shetland Islands.

IT WAS not their fault. The Shetlands suffer from being too often displayed on maps of the British Isles as a box in the corner, thus giving an entirely false impression of their true position, which is well off the top of the page. They are fourteen hours away by car ferry from Aberdeen, beyond the latitudes of Leningrad or Labrador, and on a level with the lower reaches of Greenland and Alaska. They are such a separate entity that until 1469 they belonged to Norway, their nearest large town is Bergen, and Shetlanders journeying south will talk of going, not to the mainland, but to Scotland, as though it were another country. In all but name, it is.

The shattered archipelago of Shetland consists of 117 islands, of which a mere twenty are inhabited. It is a low, treeless land, crouching in the northern sea as though ducking under the ceaseless ferocious wind. It is a drowned world, inundated by the oceans which rose with the melting ice of the last glaciation, to such an extent that nowhere in Shetland is more than three miles from the sea. The sea dominates the land, and has created some of the most intricate coastal scenery in the British Isles. It is the kind of terrain that was beloved of the Vikings for raiding and settlement, and almost every Shetland place name is of Norse origin.

The principal national scenic area of the islands is the west coast of Mainland from Fitful Head to The Deeps, where a combination of deep inlets (known locally as 'voes'), cliffs, stacks and skerries produce a dramatic oceanic landscape enhanced by a sky which, in Shetland, always seems as huge as the skies of western Russia.

Farther north on the western seaboard, not far from the oil terminal at Sullom Voe, the coastal character changes to tall cliffs where a thick layer of Old Red Sandstone sits atop the ancient gneiss, and the drama of St Magnus Bay is continued in another scenic area at Esha Ness, and again at the end of the North Roe peninsula, including the offshore reserve of the Royal Society for the Protection of Birds on Ramna Stacks.

Two of Shetland's outliers are national scenic areas in themselves. The first is Foula, fourteen miles west of the Mainland and laying fair claim to being the most isolated community in the British Isles. Forty-odd people cling to life here, often cut off for weeks at a time by wicked winter seas. Here there is no hotel, nor pub, nor accommodation of any

kind for the casual visitor, which is as well for remote communities derive neither dignity nor long-term benefit from
being turned into a day tripper's menagerie.

Foula is home to a very large number of Great and
Arctic Skuas but its outstanding feature, appreciated only by
circumnavigating the island in a small boat, is the Kame of
Foula, a stupendous vertical sea-cliff wall of ochre-coloured
sandstone rising 420 m (1,373 ft) perpendicular from the
waves, a cliff exceeded in height in the British Isles only by
the ramparts of St Kilda.

Shetland's other national scenic area outlier is the celebrated Fair Isle, midway between Orkney and Shetland. At
twenty-five miles' distance from mainland Shetland it is
further than Foula, but the distance has been greatly reduced
by the building of an airstrip. The island, once threatened
with total depopulation, has seen a healthy regeneration
since it fell under the ownership of the National Trust for
Scotland, although to discourage would-be dropouts those
who would live there are closely questioned not only on their
willingness, but their ability, to pursue the crofting life.

Fair Isle is a low-lying island save for the steep pro-
tuberance of Sheep Rock, on whose grassy top the islanders
until very recently grazed sheep, scaling the cliffs with the
animals tied to their backs. Apart from its woollen jerseys,
Fair Isle is best known for one of the foremost bird obser-
vatories in Europe lying directly on the great migration
route, where more than 300 species have been recorded since
it opened in 1948.

But those who would tread the *Ultima Thule* of the
British Isles must head north from the Shetland mainland,
hopping across two ferries to the island of Unst and the most
northerly scenic area of all at Hermaness, where the ancient
gneiss on which Scotland is founded finally fades away in a
ragged edge of coast, and makes its final appearance in the
rock of Muckle Flugga and, last of all, the sea-washed pimple
of the Out Stack. There is no more land until you cross the
ocean of the North Pole and meet the far northern edge of
Siberia on the other side.

The national nature reserve at Hermaness is one of
Britain's major breeding grounds of cliff birds: Gannet,
Puffin, Kittiwake, Guillemot, Fulmar and Shag in their
thousands, and most of all the 'bonxie', the Shetlanders'
name for the aggressive Great Skua, which will attack not
only other birds, but human visitors should they get in its
way.

The national scenic areas of Shetland are remote, that of
Orkney much less so, lying as it does on the daily car ferry
route from Scrabster to Stromness, now Orkney's principal
link with mainland Britain. Orkney is a kindlier scene than
Shetland, and is one of the most productive agricultural
counties of Britain, a rich, inhabited landscape of low rolling
hills and lush pasture. By contrast, the Old Red Sandstone of

the west side of the island of Hoy rises to a great wall of
deeply red cliffs that reach a sheer 349 m (1,140 ft) at St
John's Head. In front of the cliffs is one of the great geological curiosities of the north, the slender 450-ft pillar of the Old
Man of Hoy, a perpendicular stack of sandstone eroded
away from its parent cliff.

The Norsemen were right to name it Hoy: the High
Island. From the landward side the high plateau that ends in
the clifftop is a bare and desolate place, the home of the only
known eagles in Orkney, and so unlike the rest of the islands.
As the ferry turns east into Hoy Sound and passes the
entrance to Scapa Flow, the landscape softens to a more
typical rolling Orcadian scene, and the little town of Stromness built to the very water's edge is a welcoming harbour
after the grandeur of the cliffs.

Orkney and Shetland together form Scotland's northern
isles, but infinitely better known are the Hebrides of the
west, of which the largest of the inner islands is Skye, the
'Winged Island', so called from its long jutting peninsulas
which on the map give the impression of wings. The northernmost of those peninsulas is Trotternish; the A855 road
north from the island capital of Portree leads to the national
scenic area enclosing the finest example of landslip topography in Britain – the Quirang.

For twenty miles from Portree the road runs beneath a
high black saw-toothed escarpment of basaltic lava, a dark
frowning wall that is rarely below 306 m (1,000 ft) in height.
As the road skirts Staffin Bay it comes upon the Quirang, one
of the strangest hills in Scotland, a wild jumble of needle-
point cliffs, peaks and stacks tumbling towards the sea, the
dramatic evidence of a giant landslip which probably
occurred when the retreating Pleistocene ice cap caused
instability and large-scale faulting in the lava sheet, which at
this point is so contorted by ancient geological pressure that
its layers lie almost vertical.

The Quirang is easily reached by a path from the minor
road between Staffin and Uig, and it leads not so much on to
the hill as into it. It is possible to wander through the spires,
clefts and needles and imagine yourself in some giant ruined
cathedral, and among the jumble to come across the most
surprising feature, a high round table of brilliant green grass
as flat as a bowling green. The black lava of the hillsides is
enclosed in bright lush grass and a profusion of wild flowers.
To complete the scene the windows of the rock cathedral
offer magnificent views over the Sound of Raasay to the
mountains of Wester Ross. It is altogether improbable,
uncanny, unique.

Skye's dominant and most familiar feature is, however,
the mighty shark-toothed ridge of gabbro that forms the
Black Cuillin Hills, one of the outstanding high-level mountain walks in the British Isles which warrants a national scenic
area of its own. Many would place the Cuillins as the most

Puffin on Fair Isle

spectacular heights in Britain, for although their highest summit of Sgurr Alasdair reaches only 1,012 m (3,309 ft) – modest by Cairngorm standards – taken in their entirety they are an awesome range, with twenty peaks over 917 m (3,000 ft).

The Cuillins were formed by a large intrusion of molten rock, or magma, rising through the lavas of the Tertiary period which already covered Skye. They are formed chiefly of gabbro, a crystalline igneous rock beloved of climbers because of the way it weathers. Being harder than granite it resisted the effects of glaciation better, and the subsequent action of frost and ice has caused it to shatter in blocks rather than to rot, giving the climber ledges and handholds wherever he reaches. The shattering has produced great screes, the Great Stone Shoot which tumbles 459 m (1,500 ft) from the summit of Sgurr Alasdair to a lochan far below being the best known. There is no better illustration of the difference between gabbro and granite than between the spiky ridge of the Black Cuillin and the rounded granite humps of the Red Cuillin just to the east above the village of Broadford, their

smooth profiles looking as though they had been turned out of a pudding basin.

The Cuillin ridge is visible from a wide and far-flung arc of the Hebrides, and is the dominant geological feature of the Western Isles. The ridge is a walk for the experienced climber, who will have to move if he wants to complete it in a day; better to go equipped for a high-level bivouac. The approach is either across the peat bog from the Sligahan Hotel, whose entrance hall is well supplied with the names and telephone numbers of mountain guides, or along the minor road that leads from Carbost through the Glen Brittle forest, where there is a mountaineering centre. For the less energetic, there is no finer way to view the Cuillins than to drive the long dead-end road to the village of Elgol, take a boat excursion across Loch Scavaig, and undertake the walk, which has only one slightly tricky point, into the stupendous glacial trough of Loch Coruisk, surrounded by the sheer

Shearing near Broadford, under the Red Hills, Skye

towering walls of the horseshoe. Alternatively you can take the long, energetic but rewarding walk along the Scavaig shore to Coruisk, a return trip that will take all of a day.

The dark peaks of southern Skye look out across Cuillin Sound to an enchanting group known as the Small Isles, which together form a national scenic area mainly for their contribution to the wide and magnificent scenic vista of the western seaboard. They are easily circumnavigated, or landed upon, by the mail steamer which makes the round trip from Mallaig every day except Sunday; the Sabbath is still well kept in the west.

The largest is Rhum, an island which supported a population of 400 until the then owner, Maclean of Coll, drove them all to Canada in 1826 to make room for his sheep. The Nature Conservancy Council took over the island in 1957 and since then it has been a national nature reserve exhibiting unique geology and flora, and has been the scene of extensive experiments with the management of Red Deer and the replanting of woodland. The daily mailboat service by Caledonian–Macbrayne does not permit a short landing, but other operators run day excursions from Mallaig. Visitors can inspect the island in the immediate vicinity of the harbour at Loch Scresort and follow a nature trail, but the permission of the Nature Conservancy is required to stray further, or to stay overnight.

The north of Rhum is composed of Old Red Sandstone, but in the southern part an intrusion of igneous rocks similar to the Cuillins of Skye has raised three pointed peaks of over 765 m (2,500 ft). They are typical gabbro, sharp-edged and

Elgol, Skye, with the formidable Cuillin Hills on the far side of Loch Scavaig

splintered, but their composition is of an ultrabasic rock rare in Britain, a product of volcanic activity in the Tertiary period. The vegetation of the mountains and cliffs has lain undisturbed by man or by grazing since its formation soon after the last Ice Age, and is rich in alpine plants. Rhum has at least three unique plants, varieties of Eyebright, sedge and orchid. The island is one of the wettest in the Hebrides, and is covered with blanket bog. By the pier is the incongruous ornate pile of Kinloch Castle, built in 1907 of Arran sandstone by John Bullough, a Lancashire industrialist who then owned Rhum; it is used as accommodation for those given leave to stay on the island. The population is about forty, all of them Nature Conservancy and associated workers.

Adjoining Rhum to the south-east, and an essential element in the Small Isles seascape, is the smaller island of Eigg with its great humpback outline of An Sgurr, a basaltic lava flow which rises from a platform of Jurassic limestone to a pinnacled dome of 395 m) (1,292 ft) and then drops sharply in a steep cliff. The mixture of limestone and lava gives Eigg a highly fertile soil, and it supports an active crofting population.

Nearby Muck, equally fertile, is a low-lying green island whose shore is infested with a swarm of black volcanic dykes of hard dolerite which remain proud of the softer rocks through which they intruded, and which have been weathered away. A great mass of dykes runs up the western seaboard, long fingers of lava squeezed through fissures in the native rock at the time of intense Tertiary volcanic activity which had its centre in the Isle of Mull.

Canna is a fertile platform of Tertiary basalt which rises to 122 m) (400 ft) at its northern end in fine columnar cliffs. The island, with a population of thirty, had the good fortune to have as its owner for many years John Lorne Campbell, a committed naturalist who ensured that his land remained relatively free from modern chemical fertilizers and earned it the name 'The garden of the Hebrides'. Now the National Trust continues Campbell's good works.

There is no finer view in the Hebrides than that to be had from the deck of the Oban to Castlebay ferry, as it sails within sight of the Small Isles on an early summer evening, the three peaks of Rhum rearing in the foreground with the black-toothed ridge of the Cuillins behind.

To the north-west of Skye and the Small Isles lie the Outer Hebrides, a 130-mile chain of islands stretching from the Butt of Lewis to Barra Head. The largest is the Isle of Lewis, whose southern half is known as Harris, the home of the legendary indestructible tweed. The division used to be marked by the boundary between the old counties of Ross and Inverness, but it is also a natural boundary between the flat, featureless blanket bog of the north and the knobbly gneiss of the mountainous south, which latter forms a national scenic area along with the northern part of the next major island in the chain, North Uist.

Harris has the highest mountains in the Outer Hebrides; they are considerably less grand than those of Skye, and culminate in the 802 m (2,622 ft) peak of Clisham, to the north of Tarbert, the main ferry port of Harris which sits astride the island's narrow pinched waist.

Clear weather on Clisham will provide views from Cape Wrath to the Cuillins, and out west to the lonely pinnacles of St Kilda. The middle of Harris is an empty and infertile place, with only one per cent of the land under cultivation. Most of the settlements hug the east coast, the population having been driven from the kinder and more fertile west by rapacious Victorian landlords. The east coast is deeply indented by bays and studded with islets, a fine example of

the topography known as knock-and-lochan. The deepest inlet is the long fjord of Loch Seaforth, which carries tidal water fifteen miles inland.

The west coast is altogether softer, with miles of deserted sandy beaches backed by Machair, the unique Hebridean pasture which grows on the flat ground immediately behind the seashore, limed by ground windborne seashells. The pasture contains little grass, and is composed almost entirely of plants with showy flowers, which gives the milk a distinctive scent. The Machair has a delicate ecology which depends on its being kept free from the chemical aids to modern farming. Agriculture improvement grants from the European Community to help with the purchase of fertilizers in remote areas are putting the Machair at grave risk.

The theme of west Harris is continued in the little island of Berneray which still supports a population of about a hundred and has a magnificent sandy beach all down its western shore. The sandy scene is continued in North Uist, whose northern shore has a vast expanse of flats, while its eastern coast is a wild fragmentation of lochs and inlets, a dramatic example, with the myriad off-shore islets, of the post-glacial drowning of the land. Geologists have estimated that with the gradual thawing of the last ice cap the sea level in the Hebrides rose by three feet a century, a rise which continued until only some 6,000 years ago.

Further down the Outer Hebrides chain, the west coast of South Uist is named as a national scenic area for its

Farmhouse below Ben More, Mull

splendid expanse of Machair, from the township of Stilligarry to the southern tip of the island on the Sound of Eriskay. The A865 road which connects the Uists and Benbecula by causeway, runs the entire landward length of the area. The Machair areas are flat, rarely more than thirty feet above sea level, and although now almost exclusively used for cow pasture were once widely tilled for arable cultivation largely because of their ease of ploughing.

The Machair flowers from May until August, a colourful succession of species of Buttercup, Red and White Clover, Daisy, blue Speedwell, Dandelion, Eyebright, Birdsfoot Trefoil, Hop Trefoil, Harebell, Wild Thyme, Field Pansy and Silverweed. If, in later summer, the Machair looks merely green, it is only because the cattle have grazed it clean of its myriad flowers.

There are two approaches to the Uists by sea: by ferry from Oban to Lochboisdale in the far south, which is by far the more scenic route, or from Uig in Skye to Lochmaddy in the far north. Benbecula, which sits between the Uists, has a long-established air service from Glasgow, with the beach as a runway.

There is neither ferry nor aircraft nor any other public transport to St Kilda, the remotest, grandest, most unlikely and most awesome of all the British Isles. It rides the open Atlantic sixty miles west of the Butt of Lewis, the last giant ragged stump of the continent of Europe. Beyond there is only America. To see it for the first time, a group of towering rock cathedrals rearing impossibly from the ocean, is to gasp in wonder. Its remoteness only enhances its stupendous scale, a place born in dreams to be the fortress of giants.

Until 1930 it was the inhospitable home of thirty-six tenacious St Kildans, who finally abandoned the life and the rock to which they had so long clung by their fingernails when declining population, and the twin evils of influenza and money, brought by curious and unfeeling city tourists, finally robbed them of the tremendous will required to live in such isolation and hardship. Today it is the home of a small military detachment manning a rocket tracking station, and of 44,000 breeding pairs who make up the world's largest colony of Gannets.

The St Kilda group is a mass of Tertiary igneous rock, closely related to the gabbros of Skye and Rhum, and untouched by the mainland ice sheets of the Quaternary period. It is a small group, but its scale is huge. The main island of Hirta, whose bay provides the only safe anchorage, rises to a pinnacle of 427 m (1,397 ft) and drops sheer into the

Rushing waters near Loch na Keal, Mull

sea at Conachair cliff, the highest in the British Isles. Everything about the group is vertical. Three miles off Hirta, the great whaleback of Boreray raises its jagged spine to 398 m (1,300 ft), again to drop sheer into the sea. Beside it are the two highest and most dramatic sea stacks in British waters, Stac Lee and Stac an Armin, two dizzy fingers of rock the taller of which reaches 192 m (627 ft).

Every ledge of the stacks and cliffs is occupied by seabirds, with Gannet and Fulmar predominating. To see the entire colony rise from rest at the blare of a ship's hooter and fill the air with their supersonic diving, is a sight without equal in these islands. The little island of Soay, which is all but joined to Hirta, is home to the wild and unique Soay sheep, an ancient breed more akin to the goat, exported to the mainland and bred with success for its ability to survive in inhospitable conditions. The islands also have their own sub-species of Wren and mouse.

St Kilda is owned by the National Trust for Scotland, who lease it to the Nature Conservancy Council as a national nature reserve. Access is restricted, even for those who hire a boat to get there, although the Trust occasionally takes working parties to restore the remains of the old village. Those who have set foot on it, or who have sailed round it in fair weather or foul, never forget it. Its rocks are stupendous, its history sad, and its atmosphere eerie.

During the Tertiary geological period in which St Kilda was thrown up from the ocean floor, a mere sixty million years ago, the centre of volcanic activity in western Scotland was in what is now the Isle of Mull, and the National Scenic Area of Loch na Keal on that island's west coast provides some of the best views of volcanic landscape in Britain.

The wide bight that indents western Mull is peppered with islands, from the strangely shaped fringe of the Treshnish group, including the aptly named Dutchman's Cap with its rounded peak and flat brim, to the larger Ulva and Gometra, the historic Inch Kenneth, ancient burial place of Scottish chiefs when the onward passage to the sacred island of Iona was too rough, and the best known of all, Staffa. All are lumps of basaltic lava, which on Staffa assumes its familiar columnar form at the entrance to Fingal's Cave, a gaping hole twenty metres (sixty feet) high and over 62 m (200 ft) deep. The even crystalline structure of the lava means that, as it cooled, it tended to split with remarkable evenness into perfect hexagons, Staffa being as good an example as the equally famous Giant's Causeway in Northern Ireland.

From the volcano sited in the centre of Mull there poured, over millions of years, vast waves of lava which, at the height of igneous activity, are assumed to have been at least 1,835 m (6,000 ft) thick. Each successive layer has weathered in its own time to produce the characteristic 'trap' country, the stepped landscape which reaches from the head of Loch na Keal towards Ben More, Mull's highest peak.

That the erosion continues today is all too obvious where the road from Salen village which hugs the southern shore of the loch passes under the Gribun cliffs opposite Inch Kenneth. Here the 1,000-ft sheer edge of a lava flow, towering directly above the road, frequently sends down dangerous rockfalls as it crumbles away, made less stable by the underlying sedimentary rocks.

Just south of the Gribun cliffs the road turns sharply inland to avoid the wild peninsula of Ardmeanach. Those who attempt to walk the rocky and dangerous seashore will be rewarded by the sight of McCullough's Tree, a forty-foot high fossilized log caught up in an advancing lava flow and now exposed by the weathering of the cliffs. Loch na Keal delights because of its geology, but most of all because of its view westwards to the pattern of tiny islands whose weird shapes dance and shimmer in the dazzlingly bright Hebridean air.

Mull flanks the northern entrance to the Firth of Lorne, the beginnings of the Great Glen fault that slices the Scottish Highlands in half, while the southern flank is guarded by the Isle of Jura. Unlike basaltic Mull, Jura is built largely of hard white quartzite, a rock that can usually be relied upon to produce dramatic upland scenery. In the south of the island the quartzite rises to three elegant and distinctively shaped peaks known as the Paps of Jura, each over 734 m (2,400 ft), their likeness to upturned nipple-capped breasts spoiled only by their odd number. Their outline is a familiar backdrop to views over an extensive length of the western seaboard, as familiar in the south as the Black Cuillin is in the north.

Jura's western coast exhibits excellent raised beaches, the oldest being one hundred feet above present sea level but still strewn with shingle that looks as fresh as the last tide. The beaches are a perfect illustration of the land rising when relieved of the weight of the ice caps. Jura is largely barren and sparsely populated; George Orwell sought its solitude to write *1984* in a remote farmhouse at the northern end. But its name, which means 'deer island' is well applied; Red Deer outnumber the human population of 200 by at least ten to one.

The shattering of islands which run from the north tip of Jura to the Argyll mainland south of Oban stir the surrounding sea into some of the most dangerous waters in the Hebrides, and they form a small national scenic area for their contribution to the wider views from the mainland. Between Jura and Scarba, a circular island rising to a pyramid of 450 m (1,473 ft), lies the notorious whirlpool of Corryvreckan. Lunga, adjoining, is a dark mass of slate once worked commercially, while to the north-west lies the little chain of the Garvellachs, the holy isles of the sea, a mixture of limestone and ancient pre-Cambrian tillite, evidence of an extremely early ice age. Although now uninhabited, the Garvellachs contain the remains of what is assumed to be one of the oldest

Mist over Loch Scridain, Mull

Christian settlements in the Western Isles, the beehive cells of a monastery thought to have been established by St Columba as a retreat from his abbey on Iona.

The red and black ferries of Caledonian Macbrayne ply the Hebridean seas, but it is a pity that hardly any passenger ships now ply in and out of the great estuary of the River Clyde, surely one of the great sea approaches of the world, and made especially so by the presence in its midst of Arran, the most southerly of Scotland's principal islands.

Arran's interest is that it is a highland landscape in a lowland setting, and because of the intense variety of both its geology and topography it is often labelled 'Scotland in miniature'. In Arran we meet again the Highland Boundary Fault, which cuts the island more or less in two. The national scenic area encloses the northern part, a massive granite intrusion of the Tertiary period which has been weathered into a mountain range entirely highland in character. Only in Skye and Rhum do such high peaks tumble so directly to the shore, separated from the sea by the narrowest of coastal plains. In any view of the Firth of Clyde, the Arran peaks are inescapable.

As the car ferry from Ardrossan approaches Arran's main settlement of Brodick, capital of the island's 3,500 population, the mountains rise directly above the town. The highest is the sharp peak of Goat Fell 877 m (2,868 ft), separated from its neighbour Cir Mhor 800 m (2,618 ft) by a splendid saddle. There are two main approaches to the Arran range: from Brodick up the deeply glaciated Glen Rosa, or from further up the coast at Sannox Bay up Glen Sannox. To ascend one and descend the other makes a fine day's outing. From Sannox there is also a short walk through the forest to the Fallen Rocks, an impressive landslide of granite boulders.

Arran, sheltered and southerly, enjoys a climate mild enough to support palm trees and other lush vegetation, best seen in the gardens of Brodick Castle, a Victorian reconstruction of one of the ancient seats of the Hamilton family, where there is a spectacular display of rhododendrons from mid-April to mid-June.

Southern Scotland

SOUTHERN SCOTLAND is without the drama of the Highlands. Its hills are lower and more rounded, its coast less fretted by sea and ice, its land richer, and its charms more subtle. It is no less beautiful but in a way which tends to satisfy rather than astonish. The mind could conceivably weary of Highland superlatives, and the neck ache from gazing at so many heights.

Because there are fewer set-piece tableaux of splendour in the south, there are far fewer national scenic areas, and their choice is inevitably more arbitrary than those in the north. There are seven officially designated areas; everyone who knows southern Scotland will have his own, considerably longer, list.

The first two are properly Highland scenes, which although geographically in the south of the country lie north of the Highland Boundary Fault. The region of Knapdale lies in the far south-west of Argyll, at the start of the Kintyre peninsula, a long journey south from Oban on the A816 or from Inveraray on the A83. The area begins by the picturesque Crinan Canal, much used by yachtsmen heading for the Hebrides, and runs south to include the region of intensely folded Dalradian rocks that stretches to the mouths of Loch Sween and Loch Caolisport.

The south-east to north-west pressure of folding has given the topography a highly pronounced north-east to south-west grain; the coastline, lochs and valleys run almost perfectly parallel. It is an Appalachian-type landscape in miniature, given added attraction both by heavy afforestation, being the only use for the poor acid soils, and by the Isle of Jura off-shore, which gives both a dramatic backdrop and a shelter from the westerly winds.

Forestry plantations are frequently condemned for clothing hillsides in regimented rows of drab conifers, but Knapdale is an exception; the dense plantations have given the area of miniature glens and ribbon lochs a pleasing intimacy, and the region is further enhanced by a richness of archaeological sites. There are a number of waymarked forest walks, and a small forestry information office on the B8025 to Tayvallich, just south of the hamlet of Bellanoch.

The second southern Highland national scenic area is one beloved of Glaswegians of a generation of more ago, for it was the highlight of a trip in the days when paddle steamers used to weave a tapestry of pleasure cruises across the splendid estuary of the River Clyde. The Kyles of Bute are the narrows which separate the island of Bute from the mainland of Cowal at the mouth of Loch Ruel. The three arms of water are steeply overhung by the richly green mainland hills, and the sense of deep enclosure delivers an air of peace and calm. The Kyles can be reached by road, at the north end of Bute, or by the A886 from Strachur on the east shore of Loch Fyne, but the only proper way to appreciate them is from the deck of a paddle steamer, not an easy thing to accomplish these days.

By contrast, true southern Upland scenery is to be found along the course of the River Tweed, which rises in the high moors of the Lowther Hills near Moffat and meanders through the Border country to Berwick by way of a great wide valley that is among the best arable land in the United Kingdom, at least if we are to judge by the prices at which farms change hands. But in Upper Tweeddale, west of Peebles, the river runs through a narrower valley of high moorland hilltops which descend through a cloak of rich mixed woodland to a valley floor of parkland, pasture and riverside meadows. The national scenic area extends from Peebles upstream to the village of Broughton, and the river is easily followed by taking the A72 from Peebles westwards, then branching left along the B712 towards Rachan Mill. It is a pleasant and unified valley scene enhanced by ancient border castles, especially the fine old keep of Neidpath standing lonely sentinel on the river bank.

But the finest view of this handsome river is further downstream by the Border town of Melrose, a view which so entranced Sir Walter Scott that he made his home here, in the romantic old pile of Abbotsford House. Here the Tweed is midway between a rushing upland stream and a mature lowland river, winding in great loops through a broadening valley.

Had the selection of national scenic areas been in the hands of Scott, this one from Melrose to Newtown St Boswells would have been his first choice. It is an intensely human landscape of rich woodland and farming, ornamented by Abbotsford and Dryburgh Abbey, but its dominant feature is the triple-peaked mass of the Eildon Hills, modest in height at only 424 m (1,385 ft), but as handsome a group of summits as are to be found anywhere south of the Highlands. Rounded, feminine and isolated, they are an unusual intrusion of igneous rock into the predominating sedimentary sandstones of the Tweed valley. They are easily climbed, but they and their setting are best appreciated from Scott's View, well signposted on a minor road above Dryburgh Abbey. After the wild grandeur of the Highlands, this is a remarkably civilized scene.

The three remaining national scenic areas are all on the northern shore of the Solway Firth, that shallow and sluggish inlet that splits south-western Scotland from Cumbria. The region of Galloway is well enough known to Scots, but is generally ignored by travellers from the south in their headlong rush to the cities of Glasgow and Edinburgh, and to the alluring Highland delights beyond.

South of Dumfries, the River Nith empties lazily into the Solway Firth in a wide tidal estuary of sands, mudflats and saltmarshes of a flatness and openness unusual in the Scottish scene, particularly on the west. The large expanse of marshes is chiefly a result of the land rising slightly after the last Ice Age, when the weight of ice was removed. The flatness is relieved by the gentle granite hump of Criffell 577 m (1,886 ft) rising to the west of the estuary, the remains of a granitic intrusion into the country rock which extends for some fifteen miles to the west of the Nith. The scene is further enlivened by the handsome ruin of Sweetheart Abbey, near the village of New Abbey on the west side of the Nith, a warm and glowing pile built of rich red sandstone.

As well as being named a national scenic area for being an exceptionally fine tidal estuary, the mouth of the Nith is home to an outstanding national nature reserve at Caerlaverock, on the B725 road down the east side of the river. The reserve extends along six miles of coast from the Nith to Lochar Water, and encompasses a complete range of low-lying coastal habitats, including one of the largest remaining unreclaimed saltmarshes in Britain.

The reserve's principal attraction is as a winter roost for many thousands of geese, including the entire population of Barnacle Goose from Spitzbergen, 800 miles north of the North Cape of Norway. It is also the most northerly breeding ground of the Natterjack Toad. It should be noted that access to some parts of the reserve is restricted.

An adjoining national scenic area encloses the continuation of the tidal flats to the west, along the East Stewartry coast in the vicinity of Dalbeattie. Here the shore is still low, the water shallow, but the coastline is less open and more indented, with the triple inlets of Rough Firth, Orchardton Bay and Auchencairn Bay, separated by wooded promontories. Inland is grey granite country, quarried in the past to build the docks of Liverpool, a continuation of the granitic intrusion that raised Criffell. The open sandflats are offset by an undulating hinterland which has a pleasing intimacy; the combination has long been a magnet for holidaymakers, drawn to the coastal village of Rockcliffe. Rough Island, off-shore, belongs to the National Trust for Scotland and is a bird sanctuary where terns predominate. The Trust also owns the nearby Mote of Mark, a hundred-foot hill that once bore a sixth-century fort of the ancient Britons.

The final national scenic area is a short distance to the west, the lower valley of the Water of Fleet around the village of Gatehouse of Fleet, lying under the gentle hump of Cairnharrow 457 m (1,496 ft). The estuary attracts mainly through its combination of fine sandy beaches, among the best in southern Scotland, and the profusion of well-managed woodland, with open moorland above. Gatehouse is a child of the Industrial Revolution, a settlement built around an early cotton industry which sprang from the harnessing of the water power of the Fleet. The extensive policy woodlands were largely the creation of James Murray, the industrialist who created Gatehouse in 1760 and built his mansion at Cally, now a hotel. Extensive planting has been conducted in more recent times by the Forestry Commission, whose Fleet Forest has a number of gentle waymarked walks, and a small information office on the main A75 road just east of Gatehouse.

It is highly arguable whether the foregoing national scenic areas are in fact the jewels of southern Scotland. To name but one of many possible omissions, where is St Mary's Loch, that deeply peaceful and sequestered place in the hidden depths of Selkirkshire?

The Countryside Commission for Scotland, which

selected the national scenic areas and first published them as proposals in 1978, are the first to admit that their choice may be arbitrary, and they would admit almost as readily that beauty alone was not their sole criterion in choosing particular areas from the immense richness of Scotland for particular attention. National scenic areas are essentially areas of planning control, and one factor in the choice was undoubtedly to protect places that could at some future time suffer from unbridled development.

Scotland is still full of gloriously unspoilt tracts of land where those who seek solitude will find it with ease, and those who seek beauty will have the pleasure of discovering it.

Scotland – Useful Addresses

Scottish Tourist Board: 23 Ravelston Terrace, Edinburgh

National Trust for Scotland: 5 Charlotte Square, Edinburgh

Forestry Commission: Corstorphine Rd, Edinburgh

Nature Conservancy Council: 12 Hope Terrace, Edinburgh

Scottish Wildlife Trust: 25 Johnston Terrace, Edinburgh

Countryside Commission for Scotland: Battleby House, Redgorton, Perth

Acknowledgements

The contributors, the editors and the producers of this book would like to thank a great many people for their help. In particular they are grateful to

Susan Abbott
Eric Bartlett
G B Belton
Janet M Bleay
J H Bradley
Lindsay Colford
Andrea Cringean
The Duke and Duchess of Devonshire
Julian Duxbury
John Evans
Bernard Gilchrist MBE
J A Greenwood
R J Harvey
Alan Jones
Mr & Mrs G C Lambourne

Cynthia Lewis
Joan Morgan
Richard Muir
W H Murray
Robert Owen
Malcolm Payne
Mrs L Pickard
Michael Proctor
Marian Rees
Fiona Reynolds
Hywel H Roberts
R H (Dick) Roberts
Jacqueline Rubens
R Sands
Roger Stevens
Michael Taylor

Edward B V Tullett
Tom Weir
Richard West FRS
Nic Wheeler
Tom Williams
G W Wood
Michael Wright

The Staff of the following organizations:
Countryside Commission
Countryside Commission for Scotland
Cumbria Trust for Nature Conservation
Derbyshire County Library

Derbyshire Naturalists' Trust
Forestry Commission, Edinburgh
National Park Offices, Northumberland (Hexham) and Yorkshire (Bainbridge and Grassington)
National Trust for Scotland
Nature Conservancy Council, Blackwell, Windermere, and London
Peak Park Joint Board

Index

Further Reading

Gill, Crispin: *Dartmoor; a new study*   David and Charles 1970
Hemery, Eric: *High Dartmoor*   Robert Hale 1983

Burton, S H: *Exmoor*   Robert Hale 1978
Orwin, C S & Sellick, R J: *The Reclamation of Exmoor Forest*   David & Charles 1970
MacDermot, E T: *The history of the forest of Exmoor*   David & Charles 1973

Pearsall, W H & Pennington, W: *The Lake District* (New Naturalist Series)   Collins 1973
de Selincourt, E (Ed): *Wordsworth's Guide to the Lakes*   OUP 1977

White, J T: *The Scottish Border and Northumberland* (The Regions of Britain)   Eyre Methuen 1973
Philipson, J (Ed): *Northumberland*   HMSO 1969

Rastrick, A: *North York Moors*   HMSO 1979
Mead, H: *Inside the North York Moors*   David & Charles 1978

Edwards, K C: *The Peak District* (New Naturalist Series)   Collins 1962, Fontana 1973
Monkhouse, P (Ed): *Peak District National Park*   HMSO 1960

Wright, G N: *The Yorkshire Dales* (British Topographical Series)   David & Charles 1977
Duerden, N: *Portrait of the Dales*   Robert Hale 1978

Davies, Margaret (Ed): *Brecon Beacons*   HMSO 1967
Bartlett, E (Ed): *Breconshire Birds*   The Brecknock Naturalist's Trust
The Breconshire Naturalist   The Brecknock Naturalist's Trust

Miles, Dillwyn (Ed): *Pembrokeshire Coast*   HMSO 1978
Davies, T A Warren: *Plants of Pembrokeshire*   West Wales Naturalists' Trust 1970

Condry, W M: *The Snowdonia National Park* (New Naturalist Series)   Collins 1966
Edwards, G Rhys (Ed): *Snowdonia*   HMSO 1973